Where the Rivers Meet

The Nature | History | Society series is devoted to the publication of high-quality scholarship in environmental history and allied fields. Its broad compass is signalled by its title: nature because it takes the natural world seriously; history because it aims to foster work that has temporal depth; and society because its essential concern is with the interface between nature and society, broadly conceived. The series is avowedly interdisciplinary and is open to the work of anthropologists, ecologists, historians, geographers, literary scholars, political scientists, sociologists, and others whose interests resonate with its mandate. It offers a timely outlet for lively, innovative, and well-written work on the interaction of people and nature through time in North America.

General Editor: Graeme Wynn, University of British Columbia

A list of titles in the series appears at the end of the book.

NATURE | HISTORY | SOCIETY

GENERAL EDITOR: GRAEME WYNN

Where the Rivers Meet

Pipelines, Participatory Resource Management, and Aboriginal-State Relations in the Northwest Territories

CARLY A. DOKIS

FOREWORD BY GRAEME WYNN

UBC Press • Vancouver • Toronto

23 22 21 20 19 18 17 16 15   5 4 3 2 1

Printed in Canada on FSC-certified ancient-forest-free paper
(100% post-consumer recycled) that is processed chlorine- and acid-free.

Library and Archives Canada Cataloguing in Publication

Dokis, Carly A. (Carly Ann), 1978-, author
     Where the rivers meet : pipelines, participatory resource management, and Aboriginal-state relations in the Northwest Territories / Carly A. Dokis.

(Nature, history, society)
Includes bibliographical references and index.
Issued in print and electronic formats.
ISBN 978-0-7748-2845-1 (bound). – ISBN 978-0-7748-2846-8 (pbk.)
ISBN 978-0-7748-2847-5 (pdf). – ISBN 978-0-7748-2848-2 (epub)

     1. Mackenzie Gas Project. 2. Bearlake Indians – Northwest Territories – Government relations. 3. Environmental impact analysis – Northwest Territories – Decision making. 4. Natural gas pipelines – Environmental aspects – Northwest Territories. 5. Natural gas pipelines – Social aspects – Northwest Territories. 6. Natural gas pipelines – Political aspects – Northwest Territories. 7. Natural resources – Northwest Territories – Management. 8. Northwest Territories – Environmental conditions. I. Title. II. Series: Nature, history, society

E99.B376D64 2015   971.9'3004972   C2015-900723-2
                                                  C2015-900724-0

Canadä

UBC Press gratefully acknowledges the financial support for our publishing program of the Government of Canada (through the Canada Book Fund), the Canada Council for the Arts, and the British Columbia Arts Council.

This book has been published with the help of a grant from the Canadian Federation for the Humanities and Social Sciences, through the Awards to Scholarly Publications Program, using funds provided by the Social Sciences and Humanities Research Council of Canada.

UBC Press
The University of British Columbia
2029 West Mall
Vancouver, BC V6T 1Z2
www.ubcpress.ca

Contents

List of Illustrations / vi

Foreword: The Paradoxical Politics of Participatory Praxis / vii
Graeme Wynn

Preface / xxi

Acknowledgments / xxv

List of Abbreviations / xxvii

Introduction: People, Land, and Pipelines / 3

1 "Very Nice Talk in a Very Beautiful Way": The Community
Hearing Process / 32

2 "A Billion Dollars Cannot Create a Moose": Perceptions of Industrial
Impacts / 63

3 Life under the Comprehensive Claim Agreement / 91

4 Consultation and Other Legitimating Practices / 130

Conclusion: The Politics of Participation / 161

Notes / 175

References / 188

Index / 196

Illustrations

PHOTOGRAPHS

On the shore of Great Bear Lake in Déline / 18
Tulit'a in February / 18
Colville Lake / 21
Joint Review Panel hearing / 40
On the land at Lake Beloit / 69
Work camp in winter / 107

FIGURES

1 Effects of pipeline activities on the landscape / 75
2 SSI organizational structure / 98

MAPS

1 Sahtu region, showing the proposed Mackenzie Valley Pipeline / 13
2 The Sahtu Settlement Area / 92

TABLE

1 The pipeline corridor and wildlife habitat availability / 74

The Paradoxical Politics of Participatory Praxis

Graeme Wynn

H ALF A CENTURY AGO, as North American energy consumption increased at unprecedented rates (in Canada the rate of growth approximated 5 percent per annum through much of the 1950s and 1960s), the quest for additional sources of oil and gas led exploration and development into new and difficult locations, at considerable risk to working people, environments, wildlife, and Indigenous societies. On the east coast, companies prospected the continental shelf and discovered oil beneath the Atlantic, in an area susceptible to cyclones, rogue waves, and drifting icebergs a few hundred kilometres east of St. John's, Newfoundland. Here, extraction depended upon ocean-drilling platforms, and the dangers of the enterprise were driven home by the catastrophic loss of the *Ocean Ranger,* the world's largest semi-submersible oilrig, and eighty-four human lives, in February 1982.[1] In northern Alberta there was renewed interest in the enormous bitumen deposits, or Athabasca "tar sands," long known but for technological reasons beyond successful commercial development until 1967, and now regarded by many as a major environmental hazard.[2] And on the far northern edge of the continent, on the northern coast of Alaska and in the Beaufort Sea north of the Yukon, reserves of oil and gas were proved up in the late 1960s. In 1968, the Atlantic Richfield Company announced its discovery of North America's largest known oil field (and associated gas reserves) in Prudhoe Bay. Major gas deposits were discovered in the Mackenzie Delta three years later, and offshore drilling in the Beaufort Sea began a year after that.[3]

Bringing oil and gas to market from a location as remote and forbidding as the Arctic slope posed huge challenges, and they were addressed differently for oil and gas and by Canada and the United States, although Indigenous land claims remained unresolved in both countries. In Alaska, the US government moved quickly to strike a monumental agreement that shaped the course of development in the state. In 1971, the Alaska Native Claims Settlement Act transferred 44 million acres (180,000 square kilometres) of land to the state's seventy thousand Native people and disbursed over $900 million among them. In return, Native Alaskans ceded the remainder (almost 90 percent) of the state and gave up claims to oil, natural gas, and mineral rights in that area. By clarifying issues of title and allowing the expansion of the oil industry – which was able to construct an eight-hundred-mile-long pipeline from Prudhoe Bay to Valdez to ship oil to California – these provisions induced an economic boom.[4] They also served, as the Alaska Federation of Natives intended, to engage Alaskan tribes in corporate capitalism, and by some accounts engineered a "civil rights revolution" by affording Native Alaskans economic and political parity, and near social equality, with other residents of the state. To address the concerns of environmental groups alarmed about the desecration of wilderness by oil development, the 1971 agreement also enabled the US secretary of the interior to set aside large tracts for environmental conservation. This provision ultimately underlay the Alaska National Interest Lands Conservation Act of 1980, which selected over 100 million acres of Alaska for conservation, with over half of this area designated wilderness. Ten new national parks were established, and the Arctic National Wildlife Range (created in 1960) was doubled in size (to almost 18 million acres) and declared a refuge.[5]

Getting Prudhoe Bay gas to southern markets was considerably more difficult than moving oil by pipeline and tanker. Shipping gas requires that it be purified, cooled (to a temperature of $-162°C$), and thus compressed (to 1/600th of its gaseous volume). This entails considerable expense, in the development of plants to produce the gas/liquid phase transition (approximately $1.5 billion for every million tons of production each year), in the construction of special vessels designed to maintain the gas in a liquefied state (say $200 to $300 million each), and in building receiving terminals (about $1 billion each).[6] Wherever possible, it is vastly more profitable to move the product in a gaseous state through high-pressure pipelines, and American and Canadian interests both recognized the advantages of piping gas from the Arctic slope and linking the supply into existing pipeline networks. Various routes were explored, but the most favoured proposal was for a forty-eight-inch high-pressure pipeline from Prudhoe Bay to the Mackenzie Delta and then southward along the Mackenzie Valley to northern Alberta, to link with extant pipelines and markets in the American Midwest and California. Approaching four thousand kilometres in length, this proposed pipeline was described as the largest privately-financed project in the history of free enterprise.[7]

As oil prices climbed, Canadian prime minister Pierre Trudeau saw great public benefit in early construction of the pipeline. But conscious of the surging tide of environmentalism and the rising voices of Native peoples, he declared that the pipeline should proceed only in ways that did not "require a lowering of environmental standards or the neglect of Indian rights and interests."[8] Early in 1974, after the Inuvialuit Committee for Original People's Entitlement (COPE) asserted a claim to lands around the Beaufort Sea, and the Indian Brotherhood of the Northwest Territories filed a legal caveat claiming an interest in 450,000 square miles (1,000,000 square kilometres) of the Northwest Territories, the Canadian government appointed Justice Thomas Berger, a Vancouver lawyer, to conduct the Mackenzie Valley Pipeline Inquiry. Its mandate was to investigate the potential impacts, on this corridor, of pipeline development.

Refusing a narrow view of his assignment, Berger addressed his efforts to "the whole future of the north."[9] Conducting dozens of hearings, many of them informal, in small northern communities and seasonal encampments, Berger's inquiry gave voice to Indigenous people. Through several months, it assembled enormous quantities of testimony and information about patterns of Indigenous land use, about Indigenous conceptions of the world, about belief systems, about the aspirations and fears of Native peoples, about Indigenous relations with nature, and about land claims. Transcribed, it amounted to over forty thousand pages, assembled into 283 volumes. Those who testified did not speak with a single voice, but the weight of evidence was clear to Berger, whose recommendations, released in 1977, declared against the development of a pipeline across the northern Yukon and Mackenzie Delta and urged a ten-year moratorium on similar construction in the Mackenzie corridor.

Northern Frontier, Northern Homeland, the final report of the Mackenzie Valley Pipeline Inquiry, was a blockbuster. It sold ten thousand copies, was widely discussed, and is generally seen to have changed the terms of debate over industrial development in the North. In essence, Berger's argument was that "the unique land and water ecosystems that characterize the [Mackenzie] Delta and the margins of the Beaufort Sea," the survival of the Porcupine caribou herd, the traditional economies of Native peoples, their claims to land, and their socio-economic well-being were far more important to Canadians than any benefits that might flow from immediate exploitation of northern gas and oil reserves. Berger did not believe that the juggernaut of resource development could be stopped completely. He assumed "that, in due course, the industrial system will require the gas and oil of the western Arctic, and that they will have to be transported along the Mackenzie Valley to markets in the South." But he was convinced that Canadians should honour, "above all else ... the legitimate claims of the native people" of the region. This, he said, implied "a new set of priorities for northern development" that included "the strengthening of the traditional native economy," the development of a diversified, enduring base of economic activity, and a guarantee that when development did proceed, and necessary regulatory mechanisms were established, "the regulatory process should involve all of those interests in the North that have legitimate concerns about the impact of the project."[10]

Berger was ahead of his time in insisting on the importance of incorporating Indigenous perspectives into decision making about traditional Indigenous territories. But his ideas were soon given weight by increasingly frequent arguments for the distinctiveness and importance of Indigenous knowledge. The great French anthropologist Claude Lévi-Strauss may have set this ball rolling with his 1962 discussion of the "science du concret," or Native knowledge of the natural milieu.[11] Other scholars working in ethnoscience and ethnoecology documented the exceptionally detailed local knowledge of plants and animals developed by Indigenous people in various parts of the world, and as the distinguished Canadian resource ecologist Fikret Berkes has noted, during the 1970s workers in several disciplines began to acknowledge the "validity" of traditional knowledge.[12] In the 1980s, the idea of traditional ecological knowledge (TEK) gained widespread currency.

Despite its popularity, the phrase "traditional ecological knowledge" remains hard to define. Some quibble at the word "traditional," challenging the implication that an ever-dynamic, adaptive form of understanding is unchanging. Others, who see ecology as a branch of (Western) biological science, wonder how traditional Indigenous knowledge can be "ecological." A third critique comes from those who find the term "knowledge" too confining for something that emerges from "a complex system of social relations and institutions (social capital), founded upon particular beliefs and values (cultural capital), mediated by the practices and protocols (methods) of oral tradition."[13] With such caveats in mind, Fikret Berkes proposed a "working definition":

TEK is a cumulative body of knowledge and beliefs, handed down through generations by cultural transmission, about the relationship of living beings (including humans) with one another and with their environment. Further, TEK is an attribute of societies with historical continuity in resource use practices; by and large, these are non-industrial or less technologically advanced societies, many of them indigenous or tribal.[14]

By 1987, the importance of TEK was certified by the United Nation's Brundtland Commission Report, when it recognized (as Berger had) the interdependence of ecological, cultural, and political-economic systems. The pages of *Our Common Future* (the document that popularized the term "sustainable development") confidently asserted that Indigenous communities "are the repositories of vast accumulations of traditional knowledge and experience that link humanity with its ancient origins. Their disappearance is a loss for the larger society which could learn a great deal from their traditional skills in sustainably managing very complex ecological systems."[15]

Furthermore, the report continued, the starting point for

a just and humane policy ... [toward vulnerable groups] is the recognition and protection of their traditional rights to land and other resources that sustain their way of life — rights that may be defined in terms that do not fit into standard legal systems. These groups' own institutions to regulate rights and obligations are crucial for maintaining harmony with nature and the awareness characteristic of the traditional way of life.

By this account – and Berger would surely have agreed – dominant societies have an obligation to "give local communities a decisive voice in the decisions about resource use in their area."[16]

On a parallel track, in 1982 the United Nations Economic and Social Council tasked a working group on Indigenous populations to define human rights standards for the protection of Indigenous people around the world. This led eventually to the UN Declaration on the Rights of Indigenous Peoples. Adopted by the General Assembly in 2007, it "emphasizes the rights of indigenous peoples to maintain and strengthen their own institutions, cultures and traditions, and to pursue their development in keeping with their own needs and aspirations."[17]

Paralleling these developments, there was a rising sense that older institutionalized forms of resource management were falling short of their espoused goals – or indeed that these goals were no longer appropriate.

To reduce a complex story to its essence, management regimes rooted in turn-of-the-twentieth-century conceptions of conservation as a quest for efficient use of the earth's bounty, articulated through such notions as "sustained yield" and implemented by technocrats trained to see the world as a vast input-output system, were subject to increasing critique for their "resourcification of nature."[18] By some accounts, the ethos of "resource managerialism," so prevalent in the post-war years, ignored the intrinsic and ecological values of nature, measured policy success in simple monetary terms, and applied "corporate administrative frameworks" to the exploitation of nature for the purpose of finding "the supplies needed to feed the economy and provision society through national and international markets."[19] Worse was the mounting evidence – revealed most starkly to Canadians in the collapse of the East Coast cod fishery – that for all their reassuring rhetoric about "sustained" yields, resource managers were unable to prevent ecological disaster.[20] In a broader intellectual climate of suspicion toward Science and its claims to privileged knowledge of the world, the time was ripe for the development of new adaptive and collaborative strategies for ecosystem stewardship.[21]

Taking local knowledge seriously and listening to those whose knowledge comes from observation and experience rather than from laboratories, theories, and models quickly became important principles of environmental management. They were advocated by scholars critical of conventional practices, demanded by First Nations groups newly conscious of opportunities to exercise greater control over their lands and lives, embraced by managers aware of the shifting political climate in which they worked, and enshrined in legislation.[22] Marking the shift, Dean Bavington argued forcefully for participatory processes, or democratic decision making, and the embrace of local knowledge (as well as a moral compass) in the administration of the Newfoundland fisheries, and early in the new millennium the Irish Fishers' Knowledge Project sought to tap the wisdom of those who worked the sea in hope that it might "be utilised in Irish/European fisheries management."[23] In 2007, a review of tools found useful for incorporating community knowledge, preferences, and values into decision making accepted without qualification "the importance and necessity of including community perspectives in natural resource management."[24]

Against this evolving backdrop, as Native peoples became more assured in their claims for recognition, and the impetus to develop Canada's northern resources gained steam, politicians ceded ground and deference to Indigenous interests. The James Bay and Northern Quebec Agreement

of 1975, signed to address the concerns of resident Native peoples about
the development of massive hydroelectricity-generating projects in the
James Bay drainage, marked an important first step in this regard.[25] Under
its provisions, local Cree and Inuit groups secured a legally defined and
broadly equitable role in the management and utilization of a small frac-
tion of their traditional lands and resources (beyond the rivers dammed
and diverted, and those extensive areas flooded by dams and affected by
construction, where – said grand chief of the Cree, Matthew Coon Come
– "a wilderness so vast and beautiful" had begun to resemble a battlefield
after a bombing raid).[26]

Such arrangements – bolstered by the entrenchment, in 1982, of
Aboriginal and treaty rights in the Canadian Constitution, and subsequent
Supreme Court decisions constraining the state's power to manage resources
unilaterally – quickly became known as co-management initiatives.
Described by Claudia Notzke, a close student of one of them, as "innova-
tive management" regimes integrating local and state systems, allocating
resource control among competing interests, and facilitating the blending
of knowledge systems, these co-management arrangements established
partnerships between Aboriginal communities and governments (and in
some cases between Aboriginal communities and industry) that were
intended to share power and to overcome mutual suspicion.[27] In the
abstract, the exchange of relevant information among co-management
partners was seen as a means to incorporate local knowledge into resource
development and management activities, to ensure a heightened awareness
of ecosystem changes, and to promote compliance with mutually agreed
upon regulations.

Various forms of co-management emerged, and Berkes once categorized
them according to the extent of Aboriginal involvement. At one end of
the spectrum were those arrangements marked by full-fledged partnership and community control. Here partners were equal, procedures for
joint decision making were institutionalized, and substantial responsibilities were delegated to the local community. At the other end of the array,
locals were merely "informed" about decisions already taken. Between these
endpoints, Berkes identified an ascending hierarchy of participation levels,
from consultation through cooperation, to communication (a two-way
exchange reflected in the incorporation of local concerns into management
strategies). Between communication and full partnership there were advisory committees (through which partnership in decision making began)
and management boards that gave locals an opportunity "to participate
in developing and implementing management plans." Arrangements

cleaving to levels 1 and 2 (informing, consulting) in this hierarchy were associated with provincial settings, where earlier treaty provisions limit First Nations' opportunities to exercise management rights over lands and resources beyond the boundaries of Indian reserves.[28] Those matching levels 6 and 7 (management boards: community control) were typically found within the territories of northern land claim agreements.[29]

The Inuvialuit Final Agreement of 1984, the first "comprehensive" settlement in the Northwest Territories, was by one account where "co-management theory and practice got their impressive start."[30] It included a lump-sum compensation payment, something akin to full title to eleven thousand square kilometres around six western Arctic communities, and joint management of an additional seventy-eight thousand square kilometres. Various boards, councils, and committees – in all of which Inuvialuit make up half the membership – were set up to administer these lands and the resources they contain. Elsewhere across the North, in territories covered by the Council of Yukon Indians Agreement (1990), the Gwich'in Agreement (1992), the Sahtu Dene and Metis Comprehensive Land Agreement (1993), and the Nunavut Agreement (1993), Native peoples gained similar legally defined opportunities to establish co-management structures and play a role in resource management and development.

Taken together, these developments helped to constitute co-management as a new orthodoxy in both provincial and northern territorial jurisdictions. The value of Aboriginal knowledge was recognized in Canada's 1992 National Forest Strategy document, which noted that "the knowledge ... [Aboriginal people] have gained through their enduring relationship with the land can bring a special perspective to sustainable forest management."[31] Five years later, the Royal Commission on Aboriginal Peoples asserted that "co-management has come to mean institutional arrangements whereby governments and Aboriginal entities (and sometimes other parties) enter into formal agreements specifying their respective rights, powers and obligations with reference to the management and allocation of resources in a particular area of crown lands and waters."[32] Such arrangements have been implemented in national and provincial parks (such as Torngat in Labrador and Hay-Zama Lakes in Alberta, respectively) and, where land claims remain outstanding, in national park reserves (such as Gwaii Haanas).[33] They have been applied, through the establishment of species-specific management boards that typically include representatives of federal, territorial, and First Nations governments (e.g., the Porcupine Caribou Management Board, the Nunavut Wildlife Management Board, and the Ruby Range Sheep Steering Committee). And they have been implemented less formally through local organizations such as hunters and trappers associations, and discussions between Aboriginal hunters and trappers and state-appointed game wardens.[34]

Yet in most of these cases there was, and is, little agreement on how to strike an appropriate balance between Science and experience. The looming question, in its several variants, remains: Is it possible to find common ground between the perspectives of outport fishers and government scientists, peasant proprietors and corporate capitalists, Indigenous peoples and those largely ignorant of their homeplace and customs, or – as the anthropologist Paul Nadasdy frames it in his important book on Aboriginal-state relations in southwest Yukon – between hunters and bureaucrats? This is truly a vexing problem. Whatever good intentions may have led the parties into dialogue, whatever the goodwill on each side of these pairings, the differences between them remain enormous. The knowledge claims of Science and TEK often seem so different as to be incommensurable.

For all the promise of co-management as participatory praxis, attempts to implement it are increasingly found wanting. In the assessment of environmental historian John Sandlos, "the participatory revolution in northern parks and wildlife management remains incomplete."[35] The federal government has not surrendered significant authority in these matters to Aboriginal groups. "Co-management" arrangements are often advisory to federal government bodies or politicians. For all the lip-service paid to the importance of Aboriginal perspectives in forest management, a review of the National Forest Strategy conducted toward the end of the twentieth century concluded that the "substantial progress" evident at the "policy level" had "yet to be validated at the planning level and operational level on the ground."[36] For all the progress made in including Indigenous representation, many of those who have studied the work of co-management boards suggest that they often marginalize Aboriginal knowledge by treating it as supplementary to scientific data.

Anthropologist Paul Nadasdy's detailed ethnographic work with the Kluane First Nation and his investigation of the activities of the Ruby Range Sheep Steering Committee have done much to expose the asymmetry of power relations inherent in the struggle for and over knowledge, when hunters and bureaucrats, Aboriginals and the state engage each other on questions of wildlife management.[37] Time and again, Nadasdy shows how the environmental understanding and cultural values of Kluane people are devalued unless they can be translated into forms familiar to the Western-educated minds of government servants. The point has also been made, forcefully, by other scholars and by Native peoples themselves: "Our traditional ecological knowledge is too often taken out of context, misinterpreted, or misused. What wildlife managers, biologists and bureaucrats understand ... is interpreted within their own knowledge and value systems, not ours. In the process, our special ways of knowing and doing things ... are crushed by scientific knowledge and the state management model."[38]

The conclusion from this line of critique is clear. Co-management is not working. Failing to recognize the complexities of Indigenous-environment relations, and unable to conceive of wildlife conservation as more than an apolitical, instrumentalist, managerial task, government bureaucrats have perpetuated the imbalances of colonial power even as they appear to cooperate, collaborate, and work in partnership with Native peoples.

Joining this critical chorus, Carly Dokis nonetheless succeeds in making an important and timely contribution to the refrain. *Where the Rivers Meet* turns the spotlight on participatory environmental assessment processes in northern Canada, specifically those initiated by an October 2004 application to construct and operate a $16.2 billion, 1,200-kilometre, gas pipeline (and related infrastructure) from Inuvik southward to Alberta via the Mackenzie Valley.[39] Based on months of ethnographic fieldwork in several Sahtu Dene communities as well as observations made at a number of public hearings convened by the Joint Review Panel for the Mackenzie Gas Project, this book offers a sobering message. Despite conscientious efforts to constitute the review panel as an independent body with a judicious balance of experience and perspectives, its hearings largely failed to give due and appropriate consideration to Sahtu Dene views on the impact of pipeline construction.

Recognizing that the twenty-first-century Mackenzie Gas Project was expected to run along much the same route as the pipeline that spawned the Berger Inquiry forty years before, Dokis frames her account of the recent hearings comparatively and exposes stark contrasts between these proceedings and those conducted by Justice Berger. Whereas Berger listened – "I want you, the people who live here, who make the North your home, to tell me what you would say to the government of Canada, if you could tell them what was in your minds" (p. 4) – respected, and responded to local concerns, recent hearings have turned purported participatory processes into handmaidens of the state. Although Joint Review Panel hearings brought together two ways of knowing and communicating knowledge, they conspicuously failed to incorporate Indigenous forms of understanding into their assessment. Sahtu Dene contributions to the environmental assessment process ranged far beyond concern about the ecological impacts of industrial development to include profound expressions of identity and what it means to be "a good human being," but these sentiments were essentially ignored. Praising the Mackenzie Gas Project's potential "positive contribution towards a sustainable northern future," and declaring significant adverse impacts of the pipeline unlikely – even as it made 176 management and monitoring recommendations to mitigate ecological and socio-economic effects – the panel's recommendations paid no heed to "the moral or metaphysical effects of such a large industrial project on Dene lands or communities" (pp. xxiii, 171).

On this point Dokis is uncompromising. Although much is made of efforts to encourage Indigenous participation in resource decision-making processes, she insists that these processes serve, in practice, to reinforce existing structures of power among corporate interests, Indigenous peoples, and the state by staging the appearance of participatory decision making even as they fail to seriously consider diverse ontological, cosmological, epistemological, and cultural differences. Because even the most well intentioned of bureaucrats and managers operate within a system that is deeply committed to such ingrained "Western" ideas as the primacy of the market, the commodification of land, the importance of progress, and the dominance of humans over nature, things could hardly be otherwise. In this light, community hearings become cultural performances of a standardized, technocratic, easily replicated sort, based on Euro-Canadian ideas about truth, knowledge, property, and evidence, that reduce the "general metaphysics" (p. 168) of Indigenous people to "stories" that are included in transcripts, but largely ignored in resource management and decision-making processes.

There is much more, in the pages that follow, elaborating upon Sahtu Dene conceptions of the world and their place in it, making clear the complications involved in efforts at cooperative resource management when ideas of knowledge and truth, and about appropriate forms of decision making and governance, prove incommensurable, and revealing how deep-seated cultural commitments to generosity and sharing can make it very difficult for Indigenous people to voice dissent, especially in settings in which unfamiliar forms of technical and legal discourse predominate. Indeed, one of the most disturbing points of Dokis's analysis may be her contention that whatever its form, and whatever position individuals might take with regard to a proposed project, the participation of Indigenous people in environmental hearings is generally taken by project proponents as evidence of "consent" for the proposal. How poignant, then, one elder's reflection that "we Dene always say yes – even if we want to say no, we say yes because we do not want to be disrespectful" (p. 58).

Market conditions in 2015 have stalled development of the Mackenzie Gas Project, but *Where the Rivers Meet* remains highly pertinent to Canadians in the second decade of the new millennium. Although this book deals specifically with the Mackenzie Gas Project and the particular circumstances and beliefs of the Sahtu Dene, its basic arguments are relevant far beyond Canada's territorial North. Dokis's thoughtful assessment and critique of participatory resource management and environmental impact assessment processes – especially as these involve First Nations people – go to the heart of debates about the expansion of hydrocarbon production (be that in the manufacture of shale gas or the extraction of bitumen), and the construction of pipelines (Northern Gateway, Transmountain, Energy East, Keystone XL, or various projected gas lines) to move the products to market. Provincial and federal politicians may insist that "Canada's economic future rests in energy development and megaprojects, such as pipelines out of Alberta and liquefied natural gas terminals in B.C.," but the important message of *Where the Rivers Meet* is that the effects of such projects are not only economic or political or environmental but also profoundly moral matters.[40] That is to say – as Dokis reminds us – they involve questions about what is valuable and meaningful, consideration for the preferred modes of living of different groups within the country, and thoughtfulness about how persons and environments should be treated.

In one of the most cogent and far reaching of her critiques of the "participatory management industry," Dokis argues that thirty years of Indigenous participation in impact assessment hearings and co-management projects have been something of a charade, in the sense and to the extent that final decision-making authority has remained with the state. Drawing upon the work of political scientist Stephanie Irlbacher-Fox and Jürgen Habermas, she insists that the appearance of participation, sustained by the grant of certain non-fundamental concessions to Native peoples, has served to maintain constitutional authority and avoid a crisis of legitimation for the Canadian state. Just as Irlbacher-Fox sees land claim settlements as "symbolic" because they return only small fractions of land, resources, and authority to Indigenous people, and "to a great extent cement rather than change the fundamental" subordinate-dominant relationship between them and the state, Dokis suggests that eliciting the participation of Native peoples in environmental management helps to extend the state's efforts to rule and transform Native lives, even as it purports to hear what Native voices have to say.[41]

Following Habermas, Dokis would argue, further, that "the arrangement of formal democratic institutions and procedures permits administrative decisions to be made largely independently of specific motives of the citizens" by fostering a "diffuse mass loyalty," that – others have suggested – can be produced by such activities as impact assessments turned to envisioning a certain kind of accepted, low-risk future.[42] In this view, the illusion of participation has co-opted – and frustrated – Native peoples as it has furthered the commodification of lands and lives. Money talks, and Dokis would argue, following political scientist George Stetson, that it speaks in the language of "coloniality" – a logical structure of domination that turns on the imposition of Eurocentric conceptions of knowledge and improvement that devalue and undermine other ways of knowing and being.[43]

And here we confront, again and finally, the paradoxical implications of the trajectory traced in this Foreword and discussed in *Where the Rivers Meet*. Whatever good intentions might be ascribed to the implementation and development of participatory praxis, it is increasingly found wanting by Aboriginal people themselves. Years of state-sanctioned endeavours that purport to build solidarity between Indigenous and newcomer Canadians – such as including Native participation in Eurocentric processes of co-management – and arguments (advanced by non-Indigenous intellectuals sympathetic to the Native cause) that improvements in the democratic process, and the wisdom of the courts, can provide a path to civic solidarity between Indigenous and non-Indigenous peoples in Canada, are treated with ever more suspicion, if not disdain, by leading Indigenous thinkers.

Even if – as John Ralston Saul argued recently and hopefully – such avenues give Aboriginal peoples the capacity to shape "not just how Canada functions or will function, but how Canada imagines itself," and can help shift the relationship between newcomers and Natives from paternalism toward equality, this is no longer enough.[44] Echoing the anthropologist Michael Asch, who would invert the position espoused in law – that the purpose of constitutional rights afforded Aboriginals is to reconcile the prior existence of their societies with the sovereignty of the Crown – to argue that "it is the question of how the Crown gained sovereignty that requires reconciliation with the pre-existence of indigenous societies," a small but growing number of Indigenous intellectuals are "rejecting the colonial politics of recognition" in favour of a new politics of refusal.[45] Sometimes characterized as Indigenous resurgence, this emerging movement would radically recast Canadian society. Only a "massive transformation" of the underlying liberal capitalist assumptions of settler colonialism, says Dene political scientist Glen Coulthard, can prevent the "perpetual exploitation" of Native lands and peoples.[46] Or as Hayden King and Shiri Pasternak put it, in an important recent reflection on these matters, proponents of resurgence believe that the relationship between settlers and indigenes in Canada can truly be fixed only by reorienting "the political economy away from the mythologies of liberal capitalism toward a more sustainable and just economic and social system," by envisaging the country "as home to multiple sovereignties and jurisdictions of indigenous nations and legal orders," and by "committing to a redistribution of land, resources and power."[47]

Preface

THE FIRST TIME I saw the Sahtu region of the Northwest Territories was in March 2006, from the window of a Canadian North Airlines plane. I had caught the early morning flight from Edmonton to Yellowknife, and from there I changed planes and flew northward into the territory of the Sahtu Dene. Looking out the window, I saw vast expanses of treed lands and an astonishingly large number of lakes and waterways. The land was still frozen, even in March, and it seemed silent and still except for the occasional animal tracks that became apparent whenever we flew lower. As we approached Norman Wells, the trees became smaller and sparse. A few cutlines, the Enbridge Pipeline right-of-way, and the winter road were visible, but the land remained mostly unmarked by industrialization.

I had come to the Sahtu as a researcher interested in the input of community members in the assessment and regulation of a proposed 1,220-kilometre natural gas pipeline and related infrastructure collectively termed the Mackenzie Gas Project (MGP). My interest had begun years earlier while I was working as a research consultant in Alberta. I had learned that proponents of the pipeline and various government agencies had been engaged in Aboriginal community consultations in the Northwest Territories and had encountered both positive and negative responses there.[1] Yet, despite investing a great deal of time and money in Aboriginal community engagement, they continued to experience complications in consultation processes. I wanted to understand why. In Canada's urban South, the media regularly claimed that Aboriginal groups in the Northwest

Territories fell into two camps concerning the proposed pipeline: those who saw it as a business opportunity and a chance to profit financially, and those who feared its impact on the traditional lifestyle and were thus adamantly opposed to it. Unsatisfied with this simplistic account, I wanted to undertake a systematic analysis of local perspectives regarding the pipeline: What were local people really saying? Would their contributions be appropriately considered by decision-makers? How had the Berger Inquiry, which dealt with a mid-1970s pipeline proposal for the Mackenzie Valley, contributed to the assessment of the current project, and why was the dream of building a pipeline through the Canadian North different this time around? So, in March 2006 I began nine months of fieldwork in the Sahtu, which, along with fieldwork conducted in Calgary and Yellowknife, forms the basis of this book. As it turned out, the dynamics surrounding the pipeline decision were more complex than I could possibly have anticipated as I flew over the Sahtu on that sunny day in 2006.

This book examines the ways in which three Aboriginal communities in the Sahtu participate in decisions and activities related to non-renewable resource extraction on their lands. In particular, it focuses on the Mackenzie Gas Project, one of the largest industrial undertakings ever proposed for the Canadian North. Although the North has seen extensive oil and gas *exploration,* including over 170 test wells in the Mackenzie Delta, another 70 in the south Beaufort Sea, and further instances in the Arctic Islands and central Mackenzie Valley (Fast, Mathias, and Banias 2001), actual production has been very limited, due to marketing, transportation, logistical, and other constraints (Zavitz 1997).[2] Drilling through ice, conveying supplies and personnel to exploration sites, and shipping oil and gas to market are just a few of the challenges. In addition, there is still no licensed means to transport gas to southern markets. Thus, future production is likely to hinge on the approval and construction of the MGP or something like it.

The pipeline has been touted as the principal means of opening up Canada's northern energy frontier, not only because it has the capacity to transport current supplies of natural gas, but also because of its potential to convey gas from future exploration and production. As part owners of the pipeline, Aboriginal regional economic development corporations stand to benefit significantly from the associated capital payments and jobs. Nonetheless, the pipeline, and the cumulative effects of oil and gas activities that would probably accompany it, would bring significant changes to the very nature and culture of Sahtu communities. In 2006-07, people from across the Sahtu were given the opportunity to voice their positions regarding the pipeline at one of the largest and most complicated environmental impact assessment and regulatory reviews in Canadian history. Many were profoundly apprehensive about industrial impacts and the potential transition to a hydrocarbon-based economy, but they were also greatly concerned about identity and what it means to be a good human being.

In this book, I address the conditions under which Sahtu Dene participate in hydrocarbon decision making, and I critique some of the assumptions inherent in the regulatory, environmental assessment, and consultative processes that exist in the Canadian North. My general argument is this: although Sahtu Dene involvement in resource decision making has significantly increased, it is limited by non-local epistemological and ontological underpinnings of governance, management, regulatory, and environmental assessment institutions and practices. Indeed, these have come to reinforce the power relationships between corporate proponents, Aboriginal communities, and the state. This is achieved by staging the appearance of participatory decision-making avenues, while failing to seriously consider diverse ontological, cosmological, epistemological, and cultural differences. Basing processes in non-Dene metaphysics, knowledge, norms, and political systems requires Sahtu Dene contributors to participate in ways that are incommensurable with how they see themselves and the world around them.

For Sahtu Dene participants, the challenge is not solely to make their voices heard, but more importantly, to have them understood. This book aims to understand the ways in which Sahtu Dene people engage in the consultation, regulatory, governance, and environmental assessment processes surrounding proposed extractive industries, specifically in the context of participatory processes. It analyzes how they construct discourses regarding the impact of non-renewable resource extraction and how these are translated into multi-regional environmental assessment regimes. The intention is not to dissect people's personal motives for participation, either Dene or non-Dene, as these are often shifting and difficult to gauge. Nor do I attempt a detailed accounting of government bureaucrats and industry representatives' experiences and attempts at meaningful engagement, however laudable these may be. Rather, the point is to provide a space for Dene voices and experiences of environmental management and resource decision making, and to reveal how Sahtu Dene participation in these processes is limited *despite* the good intentions of those involved in administering them. In other words, I argue that current environmental assessment and co-management regimes are frustrated precisely because they fail to appropriately consider Sahtu Dene metaphysics, even when they are conducted by well-intentioned bureaucrats and managers. This is so because the regimes themselves are deeply rooted in the beliefs of Western industrialism, the commodification of land, the eventual triumph of the market over other ways of making a living, and the dominance of humans over nature.

The title of this book, *Where the Rivers Meet,* is the English translation of a Dene place name and community in which I conducted field research, but it also symbolizes the process of building a pipeline through the heart of the Mackenzie Valley. Flowing south toward Canadian and American consumers like a constructed river of steel, the pipeline will meet with the ancient Mackenzie and other rivers; the machines, workers, roads, and rights-of-way used during its construction will meet with Dene hunters, trappers, mothers, and grandmothers as they go about their daily lives; and throughout the environmental assessment processes, two ways of knowing and communicating knowledge met in community halls and boardrooms throughout the Northwest Territories, as people presented their visions for the future of the land.

Though some of the issues raised in this book may be unique to the Northwest Territories, many of its conclusions apply in other contexts, such as the assessment and management of the Alberta tar sands, the Northern Gateway Pipeline from the tar sands to the BC coast, and the evaluation of the proposed Keystone Pipeline project. In these cases, too, the effects of large oil and gas pipelines are not only of economic, environmental, or political concern, but also invoke ethical questions involving what is valuable and meaningful, what modes of living are preferred, and ultimately, how people and environments ought to be treated.

Scholars and policy makers alike are becoming increasingly interested in how Aboriginal communities in the Canadian North are affected by oil and gas activity, and in how Indigenous communities are participating in decision-making processes concerning resource development.[3] A growing literature is demonstrating that participation in decisions about resource and land use is framed by very specific cultural practices and that the evaluation and management of industrial impacts occur through the lens of culture. I hope that this book contributes to it. The assessment of the MGP has put the attempted integration of distinct cultural worlds, and the co-management and regulatory institutions mandated to incorporate them, to their ultimate test, and the stakes have never been higher for everyone involved.

Acknowledgments

I WOULD LIKE TO thank the people of Déline, Tulit'a, and Colville Lake for their generosity and hospitality during my stay with them, and for their willingness to so patiently and graciously share their knowledge and experience with me. I especially thank Marie and Hyacinth Kochon, Cathie Menacho, and Morris and Bernice Neyelle for opening their homes and lives to me. Thank you also to Larry and Carla at the Rayuka Inn in Norman Wells for taking me to and from the airport, and for offering me student rates during my stays. This work would not have been possible without the knowledge and experience shared by Leroy Andre, Frank Andrew, Leon Andrew, Collin Bayah, Danny Bayah, Walter Bayah, Clarence Campbell, Bobby Clement, Marty-Ann Kenny, Joseph Kochon, Richard Kochon, Wilbert Menacho, Charlie Neyelle, Jonas Neyelle, Rocky Norwegian, Gene Ouzi, Ed Reeves, Carl Yakelaya, and Alvin Yalle. Irene Betsidia's insight and skills were invaluable during my field research, and her gentle advice and support were always appreciated. I am grateful to Les Baton, Gloria Gaudet, Barry Gully, and Morris Mendo for their kindness and friendship throughout my stay in the Sahtu. It was an honour to spend time with those of you in the Sahtu.

Research funding was provided by the Canadian Circumpolar Institute C/BAR and the Indian and Northern Affairs Canada Northern Scientific Training Program grants, the Richard F. Salisbury Student Award, the International Association for Impact Assessment Western and Northern Canada Graduate Scholarship, a Doctoral Scholarship and Postdoctoral Fellowship from the Social Sciences and Humanities Research Council of

Canada, the Izaak Walton Killam Memorial Scholarship, and the Aboriginal Voice in Environmental Impact Assessment project funded through ArcticNet. I would like to thank Douglas Rae of Rae and Company for his support and advice, and for the "lift" from Colville Lake. Thank you to Thom Stubbs at Integrated Environments for his advice and reference material. Thank you also to David Livingstone at the Department of Indian Affairs and Northern Development Renewable Resources and the Environment in Yellowknife for his support of this project.

This work would not have been possible without the thoughtful guidance of Andie Palmer; I very much appreciate her professional and personal support throughout its journey. The experience and advice of Christopher Fletcher were invaluable, and I owe him a special thank you for his assistance in my field research. Mark Nuttall graciously offered his expertise in the area of northern studies, particularly in connection with resource development. A special thank you goes to Jean DeBernardi, Naomi Krogman, and Colin Scott for their valuable feedback. I would like to thank the Canadian Circumpolar Institute, and particularly Elaine Maloney, for its continued support of this project, and the staff at the Department of Anthropology at the University of Alberta, especially Liz Jobagy, Gail Mathew, and Joanne McKinnon. I would also like to thank Randy Schmidt and Ann Macklem at UBC Press for their dedication to seeing this book to press, and Deborah Kerr for her careful attention to the text. I am very grateful to the two anonymous reviewers whose insights and direction were extremely helpful in revising this work for publication.

My work benefitted from discussions with colleagues, including Greg Brown, Aaron Denham, Terry Dokis, Khosrow Farahbakhsh, Kirsten Greer, David Hackett, Benjamin Kelly, Arthur Mason, Jason McCullough, James Murton, Catherine Murton-Stoehr, Christine Schreyer, Trevor Smith, Maurice Switzer, Dan Walters, Clinton Westman, and David Zarifa. Their encouragement and friendship mean a great deal to me. Dean Bavington was instrumental in assisting me to clarify my overall argument, and his support and mentorship helped make this book possible.

My parents, Darlene and Marcus McLafferty, and my sister, Lindsey Shaw, have always urged me to follow my dreams, and I thank them for providing the guidance and opportunities that allowed me to undertake this project. Thank you to Buck and Pat Dokis for their continued love and friendship. My husband, Doug, was an incredible source of support, and I thank him for his patience and his encouragement throughout my travels and writing. Finally, I thank our children, Elijah, Miishi, and Nahanni, for providing the inspiration to finish this book.

Abbreviations

ABA	Access and benefits agreement
ANCSA	Alaska Native Claims Settlement Act
APG	Aboriginal Pipeline Group
EA	Environmental assessment
EIS	Environmental impact statement
GNWT	Government of the Northwest Territories
IGC	Inuvialuit Game Council
INAC	Indian and Northern Affairs Canada
JRP	Joint Review Panel for the Mackenzie Gas Project
MACA	Municipal and Community Affairs (Government of the Northwest Territories)
MGP	Mackenzie Gas Project
MVEIRB	Mackenzie Valley Environmental Impact Review Board
MVRMA	Mackenzie Valley Resource Management Act
NEB	National Energy Board
SDO	Sahtu Designated Organization
SLWB	Sahtu Land and Water Board
SSA	Sahtu Settlement Area
SSI	Sahtu Secretariat Incorporated
VEC	Valued ecosystem component

Where the Rivers Meet

People, Land, and Pipelines

As far back as I can remember, my ancestors have lived off of this land. It is still like that today. When we think about the pipeline we have to think about what it is going to do. We have to say something because we live off of our own land. It is our money, our food. It is who we are.

— *Dene elder, author interview, 16 September 2006*

SINCE TIME IMMEMORIAL, the Sahtu region of the Northwest Territories has been known as a rich land. Although many people imagine Canada's western Subarctic as desolate and inhospitable, the Sahtu has provided a good living for the Indigenous peoples that make it their home. After Alexander Mackenzie's 1789 expedition down the river that now bears his name in cartographic records, European merchants and traders fashioned a vision of northern prosperity that was based on fur. By the twentieth century, with fur prices declining, new commodities were sought in the oil, gas, and mineral deposits of the area. In the face of these colonial incursions, the Sahtu Dene continue to draw sustenance from their lands and to teach their young people the stories, skills, and knowledge of the elders. They have remained fundamentally engaged with a landscape that they understand as a means of survival, a principal source of identity, and a web of social and kinship relations in which human beings are merely one part.

In the 1970s, when a natural gas pipeline was first proposed to run from the Yukon through the Mackenzie Valley, the issue of Aboriginal title to the land had not yet been resolved, and there was no formalized means for Aboriginal people to participate in institutional decisions regarding the use of land and resources. Now, however, newly implemented land claim agreements have established resource co-management regimes and cooperative decision-making bodies that are intended to give Aboriginal peoples a place at the table. This form of participatory management, first heralded by Justice Thomas Berger in his famous inquiry, has become a hallmark of Canadian environmental management and has been praised, studied, and emulated in Canada and around the globe.

Leading a one-man inquiry from 1974 to 1977, Justice Berger held hearings in the ballrooms of Yellowknife hotels, at community centres across the North, at fishlakes and cabins, and along traplines, listening as northerners spoke about the proposed pipeline. Locals recall that, while flying over the vast expanse of trees and lakes, he spotted a Dene man at his trapline. He had the bush pilot land on the nearest lake so that he could have tea with the man and hear what he had to say. Berger's words at the community hearings in Déline (then called Fort Franklin) were emblematic of his mandate and of the seriousness with which he approached it:

> I want you, the people who live here, who make the North your home, to tell me what you would say to the government of Canada, if you could tell them what was in your minds. I want to hear from anyone who wishes to speak, because you have the right to speak, to tell me what you think this proposed pipeline will mean to you, to your family, and to your life. I am here to listen to you.[1]

Indeed, the inquiry was well received by many in the North, and Berger's patient demeanour and ability to listen won their trust. Dene from across the Sahtu and throughout the North came to talk to Berger and to tell him strongly that they did not want a pipeline through their lands; his published report (Berger 1977) reflected their sentiments, recommending that no pipeline be built through the Mackenzie Valley until Ottawa and the Dene could settle the issue of Aboriginal title to the land. There was a general feeling that local voices had been heard and that Berger's recommendations would encourage the establishment of a land claim in the region.[2]

Some thirty years later, many comprehensive land claim agreements had been reached in the Northwest Territories, and another participatory process was in place in the form of resource co-management. Though patterned after the Berger hearings, this process nonetheless differs fantastically from it. Now the hearings are technical; the "listeners" include many people, who are accompanied by an entourage of technicians, lawyers, transcribers, and experts. The casual approach – dropping in to someone's trapline to chat over tea – is a thing of the past. The process has become standardized, repeatable, technocratic, and quantifiable – in other words, "scientific." At the same time, the staunch resistance to the pipeline that Dene participants voiced so loudly at the Berger hearings was somehow, with this new process, translated into consent. How has this happened? In just three decades, how is it that fundamentally political statements about sovereignty and the right to decide the fate of the land have been channelled into anti-political murmurs about costs and benefits?[3] This book examines how the promise of the Berger Inquiry was transformed to become the reality of bureaucratic power and governmentality. It examines how law, and the hearings and inquiries that serve as its bedfellows, enabled participatory processes to become the handmaidens of the state.

LEGITIMATION OF THE PARTICIPATORY MANAGEMENT INDUSTRY

Participatory models of natural resource management have been emphasized in the Canadian North for some time. Aboriginal involvement in decisions related to lands and resources has been secured through jurisprudence and recently created co-management structures established as part of comprehensive land claims. Through this complex constellation of co-management boards, land corporations, quasi-judicial regulatory bodies, and government agencies, local people are expected to have an increased say in the decisions that affect their land and their lives. Yet to a large extent, they are limited to an advisory role (as are the various boards that conduct the participatory process), and final authority for resource development lies beyond local or even regional jurisdictions. In other words, the state will determine whether the Mackenzie pipeline and other pipelines will be built, though certain non-essential concessions may be offered to maintain institutional legitimacy.[4] I argue in this book that the legitimation of that authority is achieved by the appearance of public participation in the decision-making process.

It is true that, during the past thirty years, Canada has made much progress in entrenching Aboriginal land and treaty rights in its jurisprudence and national consciousness. In *Tsilhqot'in Nation v. British Columbia* (2014 at paras. 73 and 76), the Supreme Court held that Aboriginal title includes "the exclusive right to decide how the land is used and the right to benefit from those uses" and that "governments and others seeking to use the land must obtain consent of the Aboriginal title holders." However, this process has occurred only partially in Canadian law, as evident in

R. v. Sparrow (1990), *Taku River Tlingit First Nation v. British Columbia* (2004), and *Tsilhqot'in Nation* (2014). These rulings assert that constitutionally protected Aboriginal rights can be infringed as long as doing so meets a test for justification. For example, though the *Tsilhqot'in* decision outlines that the Crown must obtain consent from title-holding groups, it also finds that the Crown can undertake actions that intrude on the titled land if it "is backed by a compelling and substantial legislative objective in the public interest" (ibid. at para. 125). Thus, though the rights are accorded legal priority (are constitutionally protected), they can nonetheless be overstepped if, for example, the infringement is deemed to be in the national interest. This has significant consequences for Aboriginal people, particularly when their rights conflict with projects that the state perceives as necessary for economic development.

Prior to the mid-1970s, government and industry did little to incorporate Aboriginal perspectives into decisions regarding natural resources. For example, the James Bay Hydroelectric Project, which helped galvanize Canada's first modern land claim settlement, was announced in 1971 without consulting the James Bay Cree or the Inuit of Quebec (Mulrennan and Scott 2005). In addition, the legal duty to consult with Aboriginal peoples regarding land use and development was not established until *Sparrow*, which the Supreme Court of Canada heard in 1990. Indeed, the use of coercive state power to restrict Aboriginal involvement in resource decision making was ubiquitous in the form of imposed institutions of governance, refusal to negotiate land claim and self-government agreements, and limited state-sanctioned avenues for Aboriginal political participation (in reality, of course, Aboriginal groups did maintain some control of local resources, even if it was opaque and resistive in nature). Nonetheless, Aboriginal people continued to oppose development projects that eroded their territories, and their political organization increased throughout North America, as did international attention to Indigenous and human rights. As a result, by the mid-1970s the Canadian public no longer saw outright appropriation of Indigenous lands as an acceptable option for large multinational developers acting in partnership with the federal government. In short, the state was faced with what philosopher and sociologist Jürgen Habermas has termed a legitimation crisis.

In liberal capitalist states, the competitiveness of the domestic economy is ensured, to a large extent, by political means that, as Habermas (1975, 21) suggests, serve "to maintain the general conditions of production which make possible market regulated sustainability and expansion." In writing on public involvement in liberal capitalist will-formation, Habermas has argued that social integration is threatened when members of a society experience changes that are intolerable or incompatible with normative structures and goal values; he calls this a legitimation crisis. In the event of such a crisis, the coupling of the economic and political roles of the state is realized as an essential contradiction in the social system. That is, liberal capitalist societies are predicated on dual expectations – that some form of participatory democracy will be supported by the consent of the people and will be independent of capitalist production, and that the state will play a substantial role in expanding production and regulating markets. If social integration and mass loyalty are to be retained when the crisis arises, governing institutions must be legitimated through a political compromise in which the state gives the appearance that institutions and procedures are participatory but can also exercise sovereign administrative decisions independently of the participatory process to fulfill its economic role. The legitimation crisis cannot be adequately defused by the political system on its own. This task falls to the institutions that symbolically represent the normative structures of society; here Habermas points to public hearings, expert judgments, and judicial decisions as a mechanism to secure mass loyalty.

Thus, in the mid-1970s, during the time of the Berger Inquiry, the Canadian state revised its approach to Aboriginal involvement in resource management. It increased avenues for Aboriginal political participation in the form of comprehensive land claims, beginning with the James Bay and Northern Quebec Agreement in 1975 and continuing throughout northern Canada until the present day. Many of these claims include provisions for resource co-management and amplified Aboriginal community input via both institutions born out of land claims and consultation with Aboriginal communities in the form of public hearings. In the legal realm, Canadian jurisprudence, adapted through case law precedent, has increasingly invoked higher standards in the way in which governments and industry consider Aboriginal land and treaty rights in development decisions. For example, the *Haida Nation v. British Columbia* (2004) decision applied not only to lands covered by claims or treaties, but also to situations in which Aboriginal rights could potentially be infringed or a land claim could be adversely affected before it had been settled. All of this seems like a mighty step forward.

Yet in trying to mitigate its legitimation crisis, Ottawa has been reluctant to transfer any real resource decision-making authority to Aboriginal governments or cooperative bodies. For example, the Joint Review Panel (JRP) that was mandated in 2004 to consider the social, cultural, and

environmental impact of the Mackenzie Gas Project (MGP) was limited
to providing recommendations to the bodies that ultimately made the real
decisions. So, though the panel devoted almost two years to conducting
hearings in which northerners spoke about how a pipeline would affect
their lands and their lives, the government was not legally required to
accept or implement its report. It was at liberty to adopt some or all of
the JRP recommendations, send them back to the panel for "further
consideration," or reject them outright. The outcome of the proposed
Enbridge Northern Gateway Pipeline, which would carry bitumen from
the Alberta tar sands to the BC coast for shipment to Asian markets, will
be decided in the same manner.

In *Finding Dahshaa: Self-Government, Social Suffering, and Aboriginal
Policy in Canada,* Stephanie Irlbacher-Fox (2009, 7) argues that the negotiation of comprehensive land claims and self-government agreements in
the Northwest Territories represents a symbolic, rather than a substantive,
change in the devolution of authority to Aboriginal organizations and
governments. In her words, "Land claims can be viewed as symbolic: they
are settlements that return small fractions of lands, resources, and authorities to Indigenous peoples, and in that sense the settlements to a great
extent cement rather than change the fundamental dominant-subordinate
relationship between the state and Indigenous people." Irlbacher-Fox sees
the negotiation of claims and agreements as a move by the federal government to provide self-management opportunities that do not profoundly
reconfigure its oppressive policies regarding Aboriginal people. In a compelling example, she demonstrates that Aboriginal policy decisions are
often rooted in the assumption that Indigenous peoples must adapt to
contemporary conditions; they must "modernize" and "develop" to escape
what policy makers describe as pathologic circumstances. As Irlbacher-Fox
(ibid., 2) shows, this has significant consequences: by "positioning both
Indigenous peoples and the injustices that they suffer as non-modern and
historical, and itself as a source of social, political and material redemption,
the state manages to legitimize both injustice and its ongoing colonial-
based interventions into the lives of Indigenous people." In other words,
by characterizing Aboriginal communities as underdeveloped and in need
of modernization, the state simultaneously legitimizes its continued intervention in Aboriginal lives, obfuscates its role in the historical and contemporary oppression of local institutions and knowledge, and effectively
silences Aboriginal visions for the future.

Undeniably, specialists and experts still evaluate and transform vast
domains of daily life for northerners. The role of expert judgments and

technocratic artifacts is certainly paramount in identifying and assessing the impacts of industrial projects. The creation of new co-management boards and regulatory processes has developed into a resource management industry in the Canadian North, employing hundreds of consultants, lawyers, and experts. These "experts," and the complex apparatus and forms of discourse in which they are situated, typically subscribe to certain paradigms of thought and associated values, such as the trust placed in science and the perceived benefits of industrial development.

Even when Aboriginal people do participate in cooperative decision-making bodies, their concerns are typically reinterpreted in the language of these new institutions, and judgments are often rendered in these terms. Thus, events such as community hearings can be seen as cultural performances that reveal as much about Western conceptions of land, property, and contractual relations, and the values associated with economic development, as they do about Dene values concerning land use and relations to the environment. As legal scholar Sally Engle Merry (1991, 892) points out in an essay on law and colonialism, these cultural performances often provide authoritative interpretations of people's life situations as "everyday events and relationships are named and defined," and events are given meaning through a formalized and ritualized setting. In this way, eliciting Aboriginal participation in environmental management can be seen as an endeavour to rule and transform, even if it is done with the aim of "hearing" what Aboriginal people have to say.

Anthropologist Scott Rushforth (1994, 339) observes that Sahtu Dene people are often skeptical of non-local "expert" knowledge of the Subarctic because it is accompanied by "widespread lack of personal experience in the north." In many cases, decisions regarding resource development are based on the evaluations and recommendations of individuals in the resource management industry, rather than local people. Furthermore, expert judgments limit the ability of other types of knowledge and knowledge expression to form a basis of critique or truth making. If we recognize that technocratic artifacts such as environmental impact statements are privileged forms of truth, we can consider them as one of many narratives, told alongside those of local people, about the effects of industrial development on local lives and communities. For many Dene and other Athabaskan peoples, knowledge acquired through experience (Rushforth 1992), through generations of living on the land (Brody 1981), through dreams and other mediums (Ridington 1990), and through the transmission of stories (Blondin 1990) is a valuable form of evidence. This book explores how local people who hold such knowledge, gained through generations of living in intimate relation with the land, participate in assessment processes that are constructed around very alien technocratic forms of evidence and rationality.

ENCOUNTERS AT THE INTERFACE

Most simply, the aim of regulatory and environmental assessment boards established as a result of comprehensive land claims is to integrate the perspectives and interests of federal and territorial governments with those of Aboriginal organizations, and to provide a mechanism through which Aboriginal people have an increased say in resource development and management. Several observers have cited the Mackenzie Valley regulatory process as one of the more successful examples of collaborative decision making, with clear requirements for Aboriginal participation as well as the integration of multiple forms of knowledge. Geographer Derek Armitage (2005, 246) argues that new environmental assessment practices in the Northwest Territories have moved away from their technical orientation to incorporate what he calls "double-loop" learning, or collaborative processes that have reconfigured government-driven environmental management and decision making. Julia Christensen and Miriam Grant (2007) go even farther to suggest that the inclusion of Indigenous knowledge and political representation in land management wrests power away from the federal realm into more localized sources, though they concede that Ottawa's authority impedes the genuine integration of local knowledge. Indeed, a major contribution of the regulatory regime in the Mackenzie Valley is the acceptance of evidence presented by community members at public hearings. Hearings are intended to encourage local participation in the assessment and regulation of proposed projects where public or community concern is deemed to exist. Yet, though hearings have certainly elicited Aboriginal input in the Northwest Territories, neither Armitage nor Christensen and Grant establish that they have increased local authority in resource decision making. Complications in the attempted integration of differing epistemological foundations, linguistic and conceptual translation, and ways of viewing the land have elsewhere given rise to serious questions concerning the extent to which institutionalized joint decision making (particularly when grounded in legalistic proceedings, technocratic discourses, and non-local assumptions about the nature of the world and the inevitability of industrialism) can ever truly reflect Aboriginal views, even where traditional and land-based knowledge is genuinely considered (see Nadasdy 2005; White 2006). For example, it has been well established that the intimate connection between Aboriginal people and their environment encompasses a host of cultural, spiritual, and cosmological relationships that are not easily translated into quantifiable techno-rational categories (Stevenson 1996; Ellis 2005). Julie Cruikshank (1995, 57), for instance, illustrates how stories, and the knowledge contained therein, provide a kind of "cultural scaffolding" through which people "interpret and connect a range of events that might otherwise seem unrelated." Similarly, legal discussions of Aboriginal rights, title, and governance typically rest in Euro-American discourses of property, ownership, and long-standing beliefs about human and societal development that may not coincide with Aboriginal views (see Venne 1997; Culhane 1998; Seed 2001).

Participation in resource decision making is not simply a matter of showing up for a hearing. It rests in deeply embedded ways of thinking about the world, in the constitution of community members' knowledge, and in ideas about appropriate human conduct. Resource decision-making forums offer what anthropologist Jean-Pierre Olivier de Sardan (2005), borrowing from Norman Long (1989), calls "encounters at the interface." These can enable a systematic analysis of the interactions between members of differing cultures, where "agents who not only have different resources, but also play the games according to different rules, confront each other" (Olivier de Sardan 2005, 102). At the same time, because community hearings also exist within relationships of power, they can provide a frame to analyze interactions between local people and representatives of abstract systems such as various levels of government with diverse organizational roles.

This book examines how participation in resource decision making is shaped by very specific cultural practices and the social construction and evaluation of the associated impacts. Indeed, local discourses regarding the impacts and benefits of non-renewable resource extraction do sometimes conflict with environmental assessments that attempt to predict the effects of large-scale industrial projects. In the Sahtu, this conflict exists even when newly created environmental assessment regimes, established under comprehensive land claim agreements, fall under the rubric of resource co-management.

As a result of their interaction with bureaucratic institutions under land claim agreements, and recent case law upholding Canada's fiduciary duty to consult with Aboriginal peoples regarding development decisions, the Sahtu Dene have had to adopt new and perhaps uncharacteristic ways of speaking, making decisions, and organizing to deal with corporations and government. Ways in which decisions are made, and how positions are taken on resource development, are influenced by multiple and complex factors that are neither wholly novel nor wholly traditional. This weaving of the traditional and the novel allows interaction between Aboriginal communities, government, and industry to be sites of creativity and contestation, continually redefining conceptions of knowledge, industrial impacts, rights, governances, and models of appropriate development. Yet all these redefinitions are negotiated on unequal fields of power. This book starts from these encounters, exploring their ideas about the harms and benefits of the proposed pipeline, their power struggles between local communities and trans-local corporations, and also their ingenious use by local people to assert their own conceptions of the world.

These days, resource development projects and their assessment and regulation are not simply imposed on Sahtu Dene people without their agreement. However, the projects and their associated regulatory and conceptual apparatuses have significant effects, not only ecologically but socially and politically as well. It is no longer the case (if it ever was) that everyone in the Sahtu is opposed to industrial development, and it is important to remember that the Sahtu Dene have been proponents of industrial projects on their own lands. The ways in which people manoeuvre the economic, social, and political opportunities and constraints available to them in the face of large-scale industrial projects form an important component of decisions about land use and resource extraction.

Nevertheless, some commonalities do exist in the participatory practices of Sahtu Dene people, and important relationships and fields of power are embedded in participatory structures, which I will discuss throughout this book. Statements made in the context of public participation processes contain multiple and shifting meanings that are rooted in particular histories, past events, experiences with the state, and cultural values. In other words, they are not only deeply felt articulations of concern regarding industrial impacts or struggles to influence power structures (though these are certainly evident as well), but they are also expressions about what it means to be Dene and to pursue a way of life that is good, fitting, and proper.

THE SAHTU

A majority of the Indigenous peoples living in the Mackenzie River Valley call themselves Dene, meaning "people" in the closely related Athabaskan

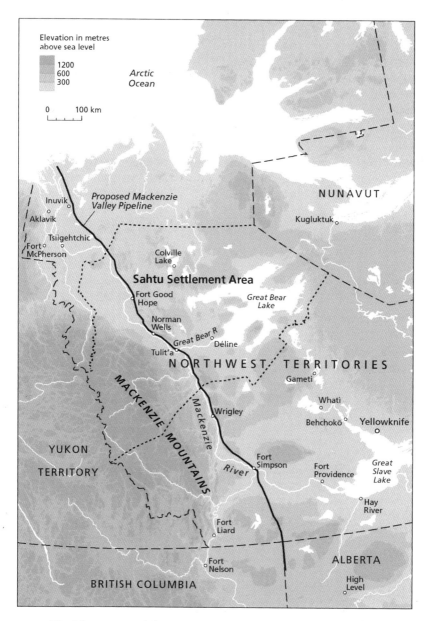

MAP I The Sahtu region and the proposed Mackenzie Valley Pipeline.
By Eric Leinberger

languages that are spoken up and down the river. The Dene have been living on these lands longer than anyone can remember; they argue that they have lived there since the beginning of the world. Their stories tell of how the world was created and of how human beings ought to conduct themselves to maintain the world as it is now. Their vast and intimate knowledge of their territory allows them to thrive in one of the coldest climates on Earth and to derive sustenance from the land.

For the past two hundred years, the Dene people of the Sahtu region have witnessed enormous changes in their landscape and their lives. As a result of the fur trade, an influx of non-Dene trappers and traders moved into their territory, and though most returned to the South after seeking their fortunes, some stayed, married, and settled in the region. They brought new goods, languages, and diseases, transforming Dene life in both positive and destructive ways. The Sahtu Dene have seen prospectors, oil companies, and miners invade their lands, and have witnessed the building of roads, pipelines, airstrips, and mine shafts to support their expansive projects. Most projects were undertaken without consultation with the Dene, and all were conducted without their consent.

What became known as the Sahtu Settlement Area (SSA) after the signing of the Sahtu Dene and Metis Comprehensive Land Claim Agreement in 1993 encompasses a large part of the central Mackenzie Valley, including Great Bear Lake, a section of the Mackenzie River, and part of the Mackenzie Mountains. Winter temperatures in the Sahtu can drop below −40 degrees Celsius. Winter is also remarkably dark, with mornings and evenings shrouded in twilight and only about three and a half hours of direct daylight. Conversely, summers are relatively bright, with almost twenty-four-hour light. Vegetation and ecozones vary in the Sahtu, but vegetation consists largely of black spruce, dwarf birch and willow, tamarack, cottongrass, lichen, moss, and some white spruce and the occasional aspen. The Sahtu has thirty watershed regions (Auld and Kershaw 2005, 37), with most waterways freezing by late November and breaking up again between May and July.

The Sahtu is home to the communities of Colville Lake, Déline, Fort Good Hope, Norman Wells, and Tulit'a, whose populations range from about 125 to 800. Except for Norman Wells, which was established largely as a result of oil fields operated by Imperial Oil, they are 91 percent or more Dene or Metis.[5] All are accessible by aircraft year-round. A daily flight links Norman Wells to Yellowknife, and air service from Norman Wells to the outlying communities is very regular: a flight goes to Déline, Tulit'a, and Fort Good Hope every day except Sunday, and the Colville

Lake flight goes on weekdays. The communities can also be reached by winter road from about the end of December to mid-April, and except for Colville Lake, they can be accessed by boat when the waterways are clear of ice.

Dene people in the Sahtu region have experienced the transition from life on the land, with perhaps intermittent visits to trading posts, to a life lived mostly in permanent communities. They can now buy their food in the Northern Store (though it can be prohibitively expensive), they can get *American Idol, Deal or No Deal,* and all the other new shows on satellite television, and they can even access the Internet, though most do so at the band or land corporation office because many homes do not yet have high-speed service.[6] When I stayed with Sahtu families, I noticed that their teenagers listened to the same songs as teenagers in the South.

Like most Aboriginal communities in the Canadian North, those of the Sahtu are characterized by a mixed economy, in which basic needs are supplied through various sources including domestic production, wage labour, transfers, and tourism and other forms of private enterprise. Peter Elias (1997), who has written extensively on mixed economies in northern Aboriginal communities, notes that most Aboriginal people in the North continue to occupy and use their traditional territories, and that a land-based economy remains a fundamental component of their lives, despite predictions that it would eventually decline in importance. Hunting, fishing, trapping, and gathering help to offset the high cost of living in the North, but they also enable people to pass on vital elements of culture and identities (Asch 1984; Hunn 1999; Adelson 2000). As Rauna Kuokkanen (2011, 217) states about mixed economies elsewhere, "Indigenous economies such as household production and subsistence activities extend beyond the economic sphere: they are at the heart of who people are culturally and socially."

Yet, the very nature of a mixed economy means that household needs cannot be met through domestic production alone and that other economic sectors also play a vital role in generating income. The degree to which northern Aboriginal communities engage in differing economic sectors is quite varied (see Elias 1997), and some scholars have pointed out that due to the interrelated nature of mixed economies, separating distinct spheres of economic activity is often futile (Brody 1981). Claudia Notzke (1999), for example, has documented that the income generated in wage labour is often used to support land-based activities, and numerous studies show that many sectors in northern mixed economies are in fact mutually supportive (Usher 1982; Elias 1997). What is clear is that the domestic economy continues to contribute significantly to the diets and the social, cultural, and economic well-being of northern Aboriginal communities (see Berkes et al. 1994), in spite of predictions that it would be subsumed under capitalism. As Scott Rushforth (1977) notes about his work in the Sahtu in the 1970s, engaging in a resource-based capitalist economy was acceptable only after provisions for securing the domestic economy were accomplished. Some thirty years later, this remains largely true, as a Sahtu Dene person stated during an interview with me: "This will be the last place; we are happy with one another because we can go out and get fish, we can go out and get everything from the land. We do not need money. We cannot eat money."[7]

Although Sahtu Dene people maintain fundamental physical, social, and moral relationships with their land, they are likewise engaged in regional and global markets and forms of exchange that require participation in commodity markets and resource production. Since about 1996, they have experienced a significant increase in oil and gas activities in their territory. For many local people, the establishment of a hydrocarbon-based economy offers opportunities for direct and indirect employment, the procurement of business contracts and partnerships, and increased revenue via access and benefits agreements.[8] For others, however, it brings significant and irreversible changes in local lifeways, including the disruption of animal-human relationships and the ability to spend time on the land. This tension between protecting an ancient and valued subsistence way of life, and fostering a growing petro-economy exists both within and between people in the Sahtu, contributing to shifting community dynamics, governance structures, and new forms of power over nature and bodies.

Yet, even with these changes, Sahtu Dene people retain many distinctly Dene elements of their lives. This is despite intensified pressure by outside forces to gain access to their lands and for the Dene themselves to assimilate into so-called mainstream Canadian educational, religious, legal, economic, political, and social institutions. Since the first contact with those who came north in search of monetary gain, Dene people have struggled to preserve and defend the life that they want for themselves and their children, often in the face of great obstacles.

In most Sahtu communities, as in other northern mixed economies, the household, and to a lesser extent a network of households connected through kinship ties, is the basic unit of production and distribution. Anthropologist Michael Asch (1984, 19) recognizes the extended household as a means of retaining a band-oriented form of production that has mediated the "individualized, self-sufficient nuclear orientation of mainstream Canadian society." In the Sahtu, members of extended households engage to different degrees in domestic production and wage labour, depending on the opportunities available in the related economic spheres, each calling on the other to provide cash or food when needed; cash and food circulate freely within and between connected households. Although cash is required to pay bills and buy services, food, gas, clothing, and other supplies (including those to engage in harvesting), it is often less valued than resources obtained and circulated in the domestic economy. For example, locals often see saving cash as a futile exercise, one that demonstrates a lack of trust that the land and Creator will provide, and that runs contrary to ideas that people have of themselves as generous and giving. Excess cash, like products of domestic production, is redistributed throughout the community through borrowing, gifting, or bingo and card games, thus creating networks of responsibility and obligation. Spending money on games such as bingo or cards demonstrates not only generosity, but can provide evidence of medicine power if one should win. Resources obtained through hunting, fishing, gathering, or trapping are not often sold between members of extended households (though they are sold to tourists and short-term residents), but are traded for items of similar value or for assurances of reciprocity in the future.

I worked mostly in the communities of Déline, Tulit'a, and Colville Lake. Déline lies on the northwestern shore of Keith Arm, on Great Bear Lake, near the head of the Great Bear River. One of the largest communities in the Sahtu, it has a population of 524, of whom 495 identify as Aboriginal (Statistics Canada 2006). Its layout along the shoreline reflects the importance of the lake to its daily activities. In summer, people keep boats at the shoreline, and in the winter the frozen lake provides an effective roadway for both cars and snowmobiles. Although all Déline residents live in fairly modern housing, many maintain teepees or other shelters for smoking and preparing fish, meat, and hides. Most homes rely on diesel furnaces and woodstoves for heat. Native-language retention rates are high in Déline, with 95.8 percent of Dene residents reporting in 2004 that they spoke Slavey (GNWT 2010b) and 58.0 percent reporting that they spoke Slavey as their primary language at home (Statistics Canada 2006).

The main employment sectors in Déline are government, health, social services, and education, and during my fieldwork, the average personal income was about $30,754 (GNWT 2010b). The Déline Land Corporation owns the Grey Goose Lodge, located at the edge of town, which caters to the few tourists and fishermen who visit, and more often to government dignitaries and bureaucrats. Déline also has a few private businesses, such as a chip stand and general contractors. Its infrastructure includes an airstrip

On the shore of Great Bear Lake in Déline. This photograph shows homes and the Great Bear Co-op overlooking sheds and boats that hug the lakeshore.

Tulit'a in February. Looking out over the old church and houses on the bank of the Mackenzie River.

and small airport, a dump, a power generation station, government offices, post office, school, community hall, hockey arena, health centre, community dock, community learning centre, and an RCMP detachment. Twice a week, water is trucked in to holding tanks in private dwellings, and sewage is removed from holding tanks twice weekly as well. Déline has two grocery stores, the Northern Store and the Great Bear Co-op, both of which sell a variety of goods, including groceries, gear, supplies, and some clothing, all at high northern prices.

Tulit'a lies at the intersection of the Mackenzie and Great Bear Rivers. Meaning "where the rivers meet" in Slavey, it sits just beneath Bear Rock, a significant place in Dene oral history and teachings. Slightly smaller than Déline, it has a population of 505, 460 of whom identify as Aboriginal (Statistics Canada 2006). Again, its layout indicates the importance of the two rivers, and most of Tulit'a is built high on the bank of the Mackenzie. The Mackenzie Mountains are visible far to the west, an important harvesting area for the Mountain Dene. The Great Bear River provides fairly easy passage to Déline and Kelly Lake, Willow (Brackett) Lake, and Lennie Lake. In years past, Tulit'a served as a summer gathering place for Dene from all over Denendeh, a Slavey language term roughly translated to mean "our land" or "land of the Dene," with people travelling to meet in the fairly centralized location. Today, the winter road connects Tulit'a to Déline, Norman Wells, and Wrigley. Language retention in Tulit'a is not as high as in Déline, perhaps due to its long history of contact with Euro-Canadian traders on the Mackenzie River.

As in Déline, the main employment sectors at Tulit'a are government, health, social services, and education. However, Tulit'a has three general contracting and slashing companies who receive contracts to clear lands to make room for the operation of extractive industries, as well as some businesses, including Mackay Range Oilfield Services, that provide various services to oil and gas industries. The Tulit'a Hotel is owned by the Tulit'a Dene Band, and there is a privately owned bed and breakfast. At the time of my fieldwork, the average personal income was $33,045 (GNWT 2010c). The infrastructure in Tulit'a is the same as that of Déline, though there is no community dock, and the new school was built in 2007. As in Déline, water is trucked in and sewage is trucked out twice a week. The new Northern Store was completed in 2006, and though Tulit'a has no Co-op store, goods in its Northern Store tend to be slightly cheaper than in the Déline outlet.

The Tulit'a District has a long experience with oil and gas exploration and production, beginning with the Norman Wells oil field in 1921. After

Imperial Oil and the federal government signed the Norman Wells Proven Area Agreement in 1944, Imperial Oil attained the exclusive right to drill for petroleum and natural gas on the agreement lands; as a partner in the project, the federal government receives a percentage of the overall production. In 1985, Interprovincial Pipeline (now Enbridge) built a pipeline from Norman Wells to Zama, Alberta. Although Imperial Oil's field is located in and around Norman Wells, some seventy-two kilometres north of Tulit'a, the Sahtu Dene and Metis Comprehensive Land Claim Agreement places it within the Tulit'a District. In addition to Imperial Oil, several other companies have been active near Tulit'a, including Husky Oil, International Frontier, Northrock Resources, and EnCana Corporation. Husky's (and Northrock's) Summit Creek activity has drilled several successful exploration wells, and the Summit Creek reserve, about fifty-five kilometres southwest of Tulit'a, is reported to be a significant discovery. In fact, in June 2011 Husky Oil paid a record high price of $376 million for two drilling licences near the Summit Creek reserve. Several mining prospecting companies are also active in the Mackenzie Mountains and downstream of Tulit'a at a location known by locals as the "smokes," a burning coal seam on the west side of·the river.

Many locals describe Colville Lake as the most "traditional" community in the Sahtu. Although it was not officially established until 1962, when Oblate missionary Bern Will Brown built a mission at the present-day townsite and several families moved there to re-establish a trapping economy, it has always been an important Dene fishing and ptarmigan-hunting site. Its Dene name, K'áhbamitué (ptarmigan net), reflects this fact. It is also the smallest community in the Sahtu, with a 2006 population of 126, 115 of whom identify as Aboriginal (Statistics Canada 2006). It nestles on a bay on the south side of the lake from which it takes its name, on a stretch of land that separates the lake from Lake Beloit. Much of it hugs the shoreline, again reflecting the importance of the lake as a travel route, for fishing, and for collecting water. Language retention in Colville Lake is less than in Déline but higher than in Tulit'a, with 65.3 percent of residents reporting that they speak Slavey (GNWT 2010a).

Land-locked and inaccessible by boat or barge, Colville Lake is one of the most isolated communities in the Northwest Territories. Food, fuel, and other supplies must either be flown in or transported via the winter road, which is open from late December until mid-April. Whereas most people now fly in and out of the community, they also travel by vehicle or occasionally by snowmobile on the winter road between Colville Lake and Fort Good Hope. Flying in and out of Colville Lake during the autumn

Colville Lake – the community docks, the church, and houses gathered on the shoreline, 12 October 2007.

is often problematic due to dense fog, produced because the two lakes, Colville and Beloit, are of unequal depths and therefore freeze at different times. Indeed, one late October I was scheduled to fly out on a Thursday but could not do so until the following Tuesday.

As in Déline and Tulit'a, the main employment sectors in Colville Lake are government, health, social services, and education. It has a small hotel that is owned and operated by Behdzi Ahda First Nation, and the late Bern Will Brown operated a lodge aimed at sports hunting and fishing. Some local people have managed to find seasonal oil- and gas-related work as environmental monitors or slashers on seismic lines – cutlines used in the exploration for oil and gas – and at drilling locations.

Colville Lake's infrastructure mirrors its size and location. The band and land corporation offices share a building, and a smaller structure houses the offices of the territorial government. An airport was built in 2012, and there is a small airstrip, a dump, power generation station, arena, learning centre, wireless Internet access, and a school. Bern Will Brown operated a small museum and a church, but these are seldom used by locals. Colville Lake has no police detachment, but RCMP officers use a small log cabin when they fly in from Fort Good Hope.

A striking feature of Colville Lake is its lack of water delivery or sewage removal services. Residents rely on the lake for all their water needs. Sewage is deposited in thick garbage bags that line toilets, are put out once a week for pickup by a band employee on ATV or skidoo, and then hauled to the dump. Many locals emphatically state that they prefer this system. As a community leader suggested during my interview with him, "It keeps us independent. If we rely on the government to get our water for us, then what else will we have to rely on them for? Besides," he added, "you are the only mola [Euro-Canadian] I know that would haul their own water, so it keeps our community Dene."[9]

Colville Lake's Co-op sells groceries and other supplies, and houses the post office. Due to its remoteness, groceries cost significantly more in Colville Lake than elsewhere in the Sahtu (in October 2007, I paid just over seventeen dollars for a one-litre bottle of water, a dozen eggs, and a can of Carnation condensed milk). Consequently, most residents depend heavily on meat, fish, and other items from the land to offset the high cost of groceries.

Like Tulit'a, Colville Lake has extensive experience with oil and gas activities. There are currently four gas fields in the Colville Hills, including Tweed Lake, Tedji Lake, Bele, and Nogha; additional exploration is under way at Turton and Tate Lakes. Petro Canada, Paramount Resources, Apache Canada, AEC West, Devlan Exploration, and Canadian Natural Resources Limited conduct exploration drilling in the area. Importantly, companies active near Colville Lake are exploring on both Crown lands and those where the subsurface rights are owned by the K'asho Got'ine District Land Corporation under the Sahtu Dene and Metis Comprehensive Land Claim Agreement. This means that the K'asho Got'ine District and thus Colville Lake could generate a substantial income from subsurface royalties, should any exploratory wells on Sahtu private lands come on-line. This places Colville Lake in the interesting position of having the highest percentage of residents who engage in hunting and trapping while at the same time standing to benefit the most from the establishment of pipeline infrastructure.

Indeed, the central Mackenzie Valley, along with the Mackenzie Delta and the Cameron Hills, has become a major area of interest for oil and gas ventures. Since 1996, the Sahtu has seen an increased interest in exploratory oil and gas activities, with the number of exploratory wells expanding from one in 1996-97 to a peak of seven in the 2003-04 drilling season (Indian and Northern Affairs Canada 2004). This reflects the belief that the Canadian North is a significant oil and gas basin, with the Northwest Territories, Nunavut, and the Arctic Islands estimated to hold 33 percent of the country's remaining conventional recoverable natural gas and 35 percent of the remaining recoverable light crude oil; approximately half of these reserves is thought to be in the Western Arctic (ibid., 8). However, as mentioned above, logistical, cost, and transportation challenges have limited oil and gas projects in the Canadian North. Exploration is a high-stakes endeavour, with company expenditures estimated at $184 million in 2004 alone (ibid., 17). And a return on this investment will not be realized until oil and gas can be shipped to southern markets.[10] Although investments in exploration and drilling remain dependent on world market prices for oil and gas, it is reasonable to predict that interest in the hydrocarbon resources of the Canadian North will remain high as long as market demand persists and particularly as more conventional reserves become depleted.

Conducting Research in the Sahtu: Learning to Hear Appropriately

I began my research in the Sahtu on a sunny day in March 2006. I had travelled to the region to attend a series of public hearings, which were held as part of the Joint Review Panel (JRP) environmental impact assessment. Getting to the Sahtu and finding affordable accommodation was not easy. With the help of a mentor who was also conducting work in Déline (and a little luck), I managed to book flights on the small airline that serviced the communities, and more importantly, to find families with whom I could stay. I would quickly learn that Sahtu people were tremendously generous, often graciously opening their homes to travellers, students, and researchers.

My primary instruction in learning to hear appropriately came from living with families in the host communities. I was very fortunate to be welcomed into the homes and lives of three gracious (and patient) households. I learned to hear via the everyday tasks of making meals and having tea, and through spending time with people on the land. For Sahtu Dene people, the land remains a significant source of dietary and economic subsistence, and cultivating its sustenance is also a vital part of what it means to be Dene. "Going out on the land" enables the intergenerational transmission of knowledge and skills as well as the preservation of cultural, community, and family ties. Indeed, spending time on the land, eating country foods, maintaining proper relationships with human and other-than-human dimensions of the landscape, and knowing how to work in the bush are strongly associated with Sahtu Dene conceptions of well-being.

Learning to hear was not always easy, especially at first, and it remained an ongoing exercise. It involved listening and taking seriously what people had to say in formal interviews, in conversations over tea, and in the context of their everyday lives. But it also involved witnessing their everyday engagement with each other and with their land. On one of my first days in Colville Lake, Thomas, a community leader and son of my host family, came by the house and said to me, "Well, if you are going to stay here, you better learn how to check fishnets."[11] Later that day, Thomas, his daughter, and I went out to check the nets, crossing the lake by snow-mobile. Though the temperature was –40 Celsius, Thomas removed his gloves, working confidently and proficiently as he pulled the nets and their contents to the surface. Having read several ethnographies about Colville Lake, I knew that touching fishnets and other items could be inappropriate for a woman, so I said, rather awkwardly, "Just let me know if I can be of any help." To which Thomas replied, "Well, you can take this stick and when I pull the fish out, you can hit them on the head with it until they are dead." Soon, I had managed to club nine whitefish and six trout to death with my stick. Thomas threw them into a sled that was attached to the snowmobile, and the fish and I went on a rather sloppy ride back to the village. On our return, Thomas looked at me, covered in fish guts, blood, and scales, and said, "Well, you did alright. You can stay. But if I find out you are with Greenpeace, I will kill you."[12] Thomas turned out to be one of my greatest teachers and friends.

In Déline, Tulit'a, and Colville Lake, working alongside various local agencies, I undertook research that was mutually beneficial to the communities and myself. In Déline, the leadership asked me to review the traditional knowledge studies that had been conducted for licensing and permitting processes. After doing so, I submitted a report to the Déline Land Corporation in October 2006, which outlined the current status and content of the studies and how they could be improved. In Tulit'a, a number of community agencies asked me to produce a semi-formal study on community perspectives regarding consultation processes, an analysis of how community members felt they might be bettered, and a community-driven consultation plan and protocol. In February 2007, I delivered a community consultation report and recommended consultation plan and protocol to the Dene and Metis land corporations in Tulit'a and to the Tulit'a Band Chief and Council. The Colville Lake leadership wished to use my preliminary research findings to support its final submission to the JRP hearings. After reviewing my findings with the community at large, I drafted a report for the Ayoni Keh Land Corporation and the Behdzi Ahda First Nation in October 2007, for incorporation into their JRP submission. My research was conducted in accordance with the Northwest Territories Scientists Act, and the Aurora Research Institute issued three Northwest Territories research licences for it (licences 14063, 14103, and 14250).

During my time in the Sahtu, I employed traditional anthropological research methodology in the form of participant observation, and I used a field journal to record detailed notes of my daily experiences, thoughts, observations, and conversations. In each community, I also conducted informal interviews with governing officials, elders, local land users, teachers, youth workers, members of resource management boards including renewable resource councils, and others. I interviewed both men and women to address any potential gendered experiences or perceptions of industrial impacts, and to gain a further understanding of the gendered nature of land use and the division of labour. Prior to the interview, I obtained informed consent from participants and asked whether I could record our conversation. Many people agreed to this, and they were given copies of the recording, as were their families on request. I also received permission from the local leadership to attend gatherings and meetings such as consultation sessions with oil and gas or mining companies, and other community decision-making forums. I was permitted to attend the September 2006 Sahtu Secretariat Incorporated General Assembly in Déline. Because many consultation sessions, access and benefits negotiations, and industry trade shows were held in Calgary or Edmonton, I often met and interviewed Sahtu people there. I commonly drove them to and from the airport, and I became very familiar with their preferred places to stay and eat in the "big city."

As part of this research, I attended all the JRP hearings held in the Sahtu in March and April 2006. I employ material from the hearings and my fieldwork to demonstrate Sahtu Dene experiences and expressions of the impact of non-renewable resource extraction, both locally and on a cumulative scale, and what Sahtu Dene people say about the way in which land use decisions should be made. Their statements, made during the JRP hearings, are contextualized against a background of local norms and expectations regarding how people come to know the things they know, how their knowledge comes to be regarded as true, how knowledge should be communicated to and considered by others, and how these variables intersect with current land use planning and environmental assessment institutional practices.

Because my research examines current environmental assessment, which employs very specific cultural practices in constructing and analyzing industrial impacts, I also engage Sahtu Dene environmental assessment discourses and explore the ways in which local experiences and expressions of industrial impacts reflect the complex physical, social, and moral relationships between the people and their land. My understanding of the relationship between Sahtu Dene people and their land, and of how they participate in environmental assessment processes, stems from witnessing what they do on the land: how they talk about their relationships with it in the context of everyday life and in the face of increased non-renewable resource extraction, and how these discourses can sometimes conflict with environmental assessments that attempt to predict the associated environmental effects. I ultimately argue that the present form of environmental impact assessment fails to appropriately consider Sahtu Dene perspectives of ecological and socio-cultural impacts, and that reconfiguring environmental impacts as sickness may have more relevance to the experiences of local people.

SAHTU DENE DECISION MAKING: THE TULIT'A HAND GAME TOURNAMENT

Life in the Sahtu taught me that one should never make travel plans or count on the plans of others. Of course, this statement is not a comment on the planning ability of Sahtu people or a minimization of their preparedness to travel; rather, it is quite simply that the land (rather than a human being) determines when and where one can travel. This occurred when a group of us planned to go by jet boat from Déline to Tulit'a to attend the Tulit'a Hand Game Tournament. On the evening before our departure, we were expecting the arrival of Jimmy, an experienced bushman from Tulit'a who had agreed to come up the Great Bear River to Déline, collect us, and take us downriver to Tulit'a. Just as night was falling, Jimmy called from a satellite phone to tell us that he was nearby but was stranded on the other side of Great Bear Lake. The whitecaps were too rough, he said, and because he was a "river" person, not a "lake" person, he was wondering if someone from Déline (who had more experience on the lake) could come and guide him over. After much debate about whether he should camp overnight where he was, or whether someone should go and get him, Jimmy decided to cross the lake himself and made it safely to Déline shortly after eleven o'clock.

At six next morning, sixteen of us gathered at the Little Lake near Déline to start our journey to Tulit'a. There were two boats, one driven by Jimmy, and after the drivers checked the gas and supplies and debated the conditions on the lake, they decided to set out, so we loaded up and motored across the Little Lake to the small mouth where it opens into Great Bear Lake. This looked calm as we approached it, but massive five-foot waves were soon battering the boats back and forth, and sometimes taking good solid shots at the hull. It is impossible to describe the height and ferocity of the waves. Water cascaded over us, and by the time we reached the other side, many of us were drenched. Once we were on the Great Bear River, the wind died down and the waves subsided.

The Great Bear River is beautiful – often glassy, sometimes with swirling pools and currents that run an amazing blue-green. I am told that it can be very shallow in places and that its safe navigation requires the ability to "read the river." Jimmy, it was explained, was one of the best river readers around, and he had travelled the river all his life. Along the banks, willows, spruce, and other vegetation were beginning to turn every shade of red, purple, orange, and yellow as fall came to the Sahtu. A woman pointed out the remnants of an old camp – it had spruce trees laid out as a drying rack – and said that a previous researcher had once stayed there during a medicine camp. About halfway down the river, we reached what people call the Rapids and the old site of Bennet Field. Now abandoned, Bennet Field once served as an airstrip and the landing place for many of the boats that carried uranium ore from Port Radium down the Great Bear River to the Mackenzie. Its old dock and the road leading from the water to the airstrip still remain. Jimmy pointed out the portage trail that Dene people once used to circumvent the Rapids when they voyaged by canoe and said that people whose boats were fitted with outboard motors were obliged to follow suit. We, however, were in a jet boat, he said smiling, so we did not need to portage.

Jimmy navigated easily through the Rapids, passed the Norman Mountain range, and got us to Tulit'a at just after one. People waited to take us to our accommodation for the next four days. As I stepped onto the dock,

I saw four butchered caribou and a moose that had been brought in from Stewart Lake, a preferred Mountain Dene harvesting area near Tulit'a. I suspected that they would feed the people who would gather in Tulit'a over the weekend.

Dene hand games involve two teams, in which every player conceals an object in one hand or the other, and opposing players must determine which hand holds the item. Any small object is suitable, and some people use coins, whereas others choose things of personal or spiritual significance. In these complex social practices, teams employ a series of elaborate hand gestures as they use their power to "know" which hand is the right one. If a team chooses correctly, it will be awarded a stick, and the ultimate goal of the game is to collect every stick. Drums and songs assist people with their power to choose correctly. In the past, Dene hand games were played spontaneously, often when groups met on the land or when neighbouring groups visited each other (Graville 1985; Heine 1999), and their purpose ranged from redistribution of wealth to amusement – not unlike the tournament that I attended. Although some hand games have been standardized and codified, largely to allow for uniform competition at sporting events such as the Arctic Winter Games (see Giles 2004, 2005a), they remain important aspects of community and intercommunity gatherings, and in the Sahtu at least, they are relatively spontaneous. For example, on several occasions during my fieldwork, an impromptu hand game was organized after locals learned that a delegation of people was visiting from outside the community.

The teams at the Tulit'a Hand Game Tournament came from various communities (both Déline and Tulit'a had two teams, and Norman Wells, Meander and Bushe Rivers in northern Alberta, and Whatì and Wekweeti in the Tlicho region each had one). I was told that people were not supposed to cheer for any particular team and that drummers were supposed to drum for everyone. The tournament was no small matter, and the stakes were significant – that year, the winning team went home with $50,000 in prize money.

Dene hand games have been well documented by anthropologists and others working with Athabaskan peoples from the Northwest Territories, northern Alberta, northeastern British Columbia, and the Yukon (see Goulet 1998; Helm 2000; Abel 1993; Giles 2005a, 2005b). Before the time of contact with European traders, they were a fundamental part of many collective gatherings. Several elders told me that, long ago, people played the games for goods such as food, clothing, and other supplies rather than for money. In fact, the Tulit'a tournament was revived in 2001 as a traditional end-of-summer gathering. Back in the old days, I was told, people travelled from their winter and spring hunting places in the Mackenzie Mountains or at Great Bear Lake, gathering in Tulit'a at the end of summer to trade their furs and get provisions before returning to their winter hunting grounds. They walked or came in moosehide boats, and reaching Tulit'a could take more than a month. Once arrived, they rekindled family ties, made new friends, traded goods, and played hand games. In those days, powerful medicine men would meet to use their power in the hand game, and the more power they had, the better they did. Occasionally, the games became too powerful and someone would be killed. One community leader from Tulit'a expressed his concern at the size of the tournament winnings: "$50,000 is too much," he said. "People might bring too much power and then something could go wrong."[13] In contemporary times, the games are played for both sport and money.

Yet even today, Sahtu participation in traditional Dene hand games involves a strengthening of family and collective ties, a formation of identity through cultural practice, and in a subtle way, a certain drawing of particular lines of authority and power. After all, those who possess power (acquired through land-based activities and conducting themselves in an appropriate manner) may be able to use it to transform the outcome of the game, just as they may apply it in other facets of daily life. David Smith (1998, 412) notes that for Chipewyan people, survival and success in life is dependent on understanding the interrelationships between human beings and the gifts of animal persons, which can be known only through a combination of practical first-hand knowledge and "supraempirical knowledge which comes mostly in dreams, but also requires being active in the bush." Working in the Sahtu during the 1970s, Scott Rushforth demonstrates Sahtu Dene associations between authority and primary knowledge acquired through personal experience. As Rushforth (1994, 336) states, "The power to inspire justifiable belief (knowledge) in others and the power to influence or determine others' conduct (having control over the actions of others) both require primary knowledge." For Rushforth, primary knowledge about the land and its resources has not been eroded by the political and economic incursion of settler states. As he (ibid., 343) argues, "Dene still control local knowledge, including primary knowledge of the land and the animals that occupy it," and consequently, associated power. At a September 2006 session of the territorial legislature that was held in Déline, the chief of Déline suggested to the premier that Déline and the government ought to "play a hand game for the land."[14] Of course, the premier took this as a joke. I, however, was not so sure that it wasn't a challenge.

The Tulit'a Hand Game Tournament began with an opening ceremony, which included a feeding of the fire, prayers, and drum songs. Following a feast, the games began in all their fury. Each team consisted of eight to ten men (unlike in other areas of the North, women do not play hand games in the Sahtu), and countless drummers created an atmosphere of excitement and sacredness as the games went on for hours. On this particular night, the matches did not conclude until one in the morning. At that point, a drum dance began. Sahtu drum dances involve a series of drummers who drum and sing particular songs. Many of these have been handed down in dreams or other prophecies; others have to do with specific peoples or places. People dance to the songs in a circle, and even the very young and the very old participate in the dancing. Drummers and dancers encourage and sometimes vie with each other as the night wears on: if the dancers begin to flag, the drummers hearten them with more songs, and if the drummers tire, the dancers keep dancing and call out for more songs. Thus, drum dances often last until the early morning, and most people stay until they end.

In the Sahtu, the events that surround hand games are as important as the games themselves. In the past, the games occurred when people from diverse groupings came together, and they are still played in that context today. Historically, Sahtu Dene social groups were flexible, and single families sometimes set off on their own to hunt or fish. At other times, multiple families might group themselves around a successful hunter or person with power who could provide food or other necessities (Abel 1993). Leadership was likewise flexible, and though recognized leaders acquired authority, they could not impose their will on others. Anyone who did not agree with the leadership (or who simply wanted to pursue different aims) was free to leave the group (Roderick Wilson 1986). As a result, decision making typically relied on persuasiveness and lengthy sifting of the issues. It was often conducted at communal gatherings such as hand games.[15] Thus, the games and their associated events were political, serving as a social space in which people made decisions about their lives and futures. Most often, the results of these decisions were non-invasive in that land use activities were not intensive, and the decisions typically did not interfere with the ability of other group members to use the land as they saw fit. Today, formal decisions affecting communities are made in band offices or land corporation boardrooms, and they can permeate every aspect of life; indeed, the decisions facing community governance bodies regarding oil and gas development on Sahtu lands have the potential to change the land and community dynamics in very profound ways.

The Tulit'a Hand Game Tournament lasted for four days. Every day, Tulit'a hosted a morning and an evening feast, and the games began at nine in the morning and continued until well after midnight. There was little opportunity for sleep, and people who were not playing hand games spent most of their time watching the games and visiting and reacquainting themselves with people who had come to Tulit'a. The final game was followed by another drum dance. This time, however, as the tournament drew to a close, a respected elder and spiritual leader from Déline addressed the crowd with a long oration, saying that the focus of the tournament was the rekindling of social ties, not the importance of money. "Even sometimes it is important to weep when we are happy," he said, "and when we meet again to show our joy."[16] Next, the grand chief of the Tlicho rose and spoke about the power of people when they come together and practise the ways of the Dene. He said that Dene culture and identity were important in keeping people strong in their struggle for self-government agreements and in ongoing land claim negotiations. In this way, speakers were engaging in the political processes of their ancestors: they were not following Robert's Rules of Order; they were talking about what people should do to be good human beings, to build strong communities, to be Dene. Several other people spoke, all of whom shared their knowledge without being asked, and the drumming began again; the Tulit'a drummers were followed by the Dogrib, the Meander, and finally the drummers from Déline. Everyone danced and sang loudly, and I was reminded of Émile Durkheim's (1915) concept of collective effervescence as the power of the drums and the singing seemed to take us to another place. Many people danced late into the night, and when the drummers tired at about three, they continued to dance, using their voices and songs to keep time. A local whispered to me, "Many people now come together only for meetings or other serious events. Decisions and other important things should be made during the contexts of celebrations, in traditional ways, rather than in boardrooms."[17] This comment made me think about how far removed the tournament was from the JRP hearings, held in this very space.

I

"Very Nice Talk in a Very Beautiful Way"
The Community Hearing Process

The view is that when the pipeline goes [in], that land is going to be worth a significant amount of money.

— *Henry Sykes, president of MGM Energy, 2011*

ON 7 OCTOBER 2004, on behalf of ConocoPhillips Canada, Shell Canada, ExxonMobil Canada, and the Aboriginal Pipeline Group, Imperial Oil submitted applications to construct and operate a $16.2 billion pipeline and related infrastructure from the Beaufort Delta through the Mackenzie Valley.[1] Called the Mackenzie Gas Project (MGP), it seeks to develop three onshore gas fields and to transport natural gas and natural gas liquids through a 1,220-kilometre pipeline from processing facilities near Inuvik into existing Alberta pipelines. The three anchor fields, Taglu, Parsons Lake, and Niglintgak, are expected to produce approximately 6 trillion cubic feet of natural gas. The pipeline is designed to carry 1.2 billion cubic feet of natural gas and natural gas liquids per day and could be expanded to accommodate gas from future discoveries (Mackenzie Gas Project 2004a).

Project proponents called it "the pipeline to the future," and industry representatives termed it "a basin-opening pipeline," citing its potential to open up new supply regions.[2] Politicians, too, made no secret of their desire to see the pipeline proceed. In a November 2006 speech to a Calgary business audience and reporters, then Indian and Northern Affairs Canada minister Jim Prentice stated that it "is an important piece of infrastructure in this country and I intend to do everything I need to as the Minister responsible" (quoted in Mahony 2006).

However, traversing the rugged northern terrain and satisfying the equally demanding assessment and regulatory regimes of the Northwest

Territories are not easy tasks. If built, the pipeline will pass through four Aboriginal land claim areas, cross five hundred bodies of water, use approximately 110 sites for acquiring granular material to use in construction, and potentially affect up to thirty-two communities in the Northwest Territories and northern Alberta (Mackenzie Gas Project 2004a). Much of its right-of-way would be built in areas that have no all-season roads, and complications posed by melting permafrost and the dramatic ice freeze-up and break-up cycles are just a few items on a long list of project challenges.

As part of its regulatory application, Imperial Oil submitted an environmental impact statement (EIS), an eight-volume overview and appraisal of the MGP. The EIS describes baseline biophysical and socio-economic conditions in the project area, assesses the direct potential impacts of pipeline activities, and presents mitigation or management measures aimed at reducing any anticipated adverse effects. It identifies the ways in which the project could negatively affect certain biophysical components: these include impacts to air quality due to increased emissions and dust generated from disturbed areas and construction camps; noise disturbances during construction stages and near compressor stations; changes in groundwater due to the removal of granular material; changes in hydrology and water quality due to increased sedimentation, water draw-downs from lakes and rivers, and expanded barge traffic; effects on fish and their habitat at pipeline watercourse crossings; changes in vegetation as a result of constructing the pipeline right-of-way; and adverse impacts on wildlife due to habitat and vegetation loss and increased access and disturbance by humans and other predators. However, the EIS reports that though the pipeline may produce some low to moderate effects, no "significant impacts" are anticipated for any element of the biophysical environment (Mackenzie Gas Project 2004a, 1:23-29).

Pipeline proponents also maintain that though the project may have some adverse effects on community well-being, it could also provide significant socio-economic benefits in the areas of job creation, procurement, and regional economic development. They suggest that it will generate "substantial" government revenue through access and benefits agreements, taxation, and royalty payments.[3] For the first time in Canadian history, the Aboriginal people of the North will be "owners of the pipeline," holding a one-third stake in it (excluding the processing and connecting facilities for the three anchor fields).[4] The Aboriginal Pipeline Group (APG), which includes shareholders from Aboriginal organizations in the Northwest Territories, would charge a toll on the gas shipped through the pipeline, which it would then distribute as dividends to its shareholders.[5]

Imperial Oil, the leading project proponent, expects that, at its peak, the MGP will provide northern residents with nearly 4,647 jobs that are directly related to pipeline activities; provisions have been put in place to hire northern and Aboriginal workers (Imperial Oil 2007, section 10, 10). The project is also anticipated to create various spin-off businesses, such as camp catering, transportation, slashing, and construction. Local and Aboriginal businesses are expected to obtain contracts to provide services and to work on the pipeline itself. The federal and territorial governments and the pipeline proponents have committed to supporting the development of northern and Aboriginal education and training programs so that workers will have the necessary skills to gain employment.

However, most of the jobs created by the MGP will exist solely during its construction phase and are expected to last only three winter work seasons. On average, only 205 jobs are forecasted for long-term pipeline and facility operations (ibid., section 10, 14). Though the pipeline may provide some short-term or seasonal employment, experience elsewhere in Canada has shown that a sudden influx of money into small communities does not always enhance their well-being, and indeed can contribute to substance abuse and increased gambling.

The pipeline EIS identifies other potential adverse socio-economic changes, including the rapid migration of foreign workers into northern communities, which would overburden their infrastructures and heighten existing strains in the areas of policing, social and health services, transportation, recreation, housing, and domestic energy supplies. Furthermore, it is expected that situating large construction camps near Fort Good Hope, Inuvik, Norman Wells, Tulit'a, and Fort Simpson will enable (mostly male) project workers to interact with local residents, creating concerns over adverse effects on community health and wellness.

The EIS also notes that the increase in foreign workers and the improved access to land due to road construction and pipeline rights-of-way could potentially intensify sport and non-local hunting, thus further straining renewable resources. It suggests that local young people might leave school prematurely to work short-term on the pipeline, and it discusses the probable effects on hunting and trapping, language and culture transmission, and use of the land. However, it asserts that the adverse socio-economic impacts will be both low to moderate and addressable: as it explains, there "will be disruptions to the people in the North, but they will be short term, and over a small area, mainly during construction.

Therefore, the disruptions will not be significant" (Mackenzie Gas Project 2004b, 7). Proponents argue that the pipeline itself would leave a relatively minor footprint on the North and would not significantly affect any part of the physical, social, or cultural environment in the Northwest Territories. Not everyone agrees: some people assert that the potential harms of the MGP are broader in scope than the EIS suggests.

In many ways, the MGP has become a symbol of northern change and contestation. Other large projects have been approved in the Northwest Territories, including the De Beers Snap Lake diamond mine northeast of Yellowknife, which processes three thousand tonnes of ore a day and was approved in 2003. Yet, at the time of writing, the Mackenzie Valley Environmental Impact Review Board had ordered that only two projects be subjected to the highest level of environmental impact assessment: the MGP in 2003 and the De Beers Gahcho Kue diamond mine in 2007 (MVEIRB 2007). Furthermore, prior to the implementation of co-management institutions, other large projects were approved in the Northwest Territories under the Environmental Assessment Act: these include the BHP Billiton Ekati and Diavik diamond mines, approved by the federal government in 1996 and 1999 respectively. And pipelines have been built in the Northwest Territories before – the Canol Pipeline of 1942 and the Norman Wells Pipeline of 1985. However, for northerners and many other Canadians, the MGP has come to represent an intersection, a tipping point of sorts, between two opposing views, which value the North either as a relatively pristine wilderness or a place of untapped resources. One perspective holds that the MGP would induce further oil and gas exploration and production, irreparably damage the land and wildlife, contribute to global climate change, and forever alter the local lifeways of northerners. The other view argues that, should the MGP *not* proceed, the northern economy would stagnate, and its existing gas wells would represent little more than missed opportunities. Advocates of both perspectives, and of many others, were given the opportunity to present their positions, concerns, and justifications in one of the largest and most complicated environmental impact assessment and regulatory reviews in Canada's history.[6]

Establishing the Joint Review Panel

One reason why the assessment and regulation of the Mackenzie Valley pipeline has received so much attention is its transboundary and transjurisdictional nature. Long before Imperial Oil filed regulatory applications, a number of agencies and government ministries were attempting to determine just how the assessment of a pipeline of this magnitude would work. A December 2000 meeting initiated by the Mackenzie Valley Environmental Impact Review Board (MVEIRB) brought together the Mackenzie Valley environmental impact assessment boards, the Inuvialuit Settlement Area Board, the National Energy Board, the Canadian Environmental Assessment Agency, the territorial government, and Indian and Northern Affairs Canada (INAC) to begin discussions to coordinate the various pieces of regulatory and environmental impact assessment legislation in preparation for an application to build the pipeline. In 2002, a Cooperation Plan for the Environmental Impact Assessment and Regulatory Review of a Northern Gas Pipeline Project through the Northwest Territories was developed between the boards and agencies that were responsible for assessing and regulating energy developments in the Northwest Territories. This plan described how the review of a transregional natural gas pipeline would be coordinated. Essentially, it expressed the desire that the relevant agencies would work collaboratively to avoid duplication in the review, and it advocated a "made in the north" process that would enhance public participation and ensure that potential impacts were thoroughly considered before project decisions were made (Northern Pipeline Environmental Impact Assessment and Regulatory Chairs' Committee 2002, 5). The cooperation plan specified that two panels should be established: The Joint Environmental Impact Assessment Panel (which later became the Joint Review Panel for the Mackenzie Gas Project, or JRP) would evaluate the potential environmental and socio-economic impacts of a proposed pipeline in the project area. The National Energy Board panel was responsible for regulatory hearings (including topics such as tolls, tariffs, engineering and design, operating safety, resource supply, and economic feasibility) and for considering the issuance of a certificate of public convenience and necessity, pursuant to the National Energy Board Act. Establishing two panels was thought necessary to provide for the distinct circumstances of the North and to establish targeted forums for public participation and debate.

As per the cooperation plan, and after receiving preliminary information packages from the pipeline proponents, the chairs of the MVEIRB (responsible for administering the Mackenzie Valley Resource Management Act), the Inuvialuit Game Council (IGC, representing the collective interests of the Inuvialuit under the Inuvialuit Final Agreement), and the federal environment minister (responsible for administering the Canadian Environmental Assessment Act) executed the Agreement for an

Environmental Impact Review of the Mackenzie Gas Project on 18 August 2004 (National Energy Board 2004). The agreement established the scope and procedures of the environmental impact review, and it set up the Joint Review Panel, which consisted of seven members. An independent body, the JRP had the authority to meet the requirements of comprehensive land claims and federal environmental impact assessment legislation. Its members were appointed by the MVEIRB (which selected three) and the environment minister (who chose four, two of whom were nominated by the IGC). All parties approved the selection of the chair. Panel members needed to be free from conflicts of interest relative to the MGP and to possess various types of knowledge "including, as appropriate, traditional knowledge, or experience relevant to the anticipated impacts of the Project on the environment" (ibid., "Joint Review Panel Membership," section 2). In the end, membership in the panel reflected the collaborative management approach instigated in the cooperation plan.

Pursuant to the agreement, a public registry was established in both paper and electronic form, under the principle that all submissions should become a matter of public record. In its evaluation of the pipeline, the JRP was to consider all evidence submitted by the public, either in writing or through hearings, and was to issue a report and final recommendations. The report would also become a matter of public record and would be submitted to the relevant government ministers, the National Energy Board, and all other boards responsible for regulating pipeline activity in the Northwest Territories. Finally, the ministers were expected to take the JRP report into consideration before making any decisions related to the approval of the MGP.

With much fanfare, the JRP public hearings began in Inuvik on 14 February 2006. Before they concluded, some twenty-one months later, the panel held more than 115 days of hearings in twenty-six communities and produced more than eleven thousand pages of transcripts.

THE JRP HEARINGS COME TO THE SAHTU

The JRP hearings reached the Sahtu Settlement Area on 3 April 2006. The day before, several people from Déline, the first Sahtu community to host the hearings, spent the unseasonably warm Sunday afternoon ice fishing. I had gone by truck onto Great Bear Lake with Jamie, a respected Déline fisherman.[7] Many people in Déline now fish from the ice road that runs across Smith's Arm of Great Bear Lake and connects on the south side of the lake to the winter road to Tulit'a. As we headed out that day, we saw several vehicles parked on the ice road. People drive along the road, select a fishing spot, drill a hole in the ice with an auger, and settle down to fish. The holes freeze over in a few days, and people either re-use them or drill new ones. As we reached two parked trucks, we stopped to say hello. Two good-sized lake trout lay in the snow beside the fishing hole.

Once we chose our spot, Jamie drilled a hole in the ice and used a badminton racket to fish out stray pieces of ice. We then tied a hook to a piece of line, secured it with a small stick, and spent the afternoon jigging. Jamie is a wonderful storyteller and a warm and open person. As he told me, he believes that knowledge and stories should be shared with everyone. That day, he talked about his late father, who was a Mountain Dene and a renowned hunter. He spoke about his late mother, who was taken to a tuberculosis sanatorium when he was just four, and how he himself was subsequently taken to residential school for a year. Jamie talked about his life and the land. He pointed to a small lake that flows into Great Bear Lake, near the western side of the townsite, and said that it was especially important to the people of Déline, as it had saved them from starvation many times. In the fall, when Great Bear Lake becomes too turbulent and dangerous for fishing, people rely on the smaller lake for fish; in the spring, when thawing ice makes Great Bear Lake unsafe, the smaller lake has already thawed, which allows people to continue fishing there. Jamie talked about the prophecies that had been told to him and about how everyone was responsible for being a good person.[8] He felt most comfortable sharing this knowledge while he was on the land. "I don't like talking about all of this when it is noisy and there is too much going on," he said quietly. "Only now should I be talking."[9]

Jamie and I were getting ready to pack up for the day when a Dash-8 landed at the local airport. As in many small northern communities, several people went to the airport to see who had arrived. The fact that the plane was a Dash-8, rather than the small Twin Otter or Grand Caravan that usually provided the daily service, meant that it had been chartered. Although people knew that the JRP hearings would begin on the following day, the everyday preoccupations of life and the beautiful weather, so perfect for ice fishing, had claimed their attention. Thus, though the arrival of the charter flight may not have been a surprise, it did feel strangely out of place on that sunny afternoon.

In the days before the hearings, life in Déline had maintained a sense of normalcy. Women attended their regular Friday night bingo game, just as always. Some secondary students were visiting from southern Canada, and locals were eager to show them a hand game and a drum dance, and to teach them about fishing. Yet, from time to time, someone mentioned what he or she planned to say in the hearings. Jamie had made a mental list of his questions, concerns, and conditions. He said, "I think I will ask them about if they can be 100 percent sure that there won't be a spill. If they can't be 100 percent sure that there won't be a spill, I don't think they should do it." Later that evening, over a cup of tea, he said, "I will say that without our land, we cannot survive. We must protect it."[10]

For the many observers and participants who were on their way to Déline, the JRP hearings were a much-anticipated event. PowerPoint presentations had been created and handouts had been printed. Journalists were on their way, and lawyers had prepared answers to anticipated questions. Representatives from numerous government departments were all converging on the Sahtu. But until the Dash-8 landed, the hearings did not attain a pronounced significance in Déline. And even after its arrival, locals inquired mostly about the time of the hearings and whether or not they would be able to attend. Only then did they learn that, for many, attendance would entail taking the afternoon off work.

The Hearing Space

The JRP held hearings in every Sahtu community, usually at the local arena, devoting two days to communities that were near the pipeline right-of-way. They employed a consistent spatial layout and followed the same general format. In this, they differed markedly from the approach of the Berger Inquiry in the mid-1970s. Justice Berger often met with people at their traplines and in their hunting cabins, sharing meals and drinking tea with them. In the JRP hearings, the seven panel members sat at a table in the front of the room, with the chair in the centre. Their table was flanked on either side by two others. One housed the transcribers and the technical and support staff whose job was to ensure that the hearing was a technical success and that it was recorded for live webcast and later transcribed for public reading. The other table was occupied by representatives from Imperial Oil. Generally, between three and five individuals sat at this table, though they often changed places with various lawyers, geologists, engineers, and scientists who sat nearby. Their table was stacked with thick binders, which contained the environmental impact statement for the pipeline. A third table, small and square, was placed directly in front of the panel's table. It was reserved for community members who wished to

Joint Review Panel hearing at Déline on 3 April 2006. The audience sits facing
the panel, and a "speak slowly" sign hangs from the panel's table.

speak to the panel or to Imperial Oil. Hanging from the panel's table was
a sign, written in English, that read "speak slowly." The rest of the room
was filled with chairs for the audience – observers from the community
and elsewhere.

In a procedure that had been established in advance, hearings began
with a prayer offered by a local elder, after which the JRP chair read a
statement that introduced the panel members and explained the purpose
of the panel and the environmental impact review. The chair read the same
statement in every community. Instructions were given to people who
wished to present their views or ask questions. Witnesses were asked to
begin by stating their names into the microphone and to identify themselves thereafter to aid transcript production. Although microphones were
provided so that they could remain seated in the audience, most opted to
sit at the small witness table while they gave their testimony. After the
opening remarks from the chair, Imperial Oil gave a presentation that
lasted about twenty minutes. This dealt with the pipeline and the anchor
fields; the environmental impact statement, including any anticipated
effects on the community, wildlife, or lands; the measures for Aboriginal
employment and safety in pipeline activities; and the mitigation measures
adopted as a result of previous input by community groups or others. The
panel then questioned Imperial Oil regarding the presentation, as did local

people. Finally, the floor was opened to community members or organizations that wished to make presentations to the panel or to address Imperial Oil. Witnesses had fifteen minutes to speak, and though I did not see anyone being cut off, and not everyone adhered to the time limit, there was a general awareness that comments must be kept within established parameters. More than once, the chair pointed frantically to the "speak slowly" sign, so that translators could reasonably keep up with the narrative. Coffee, tea, and store-bought cookies were placed on tables near the exits, and frequent health breaks provided adjournments throughout the day. During these breaks, classical music played on the loudspeakers overhead.

Anyone who has spent time in the central Mackenzie Valley, or in other rural communities in the Northwest Territories, soon discovers the significance of particular kinds of music. Important community events normally include some manner of drumming, usually as a part of drum dances. Drum songs, though often shared between communities, are associated with particular places and people: they tell stories, and most have been handed to human beings through a form of dreaming. Dene drum music is played on the radio, and many communities have their own drum groups, who make and distribute CDs throughout the territories and beyond. At certain hours of the day, local radio stations interrupt the popular country music to play drum songs, after which they return to the music of Hank Williams or another old-timer country artist. And though local youth keep up with the latest trends on the pop-chart and hip-hop scenes, and many kinds of music are appreciated, old-timer country and Dene drum music are most closely associated with times of communal festivity and feelings of a home-place.

Not once during my almost nine months in the Sahtu did I ever hear classical music. Perhaps this wasn't particularly strange. I don't generally hear it when I walk around my own city, either. However, in light of the frequency of and preference for Dene drum music, and (perhaps for disparate reasons) old-timer country music, playing classical music at the hearings seemed distinctly out of place. Although the volume was not loud, it did serve to transform the arena into another kind of place – a hearing space.

For the most part, arenas in the Sahtu are used for community-initiated activities: bingo games, band meetings, badminton, and floor hockey. Depending on the size of the event, many host talent shows, parties, feasts, weddings, and especially drum dances. In all these cases, the arena is a space created and maintained by local people; it is a community space.

However, for the purposes of the JRP hearings, the arena needed to be transformed into an unclaimed, other-than-community space, where interactions between locals, governments, regulators, and multinational corporations could be conducted. The hearing space housed entire tables of laptop computers, cables, transcription and translation equipment, monitors, and projectors, typically organized along one wall. The layout resembled a makeshift courtroom, with observers and witnesses gathered in a loose semi-circle before a central focal point (the panel table) and flanked on both sides by tables of so-called experts, all of whom came from elsewhere. Thus, on the days of the JRP hearings, the arenas were not places where folks had gathered last week for a drum dance or a feast – they were spaces created by and for outsiders.

The structural and procedural forms of the hearings were not lost on local people. Some expressed discomfort with the process itself. As one participant said, "Sometimes it is really hard for us to make speeches because, as youths and Elders we're not used to the formal Panel doing the protocol in line with making discussions."[11] Others recalled the Berger Inquiry and mentioned the informal nature of its hearings:

> What I have to say is, like, coming here, I know back in the Berger days
> – when I was just a young person then. I was just – one man was sitting
> there and seen a lot of elders speaking out ... Time have changed. A lot of
> things have changed. Like today – they didn't have those on the screen when
> Berger days now. You could see the change that happening with us.[12]

Indeed, for the particular community in question, Berger had visited people who were camped at a spring harvesting area and held a round of hearings in people's cabins at Willow (Brackett) Lake. There was a general feeling that he truly wished to understand what people were saying but that the JRP hearings were simply logging comments for the record. The informal setting on the land stood in stark contrast to the highly technocratic structure of the JRP hearings.

Nonetheless, people in the Sahtu managed to claim the hearing space as a local place. Without consulting the organizers, they frequently moved their chairs so that they could sit near children, relatives, or friends. Chairs were moved so that elders could walk a shorter distance, or to afford a better view of the proceedings. The neat regimentation of the chairs, set up in rows to focus on the panel, was disrupted, and even the aisles that gave easy access to the witness table were not immune to change. Throughout the hearings, people got up and went outside for coffee, for air or a cigarette, or to visit; they fetched tea or cookies from the small table by the door, returned to their seats, and put their Styrofoam cups on the floor or on the chair beside them. In short, they did what they always did at community gatherings. They did not wait for the panel to call a break, and they did not ask for permission to alter the space. Instead, they claimed it as distinctly their own, and in doing so they negotiated a hearing space that necessarily included a community place.

MODES OF TALKING: FORMS OF EVIDENCE

In a culture where the wisest and most competent members regard outspokenness and adamance as foolhardy, childish, and profoundly self-defeating, how can a way of life protect itself, when its protection requires outspoken and adamant protests?

– *Hugh Brody,* Maps and Dreams

Anthropologists such as Michael Asch (1997a), Dara Culhane (1998), and Andie Palmer (2000), among others, have offered insightful critiques of the cultural dissimilarities and inequity embedded in the presentation of evidence and forms of fact finding in Canadian legal systems. In no small part, the predominance of technical and specialized legal discourses at the JRP hearings limited full participation to persons who were knowledgeable of particular linguistic fields. Despite claims regarding a "made in the north" process that encouraged local participation, the technical and scientific information that formed a large part of the hearing process remained inaccessible to many people. Furthermore, the legalistic tone of the hearings was unfamiliar to people whose knowledge of Euro-Canadian courtroom proceedings and protocol was limited. In many ways, the hearings were promoted as a culture-free medium for the full and whole-hearted participation of Aboriginal contributors. However, the presentation of knowledge in the hearings (and the normative modes of talking about the things that people know) limited their ability to participate effectively.

It is worth noting that this problem is not unique to small Aboriginal communities in the Canadian North. In a case study of an environmental assessment involving a hog-processing facility and accompanying waste-water treatment plant near Brandon, Manitoba, Alan Diduck and Bruce

Mitchell (2003) state that the readability and comprehension of the environmental impact statement and other environmental assessment documents constrained public involvement in the hearing process. Consequently, the hearings often served as a kind of symbolic form of public involvement. Ciaran O'Faircheallaigh (1999, 64) has also examined a cross-section of social impact assessments in Canada and Australia, and concludes that in many cases "indigenous groups often lack the financial resources and the access to technical information and expertise to ensure effective participation." Although the illusion of widespread public or community participation in environmental issues may be more apparent in an intercultural context, it is certainly not restricted to the Sahtu.

The lack of access to technical information proved a major obstacle to Sahtu Dene participation in the hearing process. Although a public registry was maintained (including all evidence submitted to the JRP and a record of hearing transcripts), it existed in an electronic format and was accessible through the Internet. Although most Sahtu communities have dial-up Internet services at least, home computers are not common there, and some segments of the population, such as elders, virtually never use them. Thus, even people who are comfortable with computers must rely on the computer at work or at the band office, land corporation, or school to navigate the massive number of electronic documents on the JRP public registry. Using a public computer to download large files can be described as inconvenient, at best. Certainly, information is often available in print form at regional MGP offices and at local land corporation or band offices. However, in a process that changes daily, keeping up with the JRP hearings required immediate and frequent access to on-line resources. Moreover, though local people were hired to visit homes and explain the pipeline EIS and other aspects of the regulatory process, and though the proponents prepared an "Environmental Impact Statement in Brief" (Mackenzie Gas Project 2004b) in four Aboriginal languages, the "In Brief" document did not provide enough detailed information to enable people to develop well-informed arguments.[13]

Simply keeping up with the flow of information on the hearing process became immensely time-consuming. Some government departments, pipeline proponents, and non-governmental organizations engaged teams of people to track the process on a full-time basis. However, community associations (let alone community members) did not have the financial or human resources to follow suit. For the most part, they could afford only to hire lawyers or consultants who would advise them on making formal presentations to the Joint Review or National Energy Board (NEB) Panels. As one person stated before the JRP,

> Imperial Oil has tons of material for us to read, and it's really hard for us to understand that. There's no funds set aside for us to have a community workshop on the materials that's presented to us. We've been through tons of materials, yet we have a hard time understanding the materials that are before each community. We don't have the expertise. We don't have the technical help that is required to understand each material. There's volumes of tons of it that is before us, and it's really hard – even for me. I have a good education, but it's really hard for me to understand the materials in the books that are sent to each community.[14]

Local people likewise expressed their frustration with the way in which knowledge was conveyed in the JRP hearings themselves. During a round of questioning of Imperial Oil's preliminary presentation, one witness said,

> Those are just some of the questions that I wanted to ask regarding your presentation, because a lot of your wording on here won't make sense to a lot of people. It's very – a lawyer wrote it. To me you're using word tricks. And I'm not saying it in a negative way. I'm not for or against the pipeline, it's just some personal things that come to my attention and I just wanted to bring it up.[15]

Quite significantly, the incomprehensibility of environmental assessment documents has frustrated local participants. However, the situation can become even more complicated in an intercultural context, where ideas about knowledge acquisition and the most appropriate means of sharing it may not coincide.

For example, in the Sahtu, even among elected leaders, there is a general apprehension about speaking on behalf of others. The acquisition of knowledge is strongly tied to personal autonomy, and thus speaking for others implies that they cannot speak for themselves and/or that everyone shares the same repertoire of primary (and thus true) knowledge. Instead, when it comes to sharing information in large public gatherings, people with experience of the subject at hand (usually an elder) engage in long oratories, often containing specific and vivid details of personal experience along with moral instruction (Fumoleau 1977; Ellen Basso 1978), not unlike the ways illustrated at the Tulit'a Hand Game Tournament. Many elders who testified at the JRP hearings spoke in this fashion. For example, an elder at the Tulit'a hearings said,

> So as Dene, we have to go hunting. Everything we do – without it, we won't be here, we won't be eating. So that's why it's very important to live on this land, to go hunting, to survive. There is a lot of stories to it. So that's why the Higher Power put us on this earth to help each other to live well. And always the elders say: You live well when you share stories and help each other.[16]

During the 1970s, anthropologist Ellen Basso (1978, 693) worked with people at Willow Lake, near Tulit'a; as she points out, people are not asked to tell stories, but are compelled to do so because the knowledge they contain is beneficial and important to the group as a whole. What is more, it is considered inappropriate to interrupt the narrative, to ask speakers to repeat themselves, or to ask questions relating to what was just relayed.

The narrative ways in which some Sahtu Dene talk about what people know are incommensurable with the mode of fact finding that is inherent in resource co-management institutions in the Canadian North. In his work on northern Canadian land claim and co-management boards, Graham White (2006, 411) writes, "By design the Western legal system is highly adversarial, built upon the assumption that 'the truth' will come out through the cut and thrust of debate and the challenge of evidence." He suggests that cooperative resource management in the Canadian North is made difficult by the incompatibility of conceptions of knowledge and truth as embedded in Western legal systems and Indigenous forms of decision making, thought, and governance. This is most evident, I argue, in the interaction between local people and abstract regulatory systems in the context of community hearings. If, as White proposes, hearings are places where facts are questioned and truth is found via specific rules of evidence and the aggressive cross-examination of witnesses, the Sahtu Dene mode of conveying knowledge and truth will be excluded from the field of play.

This has occurred in intercultural hearing processes elsewhere in the North. Geographer Derek Armitage (2005, 241) notes that environmental assessment processes in most Canadian jurisdictions have remained "technically oriented because the primary objective of the assessment process is to offer predictive analysis and confer a degree of certainty about expected impacts of development activities." In this respect, the environmental assessment process remains proponent-driven and geared toward the demands of proof, as entrenched in the Euro-Canadian traditions of management and systems of law. Stephen Ellis points out that the incorporation of differing forms of knowledge (and particularly Indigenous knowledge) often threatens the stability of structures that are rooted in the Western industrial complex, behind which are ultimately requirements for growth, development, and capitalism. Thus, for Ellis (2005, 72), Indigenous forms of knowledge will not automatically be incorporated into environmental management and assessment when Aboriginal people are involved in the decision-making process. Rather, their knowledge is often seen as legitimate only when "it has been adapted to the specialized narrative of science." Phyllis Morrow and Chase Hensel (1992) make similar observations regarding Yupiit people in Alaska, who were obliged to use non-Native vocabulary and forms of expression to participate effectively in hearings. Working among the Kluane people of the southwest Yukon, Paul Nadasdy (2003, 139) finds that their successful involvement in resource co-management depends on adopting official linguistic fields, the consequences of which are to "tacitly agree to play by the rules of the knowledge game as set out by the state." In other words, though Sahtu Dene people were invited to speak at the JRP hearings, their effectiveness rested largely on their ability to express themselves in a way that was understandable to Western systems of knowledge and that conformed to acceptable (and foreign) norms of procedure and protocol.

In *Oral History on Trial,* Bruce Miller (2011, 114) discusses similar complications with the use of oral histories in judicial proceedings. He identifies the unavoidable antagonisms inherent in an adversarial justice system, decontextualization of oral material by Crown researchers, the differential valuation of text and narrative as legal evidence, and the abundant resources available to the Crown to "wear tribes out" as contributing to "two solitudes largely unable to hear each other." Importantly, he explains that the relevancy of oral narratives is determined by Crown researchers, who, though not pressured to favour the position of the Crown, nonetheless attempt to create a coherent storyline of relevant facts for use in litigation or negotiation. This "cherry picking" (ibid., 74), even when conducted by well-intentioned researchers, obscures not only the oral material itself, but also the meaning and knowledge systems in which it is grounded. Miller (ibid., 150) offers several suggestions to resolve this problem, such as replacing so-called neutral Crown experts with expert witnesses who are conducting research in the relevant Indigenous community, qualifying elders to serve as expert witnesses, evaluating the reliability of oral narratives by determining whether the same message appears in diverse oral accounts, and including oral narratives not only as "proof of fact" but to "show community perceptions at the time of an event or process." This would allow for a more accurate reflection of the nature and content of Aboriginal evidence. Ultimately, though, Miller (ibid., 164) strongly suggests that the process of knowledge exchange and presentation must be restructured: "However the question of the significance and feasibility of incorporating oral narratives into Western systems of knowledge and authority is understood, the adversarial legal process is clearly not the best venue to work this question out."

"These People Are Telling the Truth": Primary and Secondary Knowledge

During the JRP hearings, local people repeatedly and insistently stated that what they and other community members were saying was true. As the acting chief of Déline remarked, "What we are talking about now, about our land and that, it is all the truth."[17] Why did Sahtu Dene people so frequently and emphatically make this claim? For this, we must examine their conceptions of truth and how these differ from conceptions of knowledge as understood by pipeline proponents and environmental assessment institutions.

Ethnographers working in the Sahtu have identified strong connections between conceptions of knowledge, power, and personal experience (Savishinsky 1974; Ellen Basso 1978; Rushforth 1992, 1994). Scott Rushforth (1992, 485) argues that for Sahtúot'ine (Bearlake) people, primary epistemic evidence or personal encounters through dreaming or other means constitute a principal way of knowing. He identifies a Sahtúot'ine linguistic distinction between "'ekw'i'yek'éodehsho (she/he knows it directly – he/she knows the truth) and 'agoni'a' yek'éodehsho (she/he knows it indirectly)." Similarly, Ellen Basso writes that for K'aalo Got'ine (Willow Lake people), 'lk'óó, an important form of knowledge, is acquired during bush activities and provides the means for survival. As Basso (1978, 698) explains, "'lk'óó is not an easily interpreted word, although it can be loosely translated as 'supernatural power' or 'medicine.' As power, it can be thought of both as the source of a person's capacity for survival in the world and the strength or amount of control a person has over things in the world."

For Sahtu Dene people, the cultivation of personal experience constitutes a primary form of knowledge. "Knowing" about a particular place involves spending time there, and as a result, people may know varying amounts of things about specific places. Thus, primary experimental knowledge is not necessarily exchangeable between communities or people in the Sahtu; it is not easily extrapolated, even into regional generalizations. As one community leader said about the land around his family cabin, "I have never seen them [people from a different community] hunt or trap there. Their footprints are not on that land. But for people who have grown up and trapped in the area, what they are saying [about the land] is really true."[18]

Whereas experiential knowledge is highly valued as true, knowledge can also be shared through narrative. Most Sahtu Dene talk about listening to elders (who often have large repertoires of primary knowledge) and learning from them. However, such secondary knowledge is not automatically processed and comprehended. Often, it is fully understood only as a result of an event or through careful observation or a great deal of "thinking about it." In many respects, the general assumption is that the meaning of a story or other form of secondary knowledge will become available to people when they are morally and physically ready for it. Through much introspection, the meaning is then transformed into a kind of primary knowledge. For example, at the hearings in Tulit'a, Chief Frank Andrew spoke about some of the old-timer stories that were told to him by his elders. In legitimation of the knowledge that he had acquired, another elder said, "I believe in him, our Chief Frank Andrew. He's picking all the stories. So that's why now he's talking everything. He picking up stories. That's why he's talking to all the people. That's how we learn."[19] Thus, though secondary knowledge can be reworked and can be seen as a form of experiential knowledge, its transference to another person cannot occur without a great deal of effort.

Rushforth has addressed the role of primary and secondary knowledge in shaping Sahtu Dene participation in public hearings. Rushforth (1994, 339) describes a Berger Inquiry hearing among Sahtúot'ine at Fort Franklin (now Déline) and shows that their participation was greatly informed by perspectives about knowledge, authority, and the constitution of truth. They generally mistrusted the testimony of outsiders because they lacked widespread personal experience of the North. As justification for their mistrust, they cited their encounters with representatives from the Canadian government and industry, and the ways in which outsiders have affected the land and people in the Sahtu. As Rushforth (ibid., 346) explains, the expert witnesses from elsewhere questioned the legitimacy of local people's narratives because it was not bolstered by "college diplomas and references in academic or professional journals." Here, Sahtu Dene people cited the lack of outsiders' primary knowledge as a reason for their skepticism, whereas expert witnesses relied on the authority and power of academically recognized accreditation.

Likewise, in the JRP hearings, Sahtu Dene people recalled the impact of previous extractive projects on their lands and questioned the ability of outsiders to predict the effect of the MGP. One by one, they spoke about their experiences at Port Radium, with the Norman Wells Pipeline, and with recent exploration and drilling. They spoke about the lack of jobs and training provided for Sahtu Dene on past projects and about the failed promises of the 1921 treaty. As one person commented,

> Another thing that I want to ask about ... if the oil, or whatever, is drilled, the place that they are drilling, if they have a spill, not only the pipeline, also the vehicles. That's what it [the EIS] says. If there's an oil spill, in the event of an oil spill there could be damage to water, to the land, to our wildlife, to our fish. "Might," it says. I think that maybe that's a typo. It should be written – that typo should be taken out and it should be written "will" because that's what will happen in the event of a spill.[20]

The general mistrust of outsider evidence was based in part on Sahtu Dene conceptions about the constitution of knowledge and partly in previous experience of large-scale projects and government programs. Occasionally, both perceptions operated simultaneously. As an elder from Déline put it,

> In the old day, my elder can memorize, in those day none of them did not speak English. And they have a very poor translation. And anything that's come up like this oil company, and any other company that come along and they bring the message across to the elders and they did not receive the full information. All they do to them was a very nice talk in a very beautiful way so that they can say "yes."[21]

For many Sahtu Dene, the JRP hearings also had to do with appropriate forms of human conduct, and their participation was additionally informed by what human beings ought to do in the face of large decisions.

PROPHECY: LOOKING AT THE PAST, DETERMINING THE FUTURE

Many Sahtu Dene believe in a far distant time during which significant events occurred that now explain the modern universe. At this time, "when the world was new" (Blondin 1990), the land was inhabited by giant animals, mysterious creatures, and people who could transform themselves into other beings. Their actions, which created the world as it now exists, are often recounted in narratives that Dene storytellers and elders pass from generation to generation, and that contain instructions on proper behaviour. The stories tell of how Naácho, or giant animals, roamed and helped shape the world, and they often recall significant events surrounding culture heroes such as Yamoria, the Law-Giver, or Yamoga and Eyonecho, the Warriors (ibid.). At this time, both animate and inanimate entities (including people, animals, and places) had a great deal of power, which could be used to help others, cure people, win hand games, travel safely, and communicate with other beings. This power could be attained at birth, through dreaming, or by acquiring a spirit/animal helper.

Speaking openly about one's own power, or the suspected power of another person or being, is typically very limited. It is generally thought that talking about one's own power might result in its diminishment or outright loss.[22] To discuss another person's power, particularly that of the living, violates norms of non-interference in the affairs of others and could result in misfortune. Thus, references about who might have what kinds of power (and how strong it might be) are often indirect. People might guess that others have a form of power if, for example, they are especially adept at winning hand games, at hunting a particular animal, or at predicting the future. If someone can transform circumstances or predict events fairly consistently, this is often noted in subtle ways, and discussions of who is thought to have power persist in a very opaque manner. For example, before I went to Colville Lake, I had heard rather discreetly from people in other communities that one of its elders, named Frank, was very powerful.[23] No one in Colville Lake directly confirmed this, but as time went on, several of its leaders persisted in checking whether I had met him. "Have you spoken with Frank yet?" they would ask. "You should really go and talk to him. He knows things." Or, "You should talk to Frank. Whatever he says is the truth." People also told stories of his accomplishments: "One time Frank saved the whole community by feeding all the people when they were starving. He called the caribou back to the community by rubbing two sticks together." I sensed a collective insistence that I go and see Frank. Due to various setbacks related to translators and a community consultant with whom I worked, my visit to Frank was somewhat delayed. However, the chief of Colville Lake felt that I should meet him right away, and one snowy evening he pulled up on his snowmobile outside my cabin and told me to come with him; he would assist in the translation for my first visit with Frank. Though no one in Colville Lake ever told me that Frank was more significant than any other community member, and no one discussed his power, people's regard for it was palpable (for more on my visit with Frank, see pp. 140-42).

Although many people in the Sahtu converted to Catholicism during the past century due to missionary proselytizing, this idea of power continues to inform many stories and experiences of everyday events.[24] Interestingly, the reluctance to discuss personal power does not apply after a person with power dies. This is particularly true for people who held a great deal of power; they are sometimes referred to as prophets. In the strong prophet tradition of the Sahtu, prophets receive visions that enable them to help others and to predict future events. They can also use their acquired power to precipitate events, avoid misfortune, or communicate with and travel to unseen worlds. One of the most revered prophets in the Sahtu was ?ehtseo (Grandfather) Ayah, who lived in Déline from his birth during the 1850s to his death in 1941.[25] Often, late in the evening or on Sunday afternoons, when most houses are quiet, people spoke about Ayah and his prophecies.

According to the stories, Ayah saw everything from the beginning to the end of time. He predicted numerous local and world events, including uranium mining in Port Radium, the Second World War, and 9/11. Many people believe that some of his prophecies are yet to be fulfilled. One of them foretells a famine that will come from the South and continue to the Sahtu until nothing is left. In all the Earth, only three locations in the Sahtu will have fish. Ayah could see everything that people had done in their lives, just by shaking their hands. Wrapped in the stories about Ayah are lessons on how to be a good Dene person and how to go to heaven. The more important of these involve generosity, respect for oneself and others, and the value of non-interference and of taking responsibility for oneself. In very significant ways, the prophecies and the prophet tradition continue to inform how Sahtu Dene people view the world and their place in it.

Given that Sahtu Dene already have a well-established mode of predicting the future, participating in the JRP process, which was designed to achieve the same end, would seem rather futile. Although knowledge of the prophecies does not preclude efforts to shape the future, many Sahtu

Dene strongly believe that the words of the prophets are unquestionable. Thus, prophecies about forthcoming events are incorporated into ways of talking about the future that differ from the predictive analyses provided by Western technocratic models. One Sahtu Dene person explained,

> As an old prophet said – back then, he said a few words on behalf for the future, and I still remember. As he said about the future, an old prophet knew about it, what's going to happen in the future, because the high power already talked to him about that, and he knows about it, and he already mentioned to us so we all know about the story. And he said it's going to happen in the future. That's what has happened today with the oil pipeline.[26]

If, as the above narratives suggest, everyone (who has heard and understood the prophecies) already knows "the story," perhaps people were compelled to testify in the community hearings for reasons beyond the interrogation and presentation of knowledge.

GENEROSITY, APPROPRIATENESS, AND BEING DENE

Dene people in the Sahtu often talk about Dene law – a code of conduct handed down from the earliest times that outlines how to lead a good life. Dene law is a complex and sophisticated guide, and many of its aspects cannot be addressed here, but three of its components were important in shaping Sahtu Dene participation in the JRP hearings: helping others, non-interference, and generosity.

When I was conducting fieldwork in Colville Lake, I often stayed with some elders who spent long periods trapping on the land. When I first arrived, their son-in-law, David, picked me up at the airstrip on his snowmobile, took me to their house, and told me that they were out on the land. They would return in a few days, and until then I should make myself at home. As he drove away, David added, "Oh, and don't fill the woodstove too high; the last people to stay here burned the house down."

My first day passed without much difficulty, and I ate most of the canned food that I had brought. On the second day, I ran out of water. The house had no plumbing, and I did not know how to get water on my own, so I decided to purchase supplies at the Co-op Store on the far side of town. To my surprise, and dismay, I picked the last carton of eggs, a can of condensed milk, and a litre bottle of water from its sparsely stocked shelves, all of which came to seventeen dollars.

The temperature outside was –30 Celsius, even in April, and as I fed the stove with one measly piece of wood at a time, the house soon became very cold indeed. And perhaps most dangerously, the wood supply was getting low. On the third day, I started to panic, just a little bit, because I knew that without the generous assistance of my hosts, I would never survive in this place. I didn't know how to obtain heat, water, or the other necessities of life; I had no idea how thick the ice was on the lake, or whether I could walk on it; or which trees were good for firewood; or where (and how) I could obtain it. In short, I had no relationship with this land and thus no knowledge of how to survive there. This is in sharp contrast to the Colville Lake Dene, who have lived on the land since time immemorial and who have a deep, intimate, and reciprocal relationship with their environment. Thankfully, four days after my arrival, I came home from the Co-op Store to find nineteen frozen martens thawing before the wood-stove. My hosts had returned.

Residents of Colville Lake still live primarily off the land, through hunting, gathering, trapping, hauling their own water, and collecting their own firewood. Some locals obtain seasonal employment with oil and gas companies as slashers, environmental monitors, and labourers; others sell the furs that they trap. A few are employed full-time, largely with the band, land corporation, school, or health centre. Even they spend a great deal of time on the land, obtaining firewood and hunting and fishing to provide food that not only offsets the high cost and low nutrition of supplies from the Co-op Store, but is also a preferred taste. Thus, for example, when I first arrived in Colville Lake, the newly elected land corporation president was unable to assume his position for three months because he was out on the land. His brother took his place until he returned.

Because their work schedules tended to be flexible, and most employment was seasonal, many people in Colville Lake were able to spend at least part of their day visiting. However, public gathering spots are few in Colville Lake, so they often wandered over to the building that houses both the band and land corporation offices to share tea or coffee. I, too, found that my daily routine involved heading to the band office at about 9:30 every morning and staying until lunch time. I learned a lot from those visits and often sat in the chief's office with the band manager, the interim president of the land corporation, and others who dropped by. The chief and the interim president were brothers, two of eleven siblings from one of the largest families in Colville Lake. They were very unlike each other.

The chief, Daniel, was a large man who often smiled and told stories in low, smooth tones. Timothy was very sharp; he was business-minded and had a keen grasp of developments in the oil and gas and mining industries.[27] He said that the JRP hearings had been too formal and that though the community was trying to participate, it had been unable to do so because the hearings were so technical and the language so specific. If people wished to speak, they were required to "register" and could talk for only ten minutes. Thus, Colville Lake had been obliged to hire lawyers so that it could be heard. He added that many lawyers were being enriched by the JRP process and that though his community had tapped into the available funding, the money had been used to pay them.

Timothy talked a lot about the community and how people disliked interfering in the affairs of others. He also mentioned that, though the role of elected leaders is ostensibly to speak for the people, neither this nor making major decisions on behalf of constituents are norms in Sahtu communities. Daniel also spoke to me often and told me that his community wanted to remain independent so that it didn't rely on the government to provide things. He said that people feel better when they can live on their own and when the government can't take things from them. Timothy, too, said that Colville Lake remained Dene by employing the strategy of "keeping things difficult." No outsider would willingly cut wood or haul water, both regular activities in Colville Lake, and because of this they stayed away. As a result, outside influence was diminished, and the Dene were able to live with minimal interference.

One October morning, Daniel told me a story about how various gifts had been given to different people. Mola (those of European descent) were given the gift of money, others were given gifts to make and fix things, and Aboriginal people were given the gift of land. He said that local residents were aware of the oil and gas under their land but could not access it, so they needed the help of mola. But, he argued, because mola and the community must help each other to extract the oil and gas, Colville Lake should be a partner in the enterprise and should receive 50 percent of any profits. As he explained, if governments and the community worked together, everyone would be stronger:

> Native people need mola, and mola needs Native people because they were here first and they have all the land ... They are the keepers of the land. So, if the government worked with the communities together and they built each other up, then the community would be strong and the government would be strong. But when the government wants to keep the people down,

the community is not strong, and neither is the government. We all need to work together and share because we are all part of Canada. The government thinks that the Dene just want to block everything and that they are enemies, but this is not true – they just want everything to be fair.[28]

The importance of working together is echoed in other stories and in prophecies, and it forms a key part of how Sahtu Dene people approach environmental assessment processes. More than an instrument for predicting future impacts, the hearings became an opportunity to do what human beings should do when a big decision must be made: sit down and talk to each other. An elder from Déline said,

> This is something really big. When we work on something really big, we have to talk with each other and know what is going on then. That way, we have to really discuss things with each other. If it's in a good way, we can work on it, but if it's not good, we can't work on those kinds of things.[29]

Time and again, from community to community, people emphasized the importance of talking together. Another person described why he chose to participate: "So we're here to talk to you to help us. This is something we're concerned about. We're here to listen to each other because we are neighbors ... So this kind of issue you guys talking about, we have to help each other because we're neighbors."[30]

However, sitting down and talking with one another was accompanied by frustration and a great deal of skepticism; after all, Sahtu Dene people had already gone through a hearing process in connection with a pipeline – the Berger Inquiry. In many respects, there was a general feeling that the proponents and governments at the hearings were intent on asking for things rather than really talking with the people. Of course, this was inescapable to some extent – Imperial Oil *was* asking (in a very complicated way) for permission to run a pipeline through the Mackenzie Valley. However, Sahtu Dene people who had provided their answer to Justice Berger saw the continued pressure for a pipeline as bothersome, not because it was inconvenient, but because it involved the frequent interference by proponents and governments in other people's affairs.

Just as it is unfitting to speak on behalf of others in the Sahtu, it is also generally considered inappropriate to unnecessarily interfere in their affairs. This includes gratuitous interference with both human and other-than-human beings. For example, Sahtu Dene people frequently mention the harm done to caribou by human intrusion and note that the taste of caribou meat changes when animals are unnecessarily stressed by being chased via snowmobile or low-flying aircraft. Non-interference also characterizes appropriate human interaction and applies equally to community members (even within families) and outsiders.

During an afternoon focus group, a person from Déline told me that "Dene and mola have two different lifestyles. Even them [mola], they go up to the moon and stars. Why are they doing that? Why are they bothering things like that? It's not good to bother things like that; they should just leave it."[31] The idea that outsiders frequently involve themselves in the lands and affairs of others is grounded in past experience. People frequently asked me, "Why do they keep bothering us about this pipeline?"[32] Or, referring to the Berger Inquiry, "We already told them we don't want this pipeline, so why do they keep bothering us?"[33] Thus, in some ways, the JRP hearings were just another example of outsider interference in community affairs. As one person said to the panel, "You should think twice before you talk to us or bothering for our land here. I know where there's something under, that's what you want."[34] Many people who participated in the hearings had the impression that the pipeline plans were already in place and that asking people for their opinion at that point had more to do with the need to gain project approval than with a sincere desire to hear what people had to say. And though Imperial Oil had held several information sessions, consultation meetings, and knowledge-gathering workshops in Sahtu communities, people did not perceive these as a significant community contribution to the planning process.[35] In other words, they felt uninformed and uninvolved in meaningful planning for the MGP; they felt that they should have talked together first and begun planning for the project afterward.

The persisting request for permission to build a pipeline has an additional consequence for Sahtu Dene people: it puts them in the position of appearing ungenerous and uncooperative. Another basic component of Dene law is that one shares what one has. Working at Colville Lake during the 1960s, anthropologist Joel Savishinsky (1974, 611) documented the central role of generosity: "A person's stature and position within the community is closely related to other people's estimation of him as either a generous or stingy individual. People are consequently very sensitive about how they are regarded in this matter, and they are in turn very aware of how others behave in these same respects."

Sahtu Dene stories often emphasize sharing, and many prophecies contain instructions on the importance of generosity. Respected prophet ʔehtseo Ayah told a story of a child who came to his house, asking for food because he was hungry and people didn't have much to eat. The prophet's wife did not know what to do because she had just half a fish left for her own family. The prophet said, "If we give away the fish, it will come back to us threefold by the time the sun falls." So the woman gave away her last fish, and shortly thereafter a friend of the prophet's came back from hunting and brought him two moose. The person who recounted this story told me that it was an example of how people ought to give to others, even in hard times.[36]

Not long after I began my research in the Sahtu, I was participating in a workshop with several elders when one person said he was glad that I had come to research Sahtu Dene involvement in oil and gas decision making because, as he put it, "We Dene always say yes – even if we want to say no, we say yes because we do not want to be disrespectful. Our people need to learn to say no."[37] I heard other statements like this. In September 2006, a member of the Mackenzie Valley Environmental Impact Review Board told me that, at least once, a land use permit had been issued to an oil and gas company simply because the board had not heard a strong "no" from the community membership. Indeed, this has been a dilemma for Dene members of regulatory and resource co-management boards who suspect that a community does not want a particular development but are obliged to grant a licence or permit because they have no direct evidence otherwise.[38]

In part, the tension created by forcefully voicing dissent may rest in Sahtu Dene idioms of generosity and sharing. If people express reluctance to share the fruits of the land (or access to it), they are not acting in accordance with Dene law. However, failing to dissent may mean that an unwelcome project goes ahead. Furthermore, because the JRP hearings were part of the public record, the appearance of being ungenerous would be witnessed not solely by the panel or proponents, but by the community (and general public) as a whole.

Some Sahtu Dene, however, have developed strategies to circumvent this double bind. A common story told by many Sahtu residents again involves Prophet Ayah. Sunday afternoons in Déline move fairly slowly. Many people attend Mass at the local church and often go visiting afterward. Sitting at a small kitchen table one Sunday, I was sharing a pot of tea with some locals and discussing the possibility of the pipeline when one of them remarked, "You know, Prophet Ayah said that people from the South would come to the Sahtu and ask us for our land. He told us that we should tell them yes. He said, 'Always tell them yes, but also tell them that if they want the land, they will have to take it with them when they go.'" This tactic of saying yes while imposing an impossible condition relieves people from appearing ungenerous but also achieves the desired end. In a way, the use of this story removes people from the precarious situation of saying no when asked for their lands. At the same time, however, the effectiveness of this approach will depend on how well listeners understand its cultural context and on the ability of regulatory boards to accept alternative forms of voice as equally valid (and equally purposeful) modes of expression.

All of this is not to say that people in the Sahtu do not voice their dissent regarding industrial projects. As one person testified before the JRP, "Today, when we are speaking to you, we are talking very aggressively about our land and I feel that we have a right to do so."[39] Nor do I claim that all Sahtu Dene are opposed to extractive industries. I do, however, suggest that in expressing dissent, some were obliged to choose between proper human behaviour or complying with the foreign extraction of resources from their lands. In fact, the question of pipeline approval evoked a variety of responses, sometimes favourable and sometimes not. However, for many participants in the JRP hearings, questions of voice and of working together for the benefit of everyone (including Sahtu communities) took priority. As a witness said in Déline, "We're talking about the pipeline with them, we don't say 'yes' or 'no.' If we do it really right, then we both will say 'yes.'"[40]

PLACES OF POWER

Participants also used the JRP hearings to address issues that extended beyond the immediate impact of the pipeline. They discussed the high cost and low availability of housing in Sahtu communities, the limited access to child care and day care programs, the high cost of fuel, the lack of funding for hunting and trapping programs, and the inadequate training provided for youth in trades and in the necessary skills for a subsistence-based economy. They mentioned the lack of substance abuse programs in the North and expressed concerns about increased access to and use of drugs and alcohol. They talked about the need for a ratified land use plan and about their frustrations with government intrusions, the 1921 treaty, difficulties surrounding the current land claim agreement, and the failed promises of earlier industrial projects. In short, they used the hearings to raise issues that would otherwise have entailed the involvement of numerous other parties, such as governments, environmental groups, and extractive industries. In engaging with the panel, a government-sponsored entity, Sahtu Dene people were able to confront a face, so to speak, that simultaneously represented outside incursions but also possibilities for change. And most importantly, they were told that their words would make a difference.

In this respect, they did use the hearing space as a place of negotiation. Of course, many of the issues that they raised, such as Treaty 11 or the impact of the Norman Wells Pipeline and the Port Radium mines, were beyond the scope of the environmental impact review. Nonetheless, they could call governments and others to account regarding their failure to provide for the well-being of Sahtu communities on past projects and initiatives. They also negotiated for increased benefits (both immediate and long-term), should the pipeline be approved. For instance, they cited the example of the Norman Wells Pipeline, in which local employment was lacking, to ensure that training would be provided for local workers before the Mackenzie pipeline's construction phase, that local hiring practices would be in place, and that Sahtu businesses would be awarded contracts.

At the hearings, the pipeline proponents adjusted their appearance to look less like outsiders. The Imperial Oil representatives consistently opted for casual clothing, not the suit and tie required for business meetings in the South. One wore Dene-style moccasins. Despite efforts to transform the community arenas into neutral hearing spaces, the hearings did occur in distinctly local places. Some Sahtu Dene witnesses wore Dene vests as markers of their identity. In Colville Lake, as in other Sahtu communities, children were present for most of the hearings, and one elected leader gave his testimony while his child sat and played on his lap. In these instances, the symbolic claiming of space and identity marked the hearing space as both local and a site where Sahtu Dene people had elements of authority.

Participants also employed humour to claim the hearing spaces as their own. In Sahtu communities, humour is valued for its own sake (to make people happy – an important factor in and of itself), but it also functions as a means of moral instruction. In employing it, one can be self-deprecating or deprecating of others without telling them what to do (interfering in their affairs). Humour can also provide an element of ambiguity, which can be interpreted differently by locals and outsiders. In a process where only two options exist – to refuse to participate or to engage in something that conflicts with one's ideas of appropriate human behaviour – satirical involvement is perhaps the only way of engaging while upholding one's own values.

Humour was used to channel and voice frustrations with the technocratic nature of the hearings themselves. For example, after pointing out that people in Tulit'a were worried that their concerns would not be heard, and that promises made in the JRP process would not be kept, the chief of Tulit'a got up from the witness chair and claimed, "I think I won." To which the local audience reacted with laughter and applause. Somewhat awkwardly, the panel chair remarked, "We hope you win, I hope we can all win."[41] In another case, after a long oratory, which included stories and instruction on proper human conduct, a well-respected elder finished his testimony with a tongue-in-cheek comment about money:

> My grandma raised us – there's three of us – and at that time there's no pension, nothing. Sometimes we don't have nothing to eat, but our granny have even maybe one macaroni for us. Sometimes in the week we don't have nothing to eat. But we go hunting and get traditional food. That's why we're happy about that. But now today we're talking about lots of money. And now I want money. So that's why I'm talking to you guys. I want money.[42]

Listeners who were familiar with the character of the speaker recognized his claim to "want money" as both a partial truth and a pointed observation regarding the monetary-driven industrial complex. In joking about his reasons for participating, he was demonstrating his understanding and ability to negotiate the hearing space while also providing a serious commentary on the nature of the JRP process itself.

CONCLUSION

There tends to be a general assumption that because people are invited to participate in environmental assessments, or to voice their concerns in a community hearing, they will automatically be heard. That is to say, the overarching assumptions inherent in Western models of environmental management are rarely questioned, even when they are incommensurable with local practices. The structure and format of the JRP hearings were based on Euro-Canadian expectations about proper proceedings and ways of speaking that may not be suitable in an intercultural context. And though governments have touted the community hearing as a significant contribution to participatory and cooperative environmental assessment, it naturalizes the legalistic approach and takes Euro-Canadian institutional apparatuses as givens. Thus, industrial developments have a dual impact – that arising from the activity itself and that resulting from the *process* of environmental assessment and management. The latter comes in terms of the time and human resources necessary to participate effectively, but also because the process can call into question long-standing views about the world and negate the ways in which people think about themselves. For northern Aboriginal people, making themselves heard in the regulatory process can require choosing between collectively held values and the protocol and nature of community hearings. Sahtu Dene who opt for the former run the risk that proponents and regulators will perceive their lack of forceful dissent as acquiescence. In this way, the difference between participation and consent becomes blurred. Participatory management has taken what are fundamentally political matters and channelled them into the anti-political form of bureaucratic management, where decisions can be controlled and made predictable. Though the process is supposedly about the need for certainty and quantifiable numbers, what is really at stake here is sovereignty – whether people can make decisions that are grounded in, and consistent with, their own visions for their future.

2

"A Billion Dollars Cannot Create a Moose"
Perceptions of Industrial Impacts

One of the things that the old people always taught the
younger people is that you must always keep your food good.
If you treat your food good, the food in return will treat
you good.

— *Joe Naedzo, Berger Inquiry, 1975*

ANTHROPOLOGIST ARTURO ESCOBAR (2001, 143) writes that considering "the primacy of embodied perception, we always find ourselves in places." Given that anthropologists, human geographers, historians, sociologists, and many others have focused on the cultural construction of land and nature, this sense of place has taken on multiple and complex forms. Despite the varied approaches to place as a central aspect of human experience, the idea of place has moved decisively beyond a simple consideration of geographic, environmental, or topological significance squarely into the realm of culture.

People everywhere must come to terms with the physical reality of their experience of places, but how they conceptualize their experiences is culturally variable and structured through particular sets of lenses. Anthropologist Keith Basso (1996) suggests that for certain Apache peoples, the importance of place cannot be separated from sentiments of belonging, rootedness, and connection to collective cultural and physical landscapes. Through the recollection of places, the Apache recall the stories and knowledge contained within those places. Experiences of particular places are needed to possess wisdom — to foresee misfortune, fend off disasters, and live in harmony with human and other-than-human beings. Places serve as referential markers and as vehicles for retrieving useful knowledge. For Basso, places are not void of geographical or topological significance, but are made meaningful through the interaction between biophysical and human environments.

Anthropologist Tim Ingold (1993, 157), as well, demonstrates that binary distinctions between "natural" environments and experiences of places are often problematic because they reproduce a dichotomy between a "physical world of neutral objects" and the landscape as an ideational or symbolic construct imposed by the people who dwell there. As he puts it, human beings acquire knowledge of their environment through actions, which are themselves always shaped by the particular nature of physical landscapes. Ingold (1986, 45) writes that "our immediate perception of the environment is in terms of what it affords for the pursuit of action in which we are currently engaged." Thus, conceptualizations of our physical surroundings are shaped by what Ingold calls a "taskscape," an ensemble of interlocking actions that are inseparable from productive practices. Thus, any consideration of place must necessarily include a consideration of the mutual constitution of persons and environments, and the co-creation of perception and experience encountered through practical activities carried out on the land.

Taking the engaged nature of human interactions with the land as a starting point for how places are represented and constructed reveals how differing conceptions of environment and nature are strongly tied to productive practices. Arturo Escobar (1999) traces how the meaning of nature has shifted throughout history, according to various political and economic factors. Arguing that the concept of nature is relational and historically contingent, Escobar examines how perspectives of nature are produced through particular discourses and productive practices, including what he calls capitalist nature, organic nature, and technonature. He reveals that a capitalist view of nature entails a separation of biophysical and social facts, and is linked to the increased colonization of time, rational forms of management and surveillance, the creation of maps and other statistical data, and the association of certain landscapes with national identities. Escobar shows that engagement with non-Western constructions of nature, culture, and society must include a consideration of diverse constructions of the relationship between biological and human worlds, and that capitalist concepts of nature should not be imposed on other social orders, but must also be seen as informed by specific cultural and productive practices.

Indeed, capitalist constructions of landscape have long contributed to divergent views regarding the appropriate uses of land in colonial states, including the ways in which entitlements to the land are justified in legal and social realms, and how decisions regarding its use are negotiated. Several scholars have identified a fundamental link between conceptions of landscape, knowledge, and appropriate human development, including the ways in which notions of landscape can shape industrial processes (Brody 1981; Escobar 1999; Seed 2001). Historian Patricia Seed (2001) offers an excellent discussion of how sixteenth-century European cultural values surrounding land, gender, labour, wealth, and private property contributed greatly to the colonization of the "New World" and continue to inform the Canadian and American national present. Seed shows that long-held Western European ideas about landownership and "improvement," hunting, agriculture, the gendered division of labour, and waste or wastelands were used to justify appropriating Aboriginal lands and resources for English colonialists. David Hurst Thomas (2000) also demonstrates how conceptions of land and appropriate human development (coupled with science) helped to marginalize Aboriginal perspectives of history, knowledge, land, governance, and entitlements. In *Maps and Dreams,* Hugh Brody (1981) points to the ways in which stereotypes of Aboriginal peoples in northeastern British Columbia, combined with dreams of a resource-rich frontier, have served to rationalize European claims to "newfound" territories. Dara Culhane (1998) and Julie Cruikshank (2005) also reveal how the concept of *terra nullius* and notions of a pristine land, untouched and unused, contributed to the many industrial frontiers in western and northern Canada. The work of these scholars has contributed greatly to understanding the ways in which European cultural constructions of landscapes and peoples rationalized the expropriation of Aboriginal lands in Canadian jurisprudence and fostered multiple images of "the North" in popular national imaginations.

A capitalist orientation toward nature tends to perceive the landscape as passive, separate from people, and fully realized through labour, commodification, and the expropriation of resources. Yet, for many peoples whose livelihoods depend on an intimate knowledge of their environment, senses of place involve not only attachments to particular sites related to stories, memories, emotions, and movement (though this may often be the case), but also a keen understanding of how to live in that environment, how to locate, obtain, and sustain its riches, and how to avoid danger.

In the Sahtu, people often refer to the land as their bank, Great Bear Lake as their deep-freeze, and the environment itself as their grocery store. Important as the land is for acquiring material resources, it is also viewed in a deeply personal and spiritual manner. For Sahtu people, human beings and the landscape are implicated in intricate physical, social, and moral obligations that include relationships based on mutual respect and understanding. The land and all its components are seen as animate and sentient beings imbued with power and agency. This chapter examines how Sahtú Dene engagement with the landscape involves productive practices that contribute to senses of personal and collective well-being. Rather than seeing nature in terms of the separation of biophysical and social realms, Sahtu Dene people link the social, biophysical, and spiritual elements of the landscape. This connection exists even when people are involved in mixed economic activities, such as working at the local store, band office, or land corporation. Yet this link between the varied components of the land is subverted in environmental assessment and management practices. Rather than realizing that industrial development has real consequences for Sahtu Dene well-being, environmental assessment processes attempt to predict, monitor, and manage its effects and to provide for compensation where expected impacts occur. In this way, the determination of environmental impacts in the assessment of the Mackenzie Gas Project (MGP) and Sahtu Dene perceptions of their land are incommensurable. I argue here that despite considerations given to the social, cultural, and economic importance of the land and land-based activities for the lives of Sahtu Dene people, the means of determining and expressing the environmental impacts and risks of the MGP fail to appropriately recognize the precise nature of Sahtu Dene relationships with their land. That is, the failure of institutional environmental assessment apparatuses to take seriously the moral nature of Sahtu Dene relationships with the landscape likewise leads to an inability to accurately assess the constitution (and consequences) of industrial impacts for Sahtu Dene people.

Spending Time on the Land

Every fall, the people of the Sahtu look forward to the taste of fresh caribou meat. Most years, the caribou return to a particular spot on Great Bear Lake, and local hunters from Déline cross the lake to meet them. I was fortunate to be in Déline when this occurred. The lake had been choppy all week, and the return of the hunters was anxiously awaited. One evening the woman with whom I was staying said, "The men are coming back, let's go out and meet them." So we drove the short distance to the community dock, where their boats were expected to arrive. To my surprise, we were not alone. In fact, seven other trucks, and many more people, had also gathered at the dock in anticipation of the men's safe return with fresh caribou meat. About twenty-five of us waited apprehensively, scanning the horizon for whitecaps or lights. As the sun went down and the temperature began to drop, we saw the lights of a boat. Everyone became very excited. I was struck by the sensation of relief, gratitude, and the genuine sense of community: as the men's boats rolled to the dock one by one, people were there to welcome them home.[1]

In 2007, the Northwest Territories Bureau of Statistics reported that, on average, 59 percent of households in Colville Lake, Déline, and Tulit'a relied on country foods for most or all of their meat supplies (GNWT 2008). Indeed, local people often talk about their desire for what they call "Dene foods," meaning food obtained from the land, which is thought to be more nutritious than store-bought food. Purchased food is transported into the communities by aircraft, winter road, or barge, and the long travel times and the associated expense limit both its nutritional value and affordability. Furthermore, Dene people often associate store-bought food with artificial preservatives and are highly skeptical about the raising and processing of farmed meat.[2] However, their preference for Dene foods extends beyond nutritional and economic considerations to include what they describe as "a taste for something." People often say that their bodies "need" caribou meat and that they crave food from the land.

Country food also plays a strong role in establishing and sustaining community cohesion through the creation and maintenance of social and ancestral ties. As in the episode of the hunters' return to Déline, obtaining food from the land creates not only opportunities to travel and spend time in hunting areas, but also generates great excitement and anticipation for the consumption of seasonal delicacies. Netting spawning whitefish in the fall for their eggs or returning to a favourite duck- or goose-hunting site in the spring are anticipated not only by those who actually undertake them, but also by those who share in the harvest. The collection, preparation, and consumption of food help to recall places where Sahtu Dene have lived since time immemorial.

The circulation and sharing of Dene foods also produces intense communal responsibilities and obligations. Some Sahtu communities have greater access to fish than others, which commonly ask that fish be sent to them. Or caribou herds might be particularly accessible to a certain community, which will package and send meat to relatives and friends throughout the region and beyond. Local people often worry about the lack of Dene foods in the diet of loved ones who live away from the

Sahtu and commonly send caribou meat, fish, and particularly dry-meat to them. As I travelled to and from the Sahtu, local hunters often asked me to take dry-meat, berries, or fish to relatives living in southern cities. Dene food is exchanged and circulated throughout the region and beyond, creating a network of social responsibilities and obligations, and minimizing the possibility of going without it.

Country food is also shared within communities. If a hunter kills a caribou or a moose, the meat is distributed throughout the community to relatives, elders, lone-parent households, widows, and others who need it or who request it. Certain parts of animals, such as the caribou head, are considered especially tasty and are often reserved for elders or given away as a sign of respect. Locals are fully aware of who has set fishnets in the nearby lakes or rivers and often ask for fish for food or bait. During a visit to the Sahtu, I stayed with a family who had a fishnet in Great Bear Lake, which their oldest son checked on a daily basis. Friends and relatives often came by to visit and to ask for fish. Requests for fish or meat are made indirectly – someone will mention that he or she has a "taste for something" or is "dying for a taste of" a certain food. Most times, if the food is available, it is removed from the freezer or store-shed and shared, and there is a general conviction that because it comes freely from the land, it ought to be exchanged freely (usually without monetary payment).

In the Sahtu, where store-bought food is extremely expensive, obtaining and consuming country foods greatly offsets the high cost of living. However, spending time on the land is also very much a social act and a fundamental part of personal development. The freedom of life in the bush is strongly contrasted with that in town. The riches of the bush are free to all, and people can make their decisions free of external control, which is not often the case in a community. Some families choose to heat their homes with woodstoves not only because they must spend time on the land while gathering wood, but also because dependence on Western commodities and government programs is minimized. As the president of the Déline Renewable Resource Council said to me, "What the land provides is free. One does not pay for fish, for caribou. One has no rules, or government."[3] Alternatively, community life is often associated with non-Dene institutions and management, a climate of dependence, idleness, substance abuse, and enforcement (see Savishinsky 1974; Ellen Basso 1978, 697). In the bush, however, people must work hard for their food and other material goods; they must exercise good judgment and use personal initiative to extract themselves from sometimes troublesome situations. There is no social assistance and no time for alcohol, as a

On the land at Lake Beloit. Freeze-up in October.

Colville Lake hunter stated in the Joint Review Panel (JRP) hearings: "When you live off the land you are – because of living on the land you are an honest and straight person; but living in the community, there's a lot of negative impacts like drugs and alcohol."[4]

The ability to survive in the bush and to obtain sustenance from it is indeed a great source of pride and is seen as a strong indicator of cultural continuity. People frequently remark that their ancestors lived on the land for many generations and that they passed down their knowledge of how to find animals, good berry-picking places, and other necessities for survival; they knew the location of the good fishlakes and how to butcher and prepare Dene foods. Young people are taught how to keep warm in extremely cold temperatures, how to make emergency shelters, and how to use Dene bush medicine to heal wounds, burns, and other injuries. Life in the bush is not presented as easy, but it is seen as distinctly Dene; that is, through generations of experience, skills, and knowledge gained on the land, Dene people know it in ways that outsiders never could.

Relationships with the land form an important aspect of how Sahtu Dene people think about themselves and their place in the world. The land provides sustenance and facilitates intense connections between members of the community, ancestors, and practices that are seen as essential to being Dene. However, these relationships are also profoundly moral, in the sense that human beings and multiple components of the landscape are implicated in a series of relationships that include, yet extend beyond, taking care of the land. Via an interpreter, an elder and hunter from Colville Lake said to the Berger Inquiry in 1976,

> This is the land that we make our living on, he says. He says this land is not for us to make money out of like to dig for oil and to dig for gold or stuff like that on it, he said. Yet, we live on it to make our living the simple way, to fish on it, to hunt on it, and to trap on it and just live off the land. That's what we think this land is that, he said, but not to make money from it ... Even before the white people came, he said, we made our living off this land. He said, we were all brought up from what was from the land our parents hunted and fished and that's how we were brought up. So, he said, this land fed us all the time, even before white people came to the north. To us, he said, it's just like a mother that brought her children up, he said, that is how we think about this country. He said, it is just like a mother to us. He said that's how serious it is that we think about the land around here.[5]

Sahtu Dene people believe that a universal law informs all human and other-than-human relationships with the land.[6] As a result of this law, all living things have their places on the land and can gain physical, social, and spiritual nourishment as long as they do not break it. For many Sahtu Dene, the world is infused with power and agency. Little distinction is made between the physical and the spiritual, and consequently, nearly every aspect of Sahtu Dene life is governed by moral rules and the social and physical relationships that rely on their observation. According to historian Kerry Abel (1993, 40), "Events were not randomly caused or the result of good or bad luck. Rather the spirits were constantly at work, interacting with each other and with people." Indeed, to ensure a successful hunt, a hunter must follow the laws governing the respectful reciprocal relationships and mutual obligations between humans and animals. Otherwise, the animal might not give itself to the hunter, and the hunt would be unsuccessful. These laws cover a wide variety of subjects, from how human beings should conduct themselves in their daily lives, to how they treat the bones of the animals that they kill, to the kinds of foods that hunters eat, and to what they ought to be thinking before and after the hunt.

Today, Sahtu Dene hunters carefully ensure that Dene law is upheld, particularly in the treatment of animals or other components of the land. It is still generally thought that the mutually reciprocal relationships between humans and animals will break down if a hunter transgresses Dene law, with the result that animals will refuse to "come around any more." For example, stories in Déline tell that the people stopped conducting a ceremony called "feeding the fire," where a fire is literally fed with food, tobacco, cloth, and prayers. For some years in the mid-1980s, caribou disappeared from the Déline area, returning only when people began to feed the fire again. It is thought that feeding the fire with thanks and prayers is strongly associated with the caribou's choice to give themselves to Déline hunters.

An important aspect of the universal law involves honouring elements of the landscape by behaving with respect. Simply put, this is achieved by not offending or interfering with other creatures or the land and by making offerings to the landscape. People told me that when one travels, visits a place for the first time, or takes something from the land, one should always pay the land. Payment can consist of various valuable items, but money or tobacco are most frequently chosen. Once, when I returned from yet another unsuccessful day of fishing on Great Bear Lake, a guest at my hosts' house asked me if I was remembering to pay the land. "In order to get fish, you have to pay the land," he said. And then he asked jokingly, "Do you have one of those credit cards? Maybe you would get some fish if you put that in the water."[7]

When crossing multiple waterways, such as from Great Bear Lake to the Great Bear River, people are required to pay both the lake and the river. I myself had done this, paying with tobacco when I went from Déline to attend the Tulit'a Hand Game Tournament. The payment or offering is a request for safe passage on the water. For Sahtu Dene people, then, it is the land that determines the fate of human beings (rather than the reverse). Indeed, one of the first phrases that I learned during that trip to Déline was "Sahtu k'aowe," which means "Sahtu [Great Bear Lake] is the boss."[8] This is the most common response to questions about travel or going out on the land.

Other forms of behaviour are required to uphold the universal law. As I sat at a kitchen table with a group of hunters, an experienced hunter mentioned the posters that the Ministry of Natural Resources had recently put up in local airports. With the intent of promoting sex-specific hunting, they explained how to distinguish between male and female caribou. Hunters were to target older males and leave the females alone because their reproductive ability was seen as more important to the sustainability of the herd. However, the hunters seemed very concerned about this form of wildlife management. One man said, "It is not right for people to kill all of the old men. It would be like killing off all of the male elders in our community. If we kill off the old male caribou, then how will the herd know how to go?"[9] From this perspective, a caribou herd is like a human community: it demands the same considerations for well-being in terms of its physical and social composition. In this case, killing older males would deprive the herd of knowledge that was as important as physical reproduction for community survival.

Anthropologists working in Alaska and the Canadian North have noted the moral nature of Aboriginal people's relationships with the land and the other-than-human persons who dwell there. Irving Hallowell (1960; see also Colin Scott 1996) documents the social and kinship relations between Ojibwa (Anishnaabe) and the environment, noting that their conceptions of personhood are not limited to human beings. For example, they refer to parts of the environment as Grandfather and see its elements, such as thunder, flint, and plants, as having personhood. Importantly, not all parts of the environment are necessarily animate, but some have the potential to be so under certain circumstances. Nonetheless, when dealing with plants and animals, Anishnaabe people behave as if they were animate, with the capacity to understand and speak. Given this, human persons are expected to engage with other-than-human entities in very particular ways that demonstrate respect and appreciation.

Writing some fifty years after Hallowell, anthropologist Paul Nadasdy (2007, 25) demonstrates that these ideas persist across the North, and though they differ slightly from group to group, there are commonalities such as "food taboos, ritual feasts, and proscribed methods for disposing of animal remains, as well as injunctions against overhunting and talking badly about, or playing with, animals." Some anthropologists have focused on attempts through ritual obligations to reconcile the apparent conflict between seeing animals as persons and using them as prey (Tanner 1979; Brightman 1993), whereas others have examined the ways in which the conception of other-than-human components of the environment shape mutual interactions (Colin Scott 1996; Nadasdy 2003; Feit 2004; Kofinas 2005; Westman 2013). Yet, all these writers recognize that the Western European approach, in which humans are commonly perceived as separate from the environment, is incommensurate with Aboriginal views of the environment as a social and moral system.

Disarticulating the Landscape

What constitutes "the environment" has proven a major dilemma in environmental assessment regimes in the Canadian North and elsewhere. In 2005, the Mackenzie Valley Environmental Impact Review Board (MVEIRB 2005, 50) released its environmental impact assessment guidelines, which define the environment as "the components of the Earth including (a) land, water and air, including all layers of the atmosphere; (b) all organic and inorganic matter and living organisms; and (c) the interacting natural systems that include components referred to in (a) and (b)." The pipeline proponents employed much the same definition in their environmental impact statement (Mackenzie Gas Project 2004a, 1:section 2, 12). The environment as social space is conspicuously absent from these definitions, both of which serve to separate humanity and nature, and conceive of the environment as passive, inanimate, and unfeeling.

The dichotomy between human and "natural" elements of the environment is firmly rooted in current environmental assessment practices. Environmental assessment practitioners commonly employ what are termed valued ecosystem components (VECs) as primary variables for the evaluation of potential industrial impacts. A VEC is an environmental feature that is important to a local human population and/or ecosystem. Practitioners usually identify VECs via consultations with local communities and through the examination of ecological data.

Imperial Oil was required to submit its assessment of MGP impacts, including an identification and description of the relevant VECs. Consider Table 1, taken from its environmental impact statement (EIS), which shows how the project was expected to affect various VECs.

One afternoon, while sitting with some elders in Déline, I asked what they thought about how proponents determine the extent of industrial impacts on VECs. The community collaborator with whom I was working quickly told me that I was asking the wrong question. I should be asking what they thought about the possibility that one part of the environment could be more valuable than another. Not surprisingly, the elders replied that the idea was absurd and that all parts of the environment were equally essential. One elder said,

> You know, we know the importance of the land, we are so connected. People that come in and do the exploration and they don't know much about the land. It is so different for us Dene. A couple of years ago, they did some

TABLE 1 Significance of Potential Effects of the Pipeline Corridor on Wildlife Habitat Availability

Valued component	Phase when impact occurs	Direction	Effect attribute				Significant
			Maximum magnitude	Maximum geographic extent	Maximum duration		
Barren-ground caribou	Construction	Adverse	Low	Local	Far future		No
	Operations	Adverse	Low	Local	Far future		No
	Decommissioning and abandonment	Adverse	Low	Local	Far future		No
Woodland caribou	Construction	Adverse	Low	Local	Far future		No
	Operations	Adverse	Low	Local	Far future		No
	Decommissioning and abandonment	Adverse	Low	Local	Far future		No
Moose	Construction	Adverse	Moderate	Local	Medium term		No
	Operations	Adverse	Low	Local	Long term		No
	Decommissioning and abandonment	Adverse	Low	Local	Long term		No
Grizzly bear	Construction	Adverse	Low	Local	Long term		No
	Operations	Adverse	Low	Local	Long term		No
	Decommissioning and abandonment	Adverse	Low	Local	Long term		No
Marten	Construction	Adverse	Low	Local	Far future		No
	Operations	Adverse	Low	Local	Far future		No
	Decommissioning and abandonment	Adverse	Low	Local	Far future		No

Source: Mackenzie Gas Project (2004a, 5:section 10, 214).

exploring right across from here. When they were drilling, we could feel the ground shake. The caribou could feel it. They went in a different direction. So you can pretty well see how animals react to the exploration. All of the water, animals, even the mouse – all of the mouse dens, even the beaver. They don't see that. But we, the people who live off of the land, we see it.[10]

Of course, the notion that one part of the environment is more valuable than another is totally foreign to many Dene concepts and incompatible with them.

The premise that the landscape can be disarticulated (and then evaluated as an assortment of diverse entities) springs from capitalist thought, which distinguishes between the biophysical and the human. This was well illustrated in Imperial Oil's presentation of its EIS findings at the JRP hearings, in which it described the proposed project and its potential impacts. For the purposes of the presentation, the EIS findings were separated into two

FIGURE I   Effects of pipeline activities on the landscape

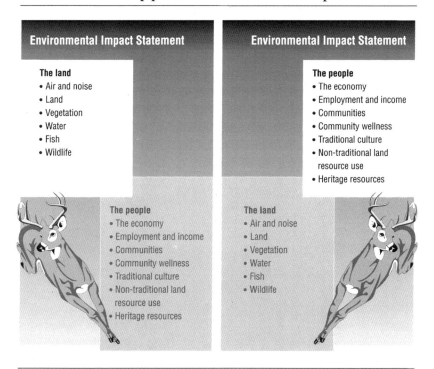

Source: Mackenzie Gas Project JRP hearing presentation, Déline, 3 April 2006.

categories: impacts on the land (including air and noise, land, vegetation, water, fish, and wildlife) and impacts on people (including the economy, employment and income, communities, community wellness, traditional culture, non-traditional land resource use, and heritage resources). Figure 1 shows how the company illustrated its approach.

At the Déline JRP hearing, a local hunter asked Imperial Oil why no people were included in the land category. A company representative replied, "On a separate chart ... we listed the items we looked at with respect to potential impacts on people ... and so we identified those concerns and measures we could take to address the kinds of concerns that you referred to."[11] Clearly, though Imperial Oil recognized the need to deal with various human components of the landscape, it did so only in terms of activities on the land (such as hunting) or the ways in which the MGP might affect tangible and thus empirically measurable aspects of the social environment (such as heritage resources, the economy, or non-traditional resource use). Importantly, it did not address the ways in which Sahtu Dene people see themselves as part of the land and the land as part of them. In other words, though it understood that impacts on the land might translate into impacts on people, it nonetheless maintained the ontological distinctions between human beings and nature.

Determining Significance

By maintaining ontological distinctions between human beings and nature, proponents of large industrial projects fail to accurately consider their impacts as experienced by Sahtu Dene people. This misrecognition can and does have profound consequences for how seriously Sahtu Dene concerns about environmental impacts are heard and considered by decision-makers, regulators, and proponents. For instance, failing to acknowledge the precise nature of Sahtu Dene relationships with the land means that the significance of industrial impacts on their subjectivities will also be misunderstood. Paul Nadasdy makes similar observations about the failure of scientists and managers to consider Aboriginal conceptions of animals as sentient beings who engage in social and reciprocal relationships with humans, even while they advocate for the appreciation and understanding of this difference. In a compelling illustration from his own work with Kluane First Nation in the Yukon, Nadasdy (2007) demonstrates that the ontological distinction between the human and the non-human is ingrained in Western European thought and how the conception of animals as other-than-human persons is marginalized in environmental management and anthropological theorizing. Nadasdy ultimately argues that we should take seriously Aboriginal people's knowledge of animals, not just as a form of metaphor or a means of understanding their cultures, but in coming to terms with the nature of animals themselves. Achieving this entails reworking the basic assumptions and concepts in Western European thought and management, those of "personhood, agency, knowledge, power, labour, and exchange" (ibid., 26). If we fail to do this, we too are complicit in dismissing Aboriginal knowledge as untrue, irrelevant, and extraneous to resource management and planning.

Environmental assessment institutional practices do examine the significance of industrial impacts on the landscape but do not genuinely consider the ways in which industrial activities disrupt Sahtu Dene relationships with it. In an environmental assessment, impacts are often seen as ecological or socio-economic, and they typically involve any change to the ecological or human environment, whether adverse or beneficial, resulting from a product, process, or approach. In assessing the impacts of the MGP, Imperial Oil used four basic questions to determine the attributes of effects: Is the effect good or bad? How intense will it be? How large an area will be affected? How long will the effect last? (Mackenzie Gas Project 2004a, 1:section 2, 26). It schematized its four questions in Table 1, under the headings of direction, maximum magnitude, maximum geographic extent, and maximum duration. Its evaluation rests in the presupposition that the significance of impacts can be captured by focusing on the intensity, geographic extent, duration, and reversibility of the effects.

As an Imperial Oil representative explained at the Déline JRP hearing,

The assessment of impacts on the land included the topics of impacts on air, and noise levels, impacts on land, vegetation, water, fish, and wildlife. In our meetings with you (the community of Déline), you told us that you had the following concerns: You told us that construction activities should be sensitive to areas of cultural and environmental significance; areas such as Bear Rock, the Great Bear River, and the Blackwater River. You told us that caribou, moose, birds, fish, and their habitats should be protected ... You told us that impacts on wildlife harvesters should be compensated ... The following are some examples of measures that the project will undertake to address these concerns. Based on the input we've received, we've modified our plans to reduce disturbances on areas that are culturally and environmentally significant. By way of example, we've eliminated the use of granular resources near Bear Rock. We've rerouted the pipeline crossing of the Great Bear River, and that crossing will be done by drilling underneath the river. We've moved the compressor station and associated facilities away from the Blackwater River, and we're applying measures to stream crossings to reduce the effects of those stream crossings on fish and fish habitat. The findings of the environmental assessment of impacts on the land were that most environmental effects will occur during the construction phase, and we believe that they can be managed so that those effects will be localized and short term. The assessment also determined that people's ability to harvest might be disrupted in the short term during the construction phase and that the project effects on air, water, land, fish, or wildlife will not last a long time or affect a large area.[12]

The assertion that the impacts on the land will be "localized and short term" is grounded in the findings of the EIS, which are themselves typically based on public and professional judgments of biophysical indicators, current abundance and distribution of wildlife populations, and the identification of important habitats that might be affected by the pipeline (Mackenzie Gas Project 2004a, 3:section 10, 1).[13] For example, in discussing the project's impact on moose, the EIS states,

> Moose use habitat along the edges of waterways. Although clearing vegetation in forested areas will produce more browse for moose, clearing areas along rivers and streams will affect moose habitat availability and might affect how moose move along these corridors and use them for overwintering. Moose might be displaced from habitat from construction noise, but once people leave disturbed sites, moose will often return to use them. Effects on moose habitat during operations should be less than construction because fewer people will be working along the right-of-way and because shrub communities cleared during construction will regrow and provide forage for moose. Access roads and rights-of-way could increase hunting pressure, particularly in remote riparian areas used by moose in winter. The largest potential effect is of moderate magnitude and long-term duration. (Ibid., 5:section 10, 3)

Thus, for Imperial Oil, the pipeline will not have a significant effect on moose: if the animals are displaced from certain areas due to construction, they will probably return; the vegetation upon which they depend will grow back; and the disturbance will be limited to the construction zones, the pipeline right-of-way, and project access roads. Although the EIS does acknowledge that the extended road infrastructure could increase hunting pressure, the disruption to moose and their habitat is ultimately described as "moderate" and is certainly not enough to justify terminating the MGP.

However, when Sahtu Dene people speak about moose, they differ fundamentally regarding the impact of the MGP. Speaking through an interpreter at the Déline JRP hearing, a local hunter and elder named Charlie Neyelle said,

> I want to talk about those stuff, which that connecting to the universal law that they [the elders] follow, the universal law of the water, they follow that. And then the universal law of the tree, and they obey that one. And the universal law of all the birds, and they obey it. And they obey the universal law of the animals, moose, and caribou and any animals. They obey the universal law. And this universal law has been destroyed with the animals. The moose have their own universal law how to go on the land. The moose are a very, very intelligent animals. They're very clever, and he [the moose] knows the area. Once you come back to that area when he was a thousand miles away, he'll come back. There's something wrong, no, I'm not going to go back there again. He going the other way ... And here the universal law that going across Mackenzie, the universal law for the animals and the waters and the minerals, we live by that a lot. And animals themselves, they live by their own law. So we both are very pleased with each other. The animals are very pleased with us and we're very pleased with them because we obey those universal law. We really respect the land. And then, the elders saying your whole land, from way up in the Arctic to all the way down south, and the whole North American and South America, they're like your whole body. And your body is all being ripped apart. It's being ripped apart and the scar all over the body. And one rip right across from the tip of your hand to all the way across your whole body to the end of the tips ... And then, the elders said they never been down South. But the elder, they have seen this prophecy. And that's all the land – the land are just like a floor tile down south. There's no room for it. And they look up this way. Only a little piece left, from your chest and up. And now the damage is coming up to your head. It is already too much to have in your body already ... These are the things we need understand the land. We didn't understand the oil company. All we understand is that addicted to oil; money. We're not looking forward to that, if there's no more fish, no more caribou, no more moose and birds.[14]

As Neyelle's words reveal, the word "moderate" cannot begin to describe the impact of projects such as the MGP. Indeed, it amounts to a breakdown in moral and physical relationships that extends beyond particular projects or isolated project effects. Neyelle sees the land as an extension of his own body and the effects of industrial activities as scars and the ripping of his flesh – a literal tearing apart of his physical and social being. On the subject of moose, Neyelle indicates that humans and animals are connected in a unique relationship that is based on mutual respect, that both parties are responsible for maintaining the relationship, that moose are intelligent and sentient beings who choose whether to return to a damaged area, and that the connection between humans and animals cannot be restored through monetary means. He adds that the universal law links animals, humans, and the landscape, and that it must be obeyed if the relationship between them is to be maintained.

Anthropologist Harvey Feit makes a comparable observation about Cree perspectives of the impacts of industrial activities on moose in the James Bay region. Citing Cree hunter Noah Eagle, who was concerned about the effect of continued logging on moose, Feit (2004, 104-5) observes, "When moose numbers have declined it is because, as he [Noah Eagle] indicates, many moose are choosing to move away from cutting areas both because their food is scarce and because they judge the land is not 'good' where there is forestry cutting." Similarly, in his analysis of the use of social impact assessment in the Alberta tar sands, anthropologist Clinton Westman (2013) finds that despite assertions by Cree hunters that the spiritual nature of a place cannot be recovered once it is disturbed, mitigation measures aimed at minimizing the impact of tar sand activities tend to disregard the relationship between the Cree and their lands. Instead, like the Imperial Oil EIS, the proponent for the Syncrude Aurora Mine argues that "while there may be some impact during construction and operations phase[s], in the long run access to the activity [in this case, gathering traditional medicines] will be improved following tar sands development and reclamation" (quoted in ibid., 138). Here again, the moral relationships between Aboriginal people and the land are mischaracterized and replaced by technical solutions that do not encompass the true costs of environmental impacts as experienced by Aboriginal people. And consequently, as Westman (ibid., 136) notes, "no tar sands project has been rejected or significantly altered" due to the inclusion of Aboriginal knowledge in its assessment.

"There Are No Doctors for the Fish":
Industrial Impacts and Sickness

One September afternoon, I was with some elders in a small cabin near the shore of Great Bear Lake, drinking tea and listening to the crackling of the woodstove when one of them commented, "We live off our land; it is our money, our food ... it is who we are. Even you, I have seen you walking around by the shore, and we have nets in that water, and we catch fish. You can see how peaceful it is here ... If the pipeline goes through, it might not be like that any more."[15] In this chapter, I have argued that Sahtu Dene and the proponents of large industrial projects differ substantially in their approach to the land and in their perceptions of the significance of industrial impacts on the land. If, as Charlie Neyelle states, industrial impacts are a scarring of physical and social bodies, what are the consequences for those who experience them? In other words, what happens, in the eyes of Sahtu Dene persons, when the universal law is transgressed?

At the 2006 Sahtu Secretariat Incorporated (SSI) General Assembly, a respected elder and hunter from Tulit'a spoke about the proposed pipeline: "All the lakes and streams are alive, so we really need to take care of the water. We eat the wildlife; those are the things I am concerned about ... We need to take care of the land, because when we damage it that causes the sickness."[16] Local concerns about the environmental impact of increased oil and gas exploration and production are acute and long-standing. Prior to the Sahtu Dene and Metis Comprehensive Land Claim Agreement, people in the Sahtu vehemently expressed their concerns regarding the lack of formal avenues for community participation in decisions related to land and resources. In 1975, when Justice Berger conducted his inquiry, Sahtu hunters bore witness to their experiences with industrial impacts. One person testified,

> Since the beginning of introducing the pipeline ... a lot of the oil companies have been making roads all over the place. In making those roads, I guess there is a lot of gas just left on the roads and stuff like that. And that caused this year – a moose was shot and usually when a moose is shot, they distribute the meat amongst the community. And the meat caused a lot of sickness. And there was one – it was one of those seismic lines. And also [a community member] was on the seismic line and saw a beaver there. But the beaver was so sick that they had to kill it.[17]

Others corroborated these sorts of statements, often emphasizing that people were speaking the truth because they had primary experiential knowledge of the land (see Rushforth 1992, 1994). Local people talked about associations between the contamination of lakes and the work conducted by oil and gas companies. One trapper said that during the spring hunt, he had seen "a whole slew of muskrats dead in" a local fishlake and added that oil companies had worked on the lake during the previous winter.[18]

Speaking through an interpreter, a Colville Lake hunter talked about the effects of seismic lines on the land and animals:

> Even now ... before anything like a pipeline is started, all these explorations being going on, (he say) the roads being cut through all over in the country (he said) ... You can see the difference in the wildlife, (he said) it is not the same because it has been disturbed. (He says) you can see. There's hardly any rabbits anymore. There used to be all kinds of ptarmigans around here. (He said) he hardly sees any of that either, (he says). (He says) even when he traps (he said) the fur that he catches, it is not it doesn't look very healthy (he said). So (he said) maybe it is on account of all of the exploration that has been going on had something to do with it.[19]

Throughout the Sahtu, locals expressed worry about young people whose lack of bush experience might result in their inability to recognize a contaminated animal, and they mentioned community members who had died from a foreign sickness that "one can't see."

Importantly, historical experiences with extractive projects and with non-local interference in animal-human relationships were also recalled. People discussed the damage caused by government-led wolf poisoning programs and the decline in fish stocks due to sports fishing. During the Berger Inquiry, a man who worked as a guide for fishing lodges on Great Bear Lake criticized the policy of throwing undersized fish back into the water:

> But you only kill a fish when it [the fish hook] touches its throat. And sometimes the fish may be more harmed than you know. The fish may be more harmed than we think but we still have to throw it back ... And sometimes there is blood coming out of the mouth and stuff like that ... But there is no doctors available for those fish in the water when you throw it back ... This is why (he says) that causes the decrease in the fish.[20]

For people who see the world as based on a universal law that upholds mutual respect and obligations between humans and animals, returning an injured fish to the water breaks that law, disrupting human-animal relations and resulting in serious consequences; the fish may choose to stay away.

Since the Berger Inquiry, Sahtu Dene people have faced increased challenges to spending time on the land. Youth now spend a majority of their time in town for school and thus go out on the land only during weekends, summers, and school-initiated events. Bingo, television, the Internet, and popular culture also play a role in the amount of time spent on land-based activities. Somewhat ironically, people who wish to hunt or trap must often engage in wage labour, simply to afford the skidoos, fuel, traps, and ammunition that enable them to do so. This, in turn, greatly influences the ways in which they use the land, the directions and distances in which they travel, and how long they hunt, fish, trap, and engage in other land-based practices. And, though some aspects of oil and gas exploration, such as the seismic lines that are frequently used for travel, have provided easier access for some hunters, others are seen to seriously interfere with animal behaviour and wellness, and with relations between human and other-than-human beings.

People who are not able spend extended lengths of time on the land continue to utilize lands closer to home, and for the most part, their actions and relationships uphold the universal law. For example, when Déline residents fish on Great Bear Lake, they pay the water in thanksgiving. To maintain relationships of mutual reciprocity, people are required to treat the remains of animals with respect and to honour and respect animals in their thoughts and actions. These expectations apply even to non-Dene, as I discovered when travelling by boat to visit relatives of my hosts at their fish camp. At midday, we beached to make lunch. My companions found fresh bear tracks along the shoreline, and I knelt down to touch them. I was reprimanded for this and was told that I risked offending the bear, which might return to cause us harm.

Since the Berger Inquiry, the amount of time spent in bush activities has changed, but local people still agree on the importance of being on the land and consuming Dene foods. Nor have co-management institutions, established as a result of comprehensive claims, changed the ways in which they express the interconnection between themselves and the landscape, and between industrial impacts and sickness. As at the Berger Inquiry, people at the JRP hearings voiced their alarm about contamination and sickness associated with pipelines and increased oil and gas work. They were concerned about noise pollution, claiming that animals and fish could hear the vibrations made by the pipeline and its infrastructure, and that they would choose to stay away. A Déline hunter explained,

> Even this winter, even all the animals are all over. It's not the same. Even they're still having a noise, but the animals all over. And all the migration. They going to different route. That's why it's happening now this winter. It happens to the caribou. If you went and hunt for caribou, it's not the same as before. Even when they shoot the caribou, they're so skinny, some of it. And now with the pipeline, if they go ahead with the pipeline, it's not going to be the same with the animals. Also, the people are like that too.[21]

A Déline resident spoke about the consequences should the pipeline leak or spill: "Fish, animals, ducks, everything, different kinds of animals, if there's an oil spill, how are they going to know it? But they're still going to drink the water if there's still oil on the land; then, too, they're going to suffer and die from it too."[22] The point here is not so much that a spill could occur, but that industrial contamination affects multiple ecological and social dimensions, and that as keepers of the land Dene people have a responsibility not only to "keep their food good" but also to maintain a moral relationship with all aspects of the landscape.

Indeed, failing to honour this relationship results in severe consequences for Sahtu Dene people. For example, as mentioned above, throwing undersized fish back into the water could produce a decline in fish stocks. In Colville Lake, where oil and gas companies have been active in the exploration and production of the Colville Hills natural gas deposits, the community noticed that caribou were no longer coming to a certain point on the lake. Local elders gave two possible reasons for this. Perhaps the industrial noise had driven them away. Or perhaps a young local, who had hit a caribou with a stick the previous fall, had broken Dene law about animal-human relations and the caribou had chosen to stay away. In both scenarios, human behaviour on the land had violated principles of how caribou ought to be treated and had disrupted human relations with them. Colville Lake requested that oil and gas work be suspended for at least a year, and the caribou did eventually return to the area.

Local residents also discussed the consequences of diminishing animal populations and the impact on human health of decreased access to Dene foods. At the JRP hearings, a Colville Lake elder and hunter observed,

In the last three years, we had a lot of development activities on our land. All our wildlife, the chickens, the rabbits, the caribou, everything started disappearing for three years. And there was many of us that went to the hospital. Now I am 72 years old and I have ... been to the hospital, and because I [ate] store bought food, that's what made me ill.[23]

He added that the emphasis on a wage economy, which would increase due to the MGP, would leave little time for land-based activities: "If everybody was employed, then – then the children are going to be discouraged to go out on the land."[24] Although community members did want their children to obtain meaningful employment, they also wanted them to acquire bush skills and to be able to maintain a land-based economy, if they so choose.

Most often, they cited sickness in referring to the industrial impacts of the pipeline. I suggest that this encompassed more than the contamination from oil spills and other associated pollution or even the loss of the high nutrition in country foods or of physical activity on the land. "Sickness" was moral sickness, which arose when people could not be fully Dene and when the universal law was not upheld. When the landscape is perceived as both an animate and feeling entity, and as an extension of one's physical and social body, industrial impacts compromise the health, well-being, and ultimately the survival of the self.

Yet, some Sahtu Dene recognize that the multiple incursions of colonial processes into the region necessitate some adaptation of land use activities, even if this is done reluctantly. The president of the Déline Land Corporation, who was supportive of the economic opportunities that the pipeline might bring and was responsible for negotiating the access and benefits agreement on behalf of his land corporation, expressed this view. Speaking at the JRP hearings, he discussed the internal conflicts that he faces personally, and as a leader of his community, in attempting to reconcile his relationship to the land with the changes facing Sahtu communities:

There is not much mention about our culture when we talk about this pipeline. I want to make sure that we can have a balance when it comes to development and protecting our way of life in the North here. I want to make sure that we can find ways to make sure that we do that. There has been a lot of money put aside for business opportunities, a socio-economic fund that was talked about a few years ago. But, to this date, I have not seen or heard of any money to help us protect our culture. We have 14 students this year that are going to graduate from high school, and I want to make sure that these kids aren't forced to go down one path, which is a wage economy. I am very concerned because my son is going to school. He loves the traditional way of life. He loves the land, the hunting, the harvesting, the stories, the sacred sites that we have on our land. Great Bear Lake is one of the best places to live. We are very grateful that we call ourselves Sahtu Tena (phonetic), Bear Lake people, and I'm very proud to be a leader for the Great Bear Lake people, but I'm very concerned that the protection of my culture is not addressed seriously at these hearings or through the different regulatory departments or bodies that were set up to help us.[25]

Some Sahtu Dene see the employment opportunities of the oil and gas sector as providing a much-needed economic stimulus, especially for youth. Even elders who spend a great deal of time on the land and who highlight the moral impacts of the pipeline know that young Sahtu Dene are unable to find work and agree that they must be given opportunities to make a living in waged employment. In taking this stance, they do not minimize the environmental impacts of the oil and gas industry or hold that they do not jeopardize the relationships between people and the land: instead, they advocate that a compromise and a balance must be found.

The idea that external forces can sometimes change environmental conditions, and that human beings must adapt to such changes, exists in Dene oral teachings. An ancient story told to me by Angus, an elder in Déline, revealed that environmental fluctuation is perceived as a normal and often inevitable part of life.[26] On a warm evening in late summer, as I sat gutting fish with Angus, he told me a story about climate change. Like most people in the Sahtu, Angus lived in a modern house, but he also maintained two teepees – one for storage and one for smoking fish and hides – and a fish shack near his home. The fish shack was made of two-by-fours and plywood, and a white tarp roof provided weatherproofing. The white tarp made the light inside the shack bright and inviting, and we sat at a small table and chairs at one side of the large room. Angus had brought in five lake trout that he had netted just offshore from his house, and he mentioned that the fish were "mushy." Only a few days earlier, four scientists from a southern Canadian university had come to Déline to tell residents that their lake was four degrees warmer that year than in the past. Angus thought that the rise in temperature was due to global warming and that it explained the mushiness of the fish. But, to my surprise, he did not express concern about the changes to the lake. Instead, he told me a story of how global warming had occurred before.

A long time ago, when the world was new, he said, two brothers were fighting. One brother was cold, and the other was warm. They fought for a long time, and the cold brother wanted to show his power, so he pushed the warm brother far down to the South, to what is now southern Canada and the United States. Then, after a while, the cold brother began to feel bad, so he slowly abandoned the fight and gradually restored some of the warmer brother's power. Thus, the cold has been retreating and will continue to retreat until it reaches the top of the globe. The compromise in this story is akin to the compromise made by Sahtu Dene to accommodate changing economies and their impacts. Thus, it is understood that environmental, social, and economic conditions are constantly shifting, that people have always adapted to this reality, and that they will continue do so in the future.

Nonetheless, people insist that human-induced changes must be conducted fairly, with due consideration of what is lost and what is gained, and with an equal share of benefits. Many Sahtu Dene are resigned to the idea that the MGP will proceed, with or without Aboriginal consent. In such a situation, participating in the process may at least secure some benefits. As a result, conflicts regarding extractive industries on Sahtu lands perhaps have less to do with contestations between domestic and waged labour, or so-called subsistence activities and capitalism, than with the ability to make decisions that are grounded in community visions, whatever those visions might be.

A New Political Landscape?

The Berger Inquiry is often cited as a high-water mark in participatory environmental management, and many environmental management regimes have been patterned after it. People in the Sahtu who spoke before Justice Berger made remarkably similar comments when they testified at the JRP hearings: that industrial impacts made them and their landscape sick. Despite the consistency of their response, the outcomes of the two processes were strikingly different: Berger recommended a ten-year moratorium on pipeline construction, whereas the JRP recommended that it be approved. The obvious question, therefore, is how could the Sahtu Dene response to the pipeline be taken as opposition in the mid-1970s but seen as consent thirty years later?

Derek Armitage (2005, 253) points out that even when Aboriginal people are represented on resource co-management boards, the politics of integrating their views into environmental assessment regimes remains driven by the proponents of industrial projects. The proponents prepare the lengthy environmental impact statement in the course of applying for regulatory permits, and though they may consult with local communities, they alone decide what kinds of knowledge will be included in their assessment – and what kinds will be excluded. Knowledge exclusion is not done with intent, but as I have argued in this chapter, it often arises from disparate views of the landscape and long-standing beliefs about appropriate human engagement with it.

Clearly, the environmental assessment of the MGP accorded serious consideration to the project's ecological impact, and some mitigation measures were recommended and adopted, such as rerouting the pipeline corridor to avoid the ecologically or culturally sensitive areas that local people identified. Socio-cultural impacts were also seriously considered, particularly the issues of employment, land use, the use of specific sacred or culturally significant sites, and the disruption of community and social ties due to rapid economic and industrial growth. However, as we saw earlier, Imperial Oil ultimately concluded that the pipeline would have no "significant" impact on the land or the people.

In assessing the effects of industrial projects on the land, proponents attempt to predict both their intensity and the most suitable means of managing them. When impacts cannot be managed, proponents have offered compensation to those who suffer as a result. In the case of Imperial Oil, mitigation measures for hunters and trappers primarily took the form of monetary compensation. For example, the company proposed a complex process for compensating trappers, who were to submit written records of the approximate seasonal yield in a particular area, provide evidence of how many traps they set, and show anticipated fur and auction values.[27] However, this approach does not address the multi-dimensional relationship between Dene people and the landscape. As a Déline hunter said, "If the oil company provide us a billion dollars, that you can use this billion dollars, but that billion dollars cannot create a fish. A billion dollars cannot create a moose. And billions and billions of dollars cannot create any other animals."[28]

Imperial Oil's assertions that the MGP would not significantly affect the environment and that sufficient compensation lay in a cash payment represent a systematic denial of the very fundamental ways in which Sahtu Dene people view appropriate human relationships with the land. Unless the company recognizes these relationships, its analysis of the project's impact will continue to subvert Sahtu Dene expressions and experiences, even in situations where local Aboriginal people are consulted. As one elder put it, "In my Dene language, if we were going to talk about an impact it would be a long, long concept."[29]

Perhaps even more crucially, the failure to appropriately consider Sahtu Dene perspectives elevated the company's views of the land (and of project impacts) to a position of power. Thus, Sahtu Dene who disagreed with its views were required to "prove" that its assessment of anticipated impacts was incorrect. Given the primacy assigned to environmental assessments, with their quantifiable and techno-rational biophysical data, and their privileged positions as artifacts of truth, this was indeed a mighty task.

The Berger hearings were conducted by one man, Thomas Berger himself. Accompanied by a translator, he visited people in their communities, their homes, their cabins, and on their traplines. He met them on their terms and listened appropriately to their opinions. He understood that, for them, the land was more than a tool that provided physical sustenance. He recognized that no amount of money could repair the universal law, should it be broken, and that numbers and charts could never accurately represent what the land meant to them. Now, however, the participatory process is not conducted on Sahtu Dene terms: it has become standardized, technocratic, easily repeatable everywhere, and based on Euro-Canadian ideas about truth, knowledge, land, and the interrogation of evidence. Although Dene people sat on the JRP and spoke at the hearings, the environmental assessment process was designed to see in just one direction: through the lens of management.

CONCLUSION

I am always struck by the smell of the houses in the Sahtu: it is a warm mix of tea, logs, freshly gutted fish, fire, and earth. It is such a familiar smell and yet so distinct to the region. This intermingling of earth and people represents the human engagement with the land but is also a very sensual expression of how Sahtu Dene people see themselves as part of the land and the land as part of them. And though their use of the land may have changed to accommodate increased pressures to engage in a cash economy and to incorporate new technologies and general practices associated with the sedentary lifestyle, their view of their relationship with the land has changed very little.

In 1995, Peter Elias (1995) wrote that in planning for industrial projects, Dene people often insisted that subsistence activities such as hunting, fishing, trapping, and gathering must be protected before the projects could proceed. I argue that this remains the case today. Sahtu Dene environmental assessment discourses frame industrial impacts to reflect the complex physical, social, and moral relationships between Sahtu Dene people and their land. Their definition of industrial impacts extends beyond ecological contamination to encompass a range of social, cultural, and metaphysical changes. Furthermore, though the ecological impacts of the MGP may be concentrated and short-term, the project also has larger and long-term consequences for the moral and social fabric of Sahtu Dene communities.

What we encounter in the various narratives regarding industrial activities are questions of voice – rival stories, as Walter Fisher (1984, 14) suggests. In seeing the impacts of the MGP as insignificant, Imperial Oil denied the stories of local people about themselves and the world. In the participatory process, the inability of Sahtu Dene to produce quantifiable data in support of their worldview and experiences – morality cannot be measured – was translated into consent for the project. Because an upheaval in the universal law could not be "proven," it could not be real. Until environmental assessment processes are more widely grounded in the views of Aboriginal people about the land, the world, and their place in it, their participation will remain an insertion into a dominant paradigm of knowledge, rather than a serious challenge to the paradigm itself.

3

Life under the Comprehensive Claim Agreement

*Has the claim made our lives better? Maybe. Some of the jobs
here wouldn't be created. But in many ways it is a strangle-
hold on the decision-making process. We know what is wrong,
and we have to have the courage to stand up and say so.*

     – Sahtu community member, Tulit'a Unity Accord

IN JULY 1993, Dene and Metis people in the central Mackenzie Valley voted to approve the Sahtu Dene and Metis Comprehensive Land Claim Agreement. Of those who voted, 85 percent of Dene and 99 percent of Metis opted in favour of the agreement (Indian and Northern Affairs Canada 1994, 1). The agreement provided the Sahtu Dene and Metis with fee simple title to 41,437 square kilometres of the 283,171 square kilometres in the Sahtu Settlement Area (SSA). Some 1,813 square kilometres of the fee simple title section include subsurface rights (see Map 2). It also provided for federal government payments of $75 million over a fifteen-year period to designated land claim organizations that are accountable to Sahtu Dene and Metis beneficiaries. Under the agreement, the Sahtu Dene and Metis secured rights to hunt and fish throughout the SSA, and they retained the exclusive right to trap there. The agreement also included provisions for an integrated system of resource co-management that sought to involve Sahtu Dene and Metis in decisions related to renewable and non-renewable resources, land use planning, environmental assessment, and the regulation of land and water use. On 6 September 1993, representatives from the federal and territorial governments and Sahtu Dene and Metis people met in Tulit'a (then Fort Norman) to formally execute the land claim. After receiving approval from Parliament, the Sahtu Dene and Metis Land Claim Settlement Act came into effect on 23 June 1994, bringing with it radically new jurisdictional and administrative boundaries, and new corporate and governance structures.

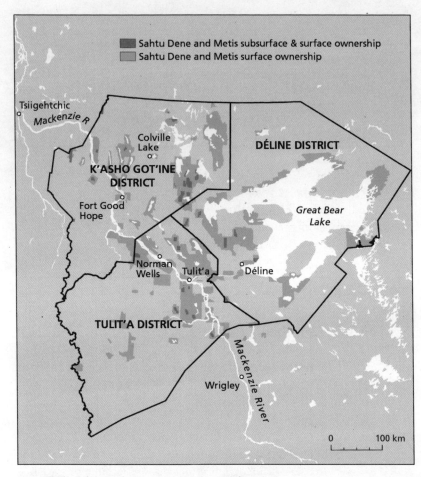

MAP 2   The Sahtu Settlement Area. *By Eric Leinberger*

The negotiation and implementation of comprehensive land claims in Canada are often held as momentous markers of governmental recognition and commitment to Aboriginal rights to land, resources, cultures, identities, and histories, as well as very tangible (and legal) expressions of the roles and responsibilities of newly created land claim institutions and governments. At the same time, the claims also produce very specific forms of knowledge and practice: they restructure and demand diverse spatial commitment and identity, and validate certain forms of governance and economies while simultaneously circumscribing others. In his analysis of claims across the Canadian North, geographer Peter Usher (2003, 379) calls them the "antithesis of the parallel canoe approach" and highlights a vision of "integration and participation rather than separation and coexistence" that is not contained in the numbered treaties. And yet, Usher (ibid.) acknowledges that in these participatory processes, the various Aboriginal signatories still do not have complete jurisdiction over their lands: "Some incidents of Aboriginal title are formally recognized on all lands ... yet nowhere are they complete. These modern treaties provide for Aboriginal involvement in the management of the entire territory, but not their exclusive governance over any of it." Although Usher sees the modern treaties as a step in the right direction, others have criticized them as simply interpolating land claim organizations into existing colonial government apparatuses. For example, in analyzing the James Bay and Northern Quebec Agreement ten years after its ratification, Vincent and Bowers (1988, 14) write that "the role of native representatives in these bodies is mostly symbolic and most of the time governments make policy decisions without consultation. Governments have maintained their administrative and political control over the Crees and Inuit."

In the Sahtu, as a result of the land claim, flexible and porous geographical boundaries became entrenched and codified through mapping and the establishment of district jurisdictions. The claim radically altered governance structures as well: the land corporation replaced chief and council as the primary decision-making authority regarding access to lands and resources. Dene forms of land tenure and political governance, even political governance that was imposed decades ago by colonialist regimes, were subsumed under the newly created structure of the land corporation. The use of the land corporation broadly transformed the ways in which Sahtu Dene communities dealt with outside interests that wished to conduct work on their lands. At the same time, land corporation presidents and management boards engaged in sophisticated strategies for the negotiation of agreements and partnerships to increase social and economic profits. These negotiations required that strategic networks be established, new terminology and skills be learned, and novel means of decision making be implemented.

Correspondingly, community dynamics shifted due to the changing governance structures, creating internal division in the Sahtu, particularly when multiple and conflicting governance institutions operated in the same arenas. For example, the land claim agreement is the only comprehensive claim in Canada that explicitly includes both Dene and Metis. Some Sahtu communities, such as Déline, have chosen to avoid distinguishing between Dene and Metis community members, asserting that all Aboriginal people whose ancestors came from the region are Dene.

After the Sahtu Dene and Metis Land Claim Settlement Act, people who had thought of themselves as belonging to larger communities, or who identified with particular spatial or social groupings, were obliged to enroll in the claim as either Dene or Metis, thus reinforcing and embedding interpersonal and political fissures in the claim itself.

Indeed, the implementation of the land claim agreement brought challenges, distress, and (at times) tremendous opportunities. In some ways, it can be seen as entrenching Sahtu Dene rights and landownership in ways that encourage economic growth and local involvement in decision making, particularly concerning lands, resources, employment, training, and business opportunities. However, some fifteen years after its ratification, people in the Sahtu increasingly questioned its ability to meet their needs, especially as certain parts of it were not yet implemented. Some even suggested that the Sahtu Dene now played a weakened role in decision-making processes because the designated Sahtu organizations, modelled on Euro-American institutional and corporate structures, opted for the bureaucratic approach and neglected local ways of reaching decisions. More than once during my field research, a local said that the Sahtu Dene were "worse off" after the implementation of the land claim agreement and that it had not brought the anticipated benefits and independence. This chapter explores the ways in which the agreement subverts local practices. Communities that once maintained a strong sense of independence and identity are now grouped into districts, generating new alliances and grievances as they negotiate and struggle for power locally, regionally, and nationally. I ask here whether jockeying for the payoffs of oil and gas activities really serves the interests of the average Sahtu Dene person. In other words, who benefits from oil and gas exploration and production in the Sahtu and why?

CREATING THE COMPREHENSIVE CLAIM AGREEMENT

When the Sahtu land claim agreement was ratified and implemented, the Sahtu Settlement Area was carved out of the central Mackenzie region. Prior to contact with European fur traders and explorers, the Sahtu Dene lived in small, self-sufficient groups that were connected through kinship ties (Savishinsky 1974; Asch 1977; Roderick Wilson 1986; Auld and Kershaw 2005). In the late eighteenth and early nineteenth centuries, the fur trade brought European traders and merchants to the area, many of whom soon returned home, but others remained to trap and manage trading posts and administrative centres. Some married Aboriginal women. Their descendants are often identified as Metis.

During the late nineteenth century, the Dene people in the central Mackenzie Valley began to petition Ottawa for a treaty to protect their land from outsiders who intended to exploit its resources, first in the form of furs and later in the form of oil and minerals (Fumoleau 1977). In 1920, after oil was "discovered" at Norman Wells, Ottawa sought to settle the land title issue and to pave the way for future resource development.[1] Though never fully implemented, Treaty 11 was signed between the Crown and the central Mackenzie Dene in the summer of 1921. Dene people regard it as a document of peace and friendship that guarantees their rights to land, not as a cession of their rights to the federal government. When exporting oil from the Norman Wells field proved unprofitable, Ottawa's interest in administering Treaty 11 lands waned considerably, and the allocation of reserves in the Northwest Territories was never executed.[2] The government was largely focused on potential resource extraction in the North and was well aware that this could not occur on land set aside for Indian reserves (Coates and Morrison 1986). For their part, the Sahtu Dene were more interested in protecting their hunting, fishing, and trapping rights than in the allocation of reserves (Berger 1977, 168). The failure to fully implement Treaty 11, certain issues regarding Dene representation at the treaty negotiations and in the treaty documents, and concerns about interpretation of the treaty terms resulted in long-standing disputes over Dene rights to land and entitlements.

From Ottawa's perspective, the land claim was a means of resolving the underlying title to the land, Dene rights to land management and harvesting access, and the failures of Treaty 11.[3] During the 1970s, political and legal pressure to resolve comprehensive land claims had mounted in the Northwest Territories. The Indian Brotherhood of the Northwest Territories (renamed the Dene Nation in 1978) and the Métis and Non-Status Native Association of the Northwest Territories (later the Métis Nation) had led the political fight, bolstered by legal rulings and quasi-judicial inquiries. By 1984, comprehensive claims had been settled with the James Bay Cree and Inuit, the James Bay Naskapi, and the Inuvialuit. The James Bay and Northern Quebec Agreement (1975), the Northeastern Quebec Agreement (1978), and the Inuvialuit Final Agreement (1984) are legal instruments that extinguish Aboriginal rights and title to the land in exchange for land, capital, hunting, fishing, and trapping rights, and a role in the cooperative management of lands. Although they differ slightly in structure, all established economic development corporations to manage the financial compensation paid to Aboriginal signatories as part of the claim.

Dene claims to lands in the Treaty 11 area gained momentum with a 1973 decision from Supreme Court justice William Morrow, which allowed the Indian Brotherhood of the Northwest Territories to file a caveat claiming an interest in more than a million square kilometres of the Northwest Territories.[4] Although the caveat was overturned on appeal in 1975 due to technical grounds, and later by the Supreme Court of Canada in 1977, neither ruling directly challenged the existence of Aboriginal rights as suggested by Justice Morrow in 1973.[5] These rulings ultimately left the door open for further negotiations between the federal government and Dene and Metis organizations regarding rights and title to traditional lands.

Also in 1977, the Berger Report recommended that no pipeline should be constructed through the Mackenzie Valley until Aboriginal land claims had been settled in the region. With the prospect of resource development again on the horizon, Ottawa entered into combined Dene and Metis comprehensive claim negotiations in 1981 and reached an agreement-in-principle for the Dene/Metis Western Arctic Land Claim in 1990. A bold proposal, the claim sought to establish a new political territory called Denendeh, or "land of the Dene," and it included Dene and Metis groups in most of the eastern Northwest Territories, with the exception of the Inuvialuit. Later that year, the Dene and Metis assemblies voted not to proceed with ratifying the agreement-in-principle, primarily because it insisted on an extinguishment clause and did not deal with the issue of self-government. At that point, Ottawa abandoned the combined claim and authorized the negotiation of separate regional comprehensive land claim settlements. The Gwich'in were the first Dene group to reach a comprehensive land claim agreement with the federal government in 1992, followed by the Sahtu in 1994, and the Tlicho in 2005. As mentioned above, the land claim agreement is unique in the Northwest Territories because it explicitly includes both Dene and Metis.

ᐁ

SAHTU DENE LAND, TITLE, AND SUBSURFACE RIGHTS

For the Government of Canada, the agreement was first and foremost an economic instrument whereby the Sahtu Dene yielded exclusive use of their ancestral territory in exchange for guaranteed rights in the form of land, participation in land management, and cash payments. The agreement recognizes the historical and cultural significance of Treaty 11, and confirms existing treaty rights that were not ceded, released, or surrendered. It also affirms that the ratification of, and enrolment in, the claim does not affect signatories' ability to participate in government programs for status, non-status, or Metis persons, or the status of SSA Indian bands under the Indian Act.

Sahtu Designated Organizations (SDOs) were established to administer the capital and land transfers from the federal government, and all beneficiaries of the claim hold a non-transferable equal interest in their respective SDO. According to the agreement, once the designated organizations receive the capital and land transfers, Ottawa is then deemed to have discharged its obligations regarding the transfer of monies and land. Its capital payments to SDOs began on the date of legislation and were scheduled to occur every year on the anniversary of the agreement for fifteen years (Indian and Northern Affairs Canada 1994, 23).

In the Sahtu, the principal SDO for the management of capital and land transfers is the land corporation. As per the terms of the land claim agreement, land in the SSA is divided into two distinct categories: Sahtu Municipal Lands, which lie within municipal boundaries, and Sahtu Settlement Lands, which are owned by the Sahtu Dene in fee simple title and are not part of Municipal Lands. The Municipal Lands are managed by the Government of the Northwest Territories through municipal organizations and the Department of Municipal and Community Affairs (MACA). However, title to Sahtu Settlement Lands is held by one of the three district land corporations: the K'asho Got'ine District Land Corporation, the Tulit'a District Land Corporation, and the Déline District Land Corporation. Sahtu Settlement Lands are considered to be privately owned by the Sahtu Dene.[6] Thus, rules regarding access and trespassing apply to them, as do specific trapping and harvesting rights.

Every district land corporation is composed of representatives from the community-level land corporations. For example, the Déline District Land Corporation has representatives from just one community-level land corporation: the Déline Land Corporation. The Tulit'a District Land Corporation is comprised of representatives from the Fort Norman Metis Land Corporation (in Tulit'a), the Tulit'a Land Corporation (in Tulit'a), and the Ernie MacDonald Land Corporation (in Norman Wells). The K'asho Got'ine Land Corporation consists of representatives from the Fort Good Hope Metis Land Corporation (Fort Good Hope), the Yamoga Land Corporation (Fort Good Hope), and the Ayoni Keh Land Corporation (Colville Lake). In this way, Sahtu Settlement Lands in the

K'asho Got'ine and Tulit'a Districts are jointly owned and administered by three community-level land corporations, some of which represent Dene beneficiaries of the claim and some of which represent Metis. The Sahtu Secretariat Incorporated (SSI), which does not own Sahtu Settlement Lands, acts as the coordinating body for the seven community-level land corporations and facilitates and implements the land claim agreement and associated services and programs for Sahtu beneficiaries. The organizational structure of the various land corporations under the comprehensive land agreement is outlined in Figure 2.

Companies that wish to conduct oil and gas development on or across Sahtu Settlement Lands must negotiate access with the relevant district land corporation. In areas where the subsurface rights are owned by a district land corporation, companies must secure its consent before undertaking exploration or production of the subsurface resources. However, where subsurface rights rest with the Crown, Ottawa is required only to notify the Sahtu Tribal Council and to consider its views on the proposed activity. In the Sahtu, this is achieved by means of a nomination process: via Indian and Northern Affairs Canada (INAC), companies nominate parcels of land that should be opened for public bidding. INAC informs them of the potential restrictions and commitments that would be required from them should their bid succeed. INAC also consults with various stakeholders, considers their recommendations, and may then open parcels for bid. A company that secures an exploration licence through the public

FIGURE 2   SSI organizational structure

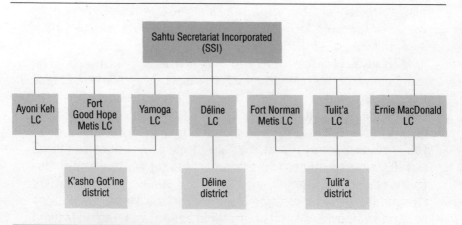

Source: Sahtu Land Use Plan background report

bidding process has a right of access across Sahtu Settlement Lands, but it must negotiate the terms of access with the appropriate district land corporation. The negotiation typically results in an access and benefits agreement (ABA), which often includes payment for surface access and the provision of business or employment opportunities for local people. According to the land claim agreement, corporations that wish to undertake work on Sahtu Settlement Lands must also consult with various district- and community-level organizations regarding environmental and wildlife harvesting impacts. Consultation is also required as part of water and land permitting applications throughout all lands within the Sahtu Settlement Area.

Incentives for district land corporations to open Sahtu Settlement Lands to oil and gas activities include the money, jobs, and business partnerships secured through ABAs but also the collection of some subsurface royalties for the extraction of oil or gas. The land claim agreement includes provisions for resource-royalty-sharing arrangements between Ottawa and the Sahtu Secretariat concerning resources extracted on Crown lands in the Sahtu. In the Northwest Territories, unlike in the oil- and gas-rich provinces of Alberta, Saskatchewan, British Columbia, and Manitoba, control over natural resources on Crown lands does not lie with the territorial government (GNWT).[7] Instead, they are managed by the Government of Canada, through the Oil and Gas Management Directorate and INAC. Accordingly, Ottawa sets and collects the royalties generated from oil and gas extraction in the Northwest Territories. Unless a resource-royalty-sharing arrangement is in place as a result of a comprehensive claim, all the monies go to Ottawa. Not surprisingly, the GNWT has pushed for devolution of these (and other) powers, but until this occurs, it remains a general stakeholder in the management of oil and gas revenues in the territory.

Although resource-royalty-sharing arrangements between Ottawa and Sahtu Designated Organizations (SDOs) are entrenched in the land claim agreement, the SDOs do not receive a total share of the royalties, or even an equal one. In fact, their portion is a mere 7.5 percent of the first $2 million of royalties that Ottawa receives each year and 1.5 percent of any additional royalties received during the same year (Indian and Northern Affairs Canada 1993, 27). The income and interest earned from royalties and capital transfers, less fees accrued, is disbursed twice a year by the Sahtu Trust to the community land corporations on a per capita basis. The Sahtu Trust, which was created by the seven community land corporations, is run by two fund managers under the direction of SSI.

The primary role of the land corporations is to administer Sahtu Settlement Lands and land use in their respective jurisdictions and to manage monies and royalties received from the Sahtu Trust. Most also have various subsidiary companies or development corporations, such as MacKay Range Development Corporation in Tulit'a, which seek and execute business partnerships with companies that wish to conduct work in the Sahtu.[8]

Land corporation membership is determined by the land claim enrolment process, and eligible persons must apply to the enrolment board.[9] At that point, they must specify the "Aboriginal Community" in which they wish to enrol. An Aboriginal Community is defined as a Dene band in Colville Lake, Déline, Fort Good Hope, or Tulit'a, or the Metis local in Fort Good Hope, Tulit'a, or Norman Wells. Thus, becoming a member of a land corporation entails self-identification, and a person must enrol in one of the seven Aboriginal Communities. Sahtu Dene and Metis land corporations are designed to be accountable to and democratically controlled by their shareholders. Land claim beneficiaries who are enrolled with an Aboriginal Community elect their community-level land corporation management board and president every two years, and the board and president direct the day-to-day operations of the corporation. District land corporations are comprised of presidents from each community-level land corporation. Although people who are enrolled in the land claim are shareholders in their particular land corporations, the corporations themselves do not pay dividends to them and thus do not generally contribute capital directly to local Sahtu beneficiaries. However, the corporations do provide some capital in the form of hunter and trapper support and other community programs, and their subsidiary companies indirectly contribute capital to local economies by generating economic activity.

Importantly, though the land corporations and other SDOs deal with land access, ownership, management, use, regulation, and Sahtu Dene hunting, trapping, and fishing rights, nothing in the land claim agreement deals directly with education, health care, political institutions established under the Indian Act, or other matters of community governance.[10] In fact, there are three local governments in the SSA: the land corporation manages the Sahtu Settlement Lands, resources, and economies; the hamlet government runs general municipal services; and the band chief and council administers rights, duties, and programs for band members under the Indian Act. Although each government has its own mandate and jurisdiction, their interests and activities unavoidably overlap, and divergent systems of community authority are created as a result. These intersections come not only at the level of stewarding community visions, but also for local people, who must locate themselves on axes of belonging and identity (as Dene persons, shareholders, band members, and members of larger communities), and who must navigate the various and sometimes competing governance authorities in the course of their everyday lives. Thus, the implementation of the land claim agreement in 1994 not only institutionalized specific lines of authority regarding rights to land and resources, it also fundamentally transformed social, economic, and political relations in the SSA.

The Comprehensive Land Claim Agreement: Restructuring Dene Life

As many Sahtu Dene people see it, the land claim agreement is a formal recognition of their rights to land, resources, and lifeways. Their primary motive for involvement in the claim was to protect their land and culture, and to ensure that their young people could find meaningful employment but also spend time on the land.

They saw the claim as an instrument with the potential to balance traditional and wage-based economies, to provide for sanctioned participation in decisions regarding lands and economic practices in their traditional territories, and to protect their relationship with their land. Although the Dene negotiators knew that the agreement did not contain self-government measures, they believed that it would protect their communities. As one negotiator said during an interview with Stephanie Irlbacher-Fox (2009, 1),

> Canada comes up with new programs and policies for Native people all the time ... And sure, we will sit with them and take those programs, that's for our People. What they haven't understood yet is that we are Dene, and nothing will change that. No policies or money or agreements or whatever ... We are Dene and that will never change.

And though the agreement did not deal with most aspects of community governance, local people felt strongly that it would (or should) provide them with more control over their lands and their lives, their economies, and their visions of the future. After all, they were now the legal owners of the land.

Nonetheless, most Sahtu Dene feel that the agreement has not lived up to its billing. As many point out, it has very little to do with Dene law or local forms of land tenure and governance. It objectifies the land as a thing that can be owned, commodified, controlled, and managed by corporate authorities. District corporate entities now own disparate parcels of land in fee simple title.[11] Sahtu Dene people, too, must now self-identify as shareholders in these corporations in ways that formalize and cement once fluid social identities and relationships into bounded political, social, and economic units. I suggest that the consequences of this are not benign; in the Sahtu, as elsewhere, peoples and practices are shaped in important ways by the structure of social relations. Forms of land tenure, governance, and social subjectivities have been restructured by the claim in a process of rupture, contradiction, and overlap.

Structuring Geographical Boundaries

As I have shown, the land claim agreement arranges the Sahtu into three distinct geographical and administrative districts (see Map 2). Suddenly, after 23 June 1994, Sahtu Dene people who had used certain areas for generations now found that their land was part of a district and subject to district administration. Prior to the implementation of the agreement, systems of land use and tenure in the Sahtu were known, recognized, and practised both within and between local families, bands, and neighbouring political groups (Savishinsky 1974; Auld and Kershaw 2005). Anthropologists and others have identified four Dene groups – the Shi'ta Got'ine, the K'aalo Got'ine, the Sahtu Got'ine, and the K'asho Got'ine – that have occupied the Sahtu since at least the time of contact with European traders, each speaking a slightly different but mutually intelligible dialect of North Slavey (Roderick Wilson 1986; Abel 1993). Each group, or regional band, is also associated with a particular land use area, although the use is fluid, and people are not restricted to harvesting in one area alone (Auld and Kershaw 2005, 5). The four groups share a common culture, often intermarry, and gather for festivals and special occasions, but each has its own unique identity, stories, and places of cultural and spiritual significance (Ellen Basso 1978, 692; Blondin 1990; Auld and Kershaw 2005).

The Shi'ta Got'ine, or Mountain Dene (now living primarily in Tulit'a, Fort Good Hope, and Wrigley), most frequently use the areas on the slopes of the Mackenzie Mountains, to the west of the Mackenzie River, and north of the Liard River.[12] Before settling in Tulit'a, Fort Good Hope, and Wrigley, they remained in the Mackenzie Mountains every fall to trap and to hunt woodland caribou and other animals during the winter months. Many visited Tulit'a at Christmas, in the spring, and in the late summer to see relatives, sell furs, and obtain supplies. Shi'ta Got'ine in

Tulit'a still maintain cabins east of the Mackenzie River and visit areas such as Stewart Lake to fish, hunt moose and caribou, and gather plants and berries. Shi'ta Got'ine people recall the important stories and prophecies of their ancestors about places in the Mackenzie Mountains, and some of the prophecies are handed down in drum songs and dances. Shi'ta Got'ine residents in Tulit'a know the best fishlakes in the mountains and how to navigate the dangerous parts of certain rivers. And every year, families return to the mountains, even if briefly, to harvest the resources of their land.

The territory of the K'aalo Got'ine, or Willow Lake people (now living primarily in Tulit'a and Déline), runs along the east side of the Mackenzie River and includes areas between Tulit'a and Déline. The people have cabins and campsites at Willow (Brackett) Lake, where they hunt, fish, trap, and gather plants. Spring is a particularly important season at Willow Lake, and Tulit'a and Déline families go to their cabins for prolonged periods to hunt migratory waterfowl as the birds return from the south.[13] A woman with whom I stayed at Tulit'a was born at Willow Lake, and she often recalled the time she spent there with her relatives. As she put it, she could truly breathe and be fully Dene at Willow Lake; her happiest moments were there.[14] Indeed, during the early May thaw, she, her children, her mother, her siblings, and their families skidooed to Willow Lake to hunt for ducks.

Sahtu Got'ine, or Great Bear Lake people (now living primarily in Déline), use the lands and waters at and around Great Bear Lake. They know the best locations to fish for spawning whitefish in the fall and where to set fishnets. Every fall, they wait with great anticipation for the first sightings of caribou as they return to the region on their annual migration from the Barrenlands. And they know the multiple and shifting temperaments of the vast lake on which they travel. In "Country Food," Scott Rushforth (1977) discusses seven Sahtu Got'ine harvesting areas, which encompass all of the Great Bear Lake area. Of these, Hottah Lake and Caribou Point are significant for caribou hunting, and the Johnny Hoe region and the areas around Porcupine River, Tuitatui Lake, and Whitefish River are important trapping sites. Though Rushforth's findings date from the mid-1970s, these locales were still important for hunting and trapping in 2006-07, when I conducted my fieldwork in Déline.

K'asho Got'ine, or Hare people (now living primarily in Colville Lake and Fort Good Hope), use the most northern and eastern parts of the Sahtu, including areas east of Colville Lake extending onto the Barrenlands and between Fort Good Hope and Colville Lake. Every fall, they participate in a community caribou hunt at Horton Lake. As many as thirty Colville Lake residents charter flights into the lake, where they hunt caribou as they migrate from the Barrenlands. They set up camps, hunt, butcher, and prepare caribou meat, and gather berries.[15] Colville Lake residents talk about other seasonal hunting, fishing, and gathering locations, including a small creek where whitefish spawn in late fall. After Colville Lake freezes, people set fishnets at the creek, and the fish and their eggs are considered a special delicacy; the eggs are often described as "candy for the kids."[16]

The people of Colville Lake insist that their ancestors "knew this land": they knew the good places to hunt and trap, the good fishlakes, where and when the caribou came, and the very texture and substance of the land. The hamlet of Colville Lake lies at the base of a point that juts into the lake. The point resembles a caribou head in profile, and as a community leader explained to me, his ancestors were fully aware of this fact. He said that the name of the Colville Lake First Nation (Behdzi Ahda) came from this point. He showed me an aerial photograph, in which the caribou head, complete with a lake for the eye and a small point for the ears, was clearly visible. He said that hundreds of years ago, his ancestors did not have airplanes, but they knew exactly what the point looked like from above. In a very real way, they are still present: their transference of knowledge to subsequent generations shapes the ways in which people use the land today, and their names for significant places continue to serve as referential markers.

In the Sahtu, each regional band maintains its own unique identity, and each has different stories, places of cultural and spiritual significance, prophets and prophecies, and songs. For example, Colville Lake's Ayoni Keh Land Corporation takes its name from an ancient story of how the people came to live in the area. Ayoni Keh is a tall mountain just northeast of Colville Lake. One cold fall day, while several of us sat in the band office, the chief told its story. Long ago, a group of people lived on the top of Ayoni Keh. One day, two young boys were playing with an owl feather. One boy made the other cry, and then the father of the crying boy came and made the first boy cry. The two fathers began to fight, and one was killed. According to the story, the relatives of the two men fought a big war, in which many people died. Even today, I was told, a lake of blood lies at the top of Ayoni Keh. Eventually, the people parted ways and went in different directions. The young men went south and became the Chipewyan people. The adult men went north and became the Inuit, and the dogs went west and became the Gwich'in. But the older people who couldn't walk and the very young babies stayed in the Colville Lake area. As the story goes, this is why the K'asho Got'ine are wise and strong with their minds, just as the elders who stayed in the area.[17]

Within communities as well, certain families became associated with particular areas, places that they know best and on which their ancestors trapped, hunted, gathered, fished, and secured economic, nutritional, and spiritual sustenance for generations. They can point out the exact spots that their fathers and mothers and grandparents frequented, and where they themselves trap, hunt, and fish. On the rare occasions that we went by truck on the winter road, they would point toward locales where they had spent many seasons and recall stories by markers on the land-scape (see Palmer 2005).

One crisp day in February 2007, I went with David to check on several oil and gas exploration camps along the winter road south of Tulit'a, near Blackwater River.[18] David worked as a full-time administrator for the Tulit'a District Land Corporation, and his brother was the president of the Fort Norman Metis Land Corporation. Part of David's job was to facilitate consultation and access and benefits negotiations between the land corporation and oil and gas companies, with the aim of creating more local jobs. He was also responsible for seeing that the companies were honouring their economic and environmental commitments, and did not "make a mess" of their field-sites. So on that day, we set off to check a few sites where Husky Oil was conducting winter work. After several kilometres of silence, David interrupted the soft drone of the country music on the satellite radio to point out specific landmarks. He spoke about the trails that wove through the landscape; they had existed for centuries, and he had travelled them by dog team as a young boy. He told me where they went: "If you follow this one, it will lead you to a good fishlake way in the back there." Or, "This one heads down to the Mackenzie River." Every trail had a specific destination and purpose. David talked a lot about his childhood, as the markers on the landscape stood as remind-ers of his father's and his grandfathers' traditional hunting and trapping areas. "My dad," he said, "he had traps all over here. Me, I spent time out here as a kid. I never went to school until I was eleven years old. My edu-cation was out here, with my dad." He pointed out old camps that they had used and trails that they had followed by dog team. He could name almost every creek, although he did not recall their Slavey names. As I got to know David during my fieldwork, he often talked about the challenges of his paid employment. David had a job – and he needed it, as he, like others, had bills to pay. He was determined to use his position with the land corporation to create meaningful employment in his community. And yet, he often recalled that his father and other elders had instilled in him an insistence that the land was his community's only real security: that it needed to be treated according to Dene law, that it must be protected, and that survival (social, physical, and spiritual) was possible only if proper relationships were maintained with it. As we drove on that sunny February day, and the land evoked memories for David, we often passed animal tracks – some small marten tracks, some large moose tracks. In almost every instance, David could tell what species had made them and whether they were fresh or old. He always saw them before I did. Several kilometres later, we stopped at some of David's traps set along the highway. At one place, he jumped out of the truck and ran into the bush. A few seconds later, he emerged with a frozen marten in a trap. He held it up, grinning, and threw it into the back of the truck.

On the way home, David suggested that we visit Imperial Oil's Peele River work camp, which would soon move to just four miles outside of Tulit'a. I was amazed by the large amount of equipment, and by the effort required to bring it in via the winter road. Knowing that everything would be packed up in just a few short days was equally amazing – only the large cleared area would remain to show where the trailers had rested. We went into the supervisor's trailer, and David questioned him on the camp's security measures. He wanted to ensure that the mostly male workers could not take advantage of their new location to spend too much time in Tulit'a. After a whole day on the road, we were hungry, so we went to the camp kitchen to eat. Five other Tulit'a men were there as well; they were on a two-week rotational schedule and, like other workers, were prohibited from leaving camp during that time, so they were eating in the kitchen. I later learned that the camp prepares extra food, in case people come by on the winter road; how like northern hospitality always to have a hot meal waiting.

Although common land use patterns and preferred harvesting areas are generally known and acknowledged, they remain flexible, fluid, and stewarded according to unwritten laws. It is widely believed that the land is not owned (in the sense of common property law); instead, it is known. That is, certain people and families have acquired more primary experiential knowledge of some areas through continued and frequent use and are thus best equipped to obtain sustenance there and to employ conservation tactics to ensure sustainability for the future. However, traditional land use areas are not sectioned into tidy bundles: they often overlap, intersect, and change as animals migrate or conditions vary. Indeed, some hunting areas are frequented by entire communities, as in the case of Horton Lake,

Work camp in winter. The trailers pictured here serve as housing and portable offices for workers.

where the people of Colville Lake hunt caribou every fall. Other sites (such as fish-spawning locations) are particularly rich in seasonal resources and are frequented by selected hunters for a short time.

As a consequence, deriving sustenance from the land has not customarily hinged on asking permission or obtaining some form of landownership or proprietary rights. Instead, it accrues through acquiring intimate knowledge of the land and by conducting oneself in an appropriate manner. Most frequently, this knowledge is learned through close family members, but it can also be acquired through extended kin and social networks, thus interlinking people and communities through comprehensive networks of land use and practice. To a large degree, land use boundaries were negotiated through economic and social ties with people and groups in both the Sahtu and nearby regions.

Now, however, with the implementation of the land claim agreement, the spatial and administrative distribution of the land has become marked with permanent and artificially constructed boundaries that do not necessarily represent how the land is conceptualized or used by local people. As a Colville Lake elder remarked, "In looking at the map of the Sahtu region, I am concerned about the fragmentation of the land into districts. It doesn't reflect our use of the land" (Sahtu Land Use Planning Board 2004, 31). Indeed, because intercommunity linkages and governance saw land use practices as fluid and boundaries as porous, land use and travel in the Sahtu remained flexible and overlapping.

Under the land claim agreement, Sahtu Settlement Lands are now owned by corporate entities, which have corresponding rights and obligations under Canadian property law. Decisions about who is permitted to use the land and for what purposes now come under the authority of district land corporations and regional co-management boards, such as the Sahtu Land and Water Board (SLWB), which is responsible for issuing land use and water permits throughout the SSA. The boards and presidents of all the land corporations are elected by Sahtu beneficiaries, and two of the SLWB members are nominated by the Sahtu Secretariat (the remaining two are nominated by the GNWT and the federal government). Despite this, many local people see the overall permitting process as an attempt to assert non-local jurisdiction and control over their territory. Although Sahtu Dene who wish to construct camps or cabins for hunting or trapping are not required to obtain land use permits, local people commonly feel that decisions regarding the land are no longer theirs to make. Instead, due to the permitting process, such decisions now come under district or regional control. They also feel that this process has contributed to heightened tension, and sometimes overt conflict, should local and regional levels of authority disagree regarding the legitimacy of decisions.

For example, a land corporation employee once contacted the SLWB to determine whether he needed a permit to build a cabin on Sahtu Settlement Lands that were owned by the district land corporation of which he was a beneficiary. According to him, the SLWB replied that yes, he did need a permit. He then asked the SLWB what it would do if he did not apply for the permit and was informed that he would be fined $5,000 for taking the logs to make the cabin. In response to this, he

> told all the people to go out on the land and build cabins. I am doing that so that people will understand that it is their land. When they [the SLWB] ask whether or not they have permits for their land, they will tell them that they were built before the permitting system. But this will make everyone understand whose land it is, because people have cabins there. When they ask who owns this land, the community can reply, "We do, because we have been trapping on this land for as long as anyone can remember."[19]

So, though local forms of land tenure require the involvement of people who have primary and intimate knowledge of the landscape, non-local forms of management require elaborate bureaucratic policy to determine, regulate, manage, and enforce who will have access to the land and for what reasons. Situations like the one discussed above, in which a Sahtu beneficiary hoped to build a cabin, have meaningful consequences for the people involved.[20] However, when a company applies for a permit to undertake oil or gas exploration or production, the situation is considerably larger in scale, and the issue of who has the authority to grant the permit is magnified proportionately. It is true that Sahtu Dene people sit on the management boards that influence these decisions. Nonetheless, a comment from James C. Scott (1998, 87) regarding the "transformative power" of maps is germane here. Scott reminds us that this power resides not in a map per se, "but rather in the power possessed by those who deploy the perspective of that particular map." This applies whether the reader of the map is Sahtu Dene or not. And in mapping what became the Sahtu Settlement Area, the physical, metaphorical, and jurisdictional lines were drawn and firmly imprinted according to corporate standards and those of private property law. The enforcement of the particular map of the SSA rests in legislation and bureaucracy rather than in local practice – with the settler state, rather than in Dene law.

Structuring Collective Identities

Just as the land claim restructured formerly fluid geographical boundaries, enrolling as a beneficiary encodes social identities. As explained earlier, people can enrol with only one community-level land corporation and must identify their Aboriginal Community in doing so. In other words, they must choose whether they are Dene or Metis. For example, Tulit'a residents must choose between its two community-level land corporations: those who identity as Dene will belong to the Tulit'a Land Corporation, whereas those who identify as Metis will belong to the Fort Norman Metis Land Corporation. The exception to this is Déline, which does not distinguish between its Dene and Metis residents, and thus has just one local land corporation. As a Déline elder explained, "We are all Dene."

The establishment of two local land corporations in Tulit'a caused tremendous bureaucratic complications in the negotiation of access and benefits agreements, consultation processes, approval and permitting of extractive projects, and other jurisdictional issues. For instance, if an oil and gas company wants to conduct work near Tulit'a, it must obtain permission from both the Dene and Metis land corporations, and must negotiate an access and benefits agreement that is acceptable to both.[21] However, in reality, the complexity and layers of bureaucracy often mean that companies consult with just one land corporation, resulting in tensions between the local land corporations and community members. In

Tulit'a, as in other communities, the Dene and Metis land corporations have separate offices, across town, and they conduct their business separately. As a Tulit'a leader put it, "The land claim in Tulit'a has split the community and has established all kinds of organizations that operate on their own and don't know what the other one is doing; this has split the operating money and any money that people might get in benefits."[22]

During my stay in Tulit'a, I tried to determine how people decided to enrol in the land claim as either Dene or Metis. For the most part, families and their closest relatives enrolled in the same land corporation, though half-siblings sometimes departed from this pattern: one sibling might choose the Metis corporation, whereas the other opted for its Dene counterpart. Dene and Metis relationships have a long history in Tulit'a, with certain families identifying as Metis and others as Dene. Interaction between the families has sometimes been inharmonious. Dene families have expressed misgivings about Metis families occupying certain jobs or places on the landscape, and Metis families have been concerned about securing Aboriginal rights to lands and resources or about fully participating in comprehensive land claims and treaties. Yet, though friction may occasionally have arisen in the small community, people collectively thought of themselves as being from Tulit'a, and given the cultural value placed upon generosity and helping others, Dene and Metis families would often find mutual support in one another.

After 1994, however, these political fissures became entrenched in the land claim itself. Though they tend to be only slightly palpable at the interpersonal level, they are very obvious in community politics. The discord is reflected in the fact that the two land corporation offices are on opposite sides of town, but it also appears in community meetings, especially when one corporation is negotiating business contracts of which the other has no knowledge. As a Tulit'a resident put it, "For such a small community of five hundred people, we can't seem to get along. The electoral system divides people, and once people are divided it is hard to work together and hard to get things done."[23]

Many people in Tulit'a recognized the structuring practices of the land claim agreement and the growing tension that it created between Dene and Metis beneficiaries. In late 2006, with the pipeline potentially on the horizon and Husky Oil wishing to conduct further exploration south of Tulit'a at Stewart Lake, the community decided that something must be done to repair the rift. So, in February 2007, Tulit'a hosted what it called the Tulit'a Unity Accord, an agreement between its Dene and Metis residents to work together under the terms of the land claim agreement. The accord brought together Dene and Metis community leaders, beneficiaries, elders, and other dignitaries from across the Northwest Territories, including then premier Joe Handley and Sahtu MLA Norman Yakeleya, to engage in celebrations and workshops to improve community cohesiveness. The late Leslie Nielsen, a celebrity and actor who lived in Tulit'a during his youth, came and spoke, as did Clarence Louie, the chief of the Osoyoos Indian Band. Expert fiddlers were brought in to run workshops for community youth, and professionals on building self-esteem worked with the kids. Elders participated in storytelling programs at the local school, and the chair of the Mackenzie Valley Environmental Impact Review Board came to Tulit'a to give workshops on how to better understand the land and water regulatory process. The celebrations lasted for four days, with drum dances, feasting, and old-timer dances. On 17 February, Rocky Norwegian, president of the Fort Norman Metis Land Corporation, and Grand Chief Frank Andrew from the Sahtu Dene Council exchanged gifts of a fiddle and a drum, respectively, and signed the accord in an emotional ceremony, vowing to work together in the spirit of cooperation.

The Tulit'a Unity Accord marked a public recognition of the land claim agreement's social and political structuring power. I had heard private discussions of the topic, but the tensions inherent in the claim were widely acknowledged and openly treated at the accord celebrations. Former Sahtu MLA Steve Kakfwi stated,

> The land claim was organized to keep people separate – the Dene land corporation, the Metis land corporation, the chief and council. The companies come in and they meet with the different organizations separately. We have different offices, and sometimes one group will make a deal and support a project, and one will not support it. I mean, how many organizations does one community need? The band and the land corporations try to do a good job, but it is very difficult. It [the land claim] is meant to divide and conquer.[24]

Others mentioned that, where land use is concerned, the decision-making process did not represent the views of community members. A local man who worked for the Protected Areas Strategy made this clear:

> The district land corporation is the administrator of the lands in the Tulit'a District. What that means is that basically nothing happens until the district land corporation approves it. And the district land corporation gets its marching orders from the people – or at least that is supposed to be how

it works. The land claim is supposed to give us more say from the bottom up, not from the top down. We were trying to get away from that. But it is happening from the top down.[25]

People commonly spoke about leadership and the need for community members to participate in decisions about land use. Again, Steve Kakfwi very honestly stated,

The communities could have a lot of money, they have a lot of staff, but we have different leaders who have their own interests. Some are after money, and jobs, and contracts. Some are after protecting the land or social services. What do you want your leaders to do? Do you just want them to go after jobs, money, and contracts? Do you want to protect the land? Do you want a balance? You need to stand up and say that. You need a common vision as to what Tulit'a wants to do.[26]

The Tulit'a Unity Accord was an agreement of hope and optimism; it celebrated the possibility of community cohesion and collective promise. At the same time, it was an honest recognition of the shortcomings of both the land claim agreement itself and of the participants in the claim who had not upheld its collective spirit and intent: to increase benefits and control for all beneficiaries. After the accord was signed, Dene and Metis land corporations (and the chief and council) did schedule bi-weekly meetings to better coordinate their activities and did contemplate centralizing the various political offices in one building. The extent to which the accord has mended Dene and Metis relationships in Tulit'a still remains to be seen. Regardless, it is an exceptional example of a treaty signed between two Aboriginal groups, one Dene and one Metis, in an attempt to put collective interests before those of political factions.

The implementation of the land claim agreement also affected relationships between communities. With its tiny population, Colville Lake hesitated to enter into the claim at all, fearing that larger communities might dominate decision-making processes.[27] Thus, it insisted that it be granted a veto on all land that it claims. However, Colville Lake is part of the K'asho Got'ine District, which means that it must negotiate access and benefits agreements in tandem with the two other local land corporations of the district – the Yamoga Land Corporation in Fort Good Hope and the Fort Good Hope Metis Land Corporation. Business contracts, employment opportunities, and payment for access to land must be agreeable to all three, even if the work will be situated near Colville Lake alone. This has caused a number of open conflicts; in the most prominent, a lengthy access and benefits negotiation, Petro Canada finally attempted to take the three corporations to arbitration. Apparently, Fort Good Hope and Colville Lake could not agree regarding which should be entitled to contracts and other financial resources. As a person who worked for one of the corporations explained to me, the failure of the negotiations was "actually not Petro Canada's fault; they are just caught in the middle of a battle for power between Fort Good Hope and Colville Lake."[28]

Other communities have conveyed their frustration with the allocation of business contracts to one community rather than another. Some voice concern regarding projects that are approved (or supported) in one district but are perceived to have impacts on another. For example, a proposed hydroelectric dam on the Great Bear River would affect both Tulit'a and Déline. And a bridge over the Great Bear River, part of the proposed all-weather highway to connect Wrigley and Inuvik, would also have an inter-jurisdictional impact. In these cases, the effect on wildlife is a significant concern, but so are the questions of who will receive business contracts for activities such as slashing and catering, and which Northern Store will supply groceries and other goods to work camps.

Friendly rivalries do exist between communities – often expressed in collective teasing about which speaks more Slavey or eats more Dene food – but many maintain intense social, historical, and kinship ties. This is particularly true for Déline and Tulit'a, and for Colville Lake and Fort Good Hope, where family members and friends often travel back and forth to visit each other. In regional celebrations or tragedies, all the communities come together to offer mutual support. For example, following a tragic plane crash near Fort Good Hope in 2006, people from all over the Sahtu immediately came to prepare food, sit with mourners, and assist the community during that very difficult time.

Recent anthropological literature suggests that the consequences of territorialized boundary making may have relevance for First Nations in other jurisdictions as well. Paul Nadasdy (2012) points to consequences of land claim processes in the Yukon and argues that the establishment of territorialized socio-political units goes beyond formalizing jurisdictional boundaries to reflect (and bring into being) a particular conceptualization of bounded political territories that are closely tied to modern statecraft. Nadasdy shows that land claim processes involve inscribing bounded geographical areas into distinct political units that may not mirror local land use, governance, and identities. Drawing from his analysis of efforts by the Kluane and White River First Nations to resolve overlaps in their traditional territories for land claim purposes, Nadasdy notes that their concepts of land use and tenure emphasize relatedness and sharing rather than firm territorial boundaries. As he explains, reframing Kluane and White River territorial ordering in land claim processes goes beyond redefining (and resetting) territorial jurisdiction to create ethno-territorial identities that are not grounded in the flexible and kin-based networks that customarily defined social groups.

Brian Thom, as well, has demonstrated that land claim processes for Coast Salish people have tended to express territoriality in terms familiar to the modern state. As Thom (2009, 194) writes, some Coast Salish see "boundaries and borders [as] arbitrary and artificial at best, and at worst a part of a recurring colonial mechanism of government to create divisions between communities and kin and weaken the potential for a future where all Coast Salish people are a politically unified, self-determining indigenous Nation." Thom (ibid., 201) explains that the Cartesian mapping techniques that are used to identify territory for land claims function to exclude and enclose, and have little to do with Coast Salish concepts of relatedness and community. He suggests that developing a "radical cartography" that better reflects Coast Salish flexibility of group membership and kinship would improve both political relations and resource management.

In the Sahtu, the animosity generated by access and benefits agreements, business contracts, and other jurisdictional issues related to the land claim appears to remain at the level of community politics. That is, it results from land-claim-based political territorialization. This suggests that two interesting and often contradictory forces are at work in the lives of Sahtu Dene people: what should be done to support kinfolk (and thus be a good human being), which plays out in interpersonal relationships; and what must be done to maintain some form of economic or jurisdictional benefit, which can be seen at the level of community politics. At least in part, these contradictory forces spring from the lack of integration between Sahtu Dene values of generosity and mutual support, on the one hand, and the decision-making processes, lines of authority, and economic relations established in the land claim agreement, on the other. Thus, political friction, both between Dene and Metis beneficiaries and between Sahtu communities, is heightened as a result of the land claim primarily because it does not take into account local normative practice. None of this is to suggest that conflict never occurred in Sahtu Dene communities before the advent of the land claim or that, had the claim never existed, they would have remained discord-free, especially given the recent pressure to "develop" non-renewable resources in the region. However, what the land claim has done is fix the fissures and contradictory forces into permanent composition; it has entrenched distinctly non-local forms of land tenure, governance, and social relations in solid form.

THE LAND CORPORATION
AS PRIVILEGED FORM OF MANAGEMENT

From the outset, the land claim agreement required Sahtu Dene people to set aside local values regarding lands, economies, and forms of exchange in favour of motives for profits, money, and business contracts. The conceptualization of Sahtu Settlement Lands in the form of private property rights, and the use of a corporate framework to manage them, serves several purposes. First, the Sahtu Dene are now shareholders in a corporate structure, which, if it expects to be profitable, must use the land as an economic instrument to generate wealth. Second, vesting title to SSA lands in district land corporations fundamentally limits political institutions such as chief and councils in important decisions about the land. Thus, the political body that once represented the interests of the Indian band is now on the periphery when it comes to decisions about essential aspects of Sahtu Dene life: hunting and trapping rights and other forms of land-based economic and/or community development practices. Finally, the establishment of Sahtu Dene land rights in the form of private property law endorses particular ways of viewing relationships between human beings and the world. To put it simply, though the agreement secured a central place for the Sahtu Dene in the management of lands and resources, it has done so in a very particular way: via a corporate structure that is designed to generate profits from the exploitation of land.

At the same time, Sahtu Dene people are now landowners, and the land corporations that make the decisions about land use are composed of Sahtu Dene presidents, staff, and shareholders. Sahtu Dene people now have rights to hunt, trap, and fish throughout the SSA and to partake in environmental assessments and regulatory processes. Thus, beneficiaries of the claim find themselves in the uncomfortable position of participating in institutions that both protect Sahtu Dene rights and endorse the commodification of land and land-based resources. They are enmeshed in a paradox: they now own their land, but the associated form of management undermines their relationship with it.

The establishment of a corporate structure to manage private land holdings required land corporation presidents, board members, and staff to develop sophisticated negotiating skills and become experts in regulatory processes and oil and gas vernacular. To bargain effectively with oil and gas companies, land corporation staff had to absorb complex documents and become skilled in contract and proposal writing. They also had to cultivate strategic links with people in various industries, such as suppliers and oil and gas service companies. In many ways, land corporation offices have become the technological hubs of communities, with access to resources such as sophisticated maps and mapping tools and high-speed Internet. The Colville Lake land corporation acquired wireless Internet services via satellite because high-speed communication was necessary in its dealings with the many gas companies that are interested in exploring the Colville Hills.

Importantly, engaging with outside interests that wish to conduct work on Sahtu lands has also required land corporation leaders and staff to apply novel means of making decisions and lines of authority. A number of factors play a role here, including the complexity of the regulatory and negotiation process, the limited familiarity of most beneficiaries with the oil and gas industry, the need to make decisions quickly and remotely (with companies in Calgary, rather than in the Sahtu), and the nature of the closed "boardroom meetings" as the primary decision-making arena for granting land access. All of these have significant implications for community dynamics.

MAKING DECISIONS: ACCESS AND BENEFITS AGREEMENTS

The primary means through which extractive companies obtain permission to work on Sahtu Settlement Lands is the access and benefits agreement (ABA), or impact benefits agreement as it is sometimes called. This common type of contract is negotiated and signed between development corporations and Indigenous communities in Canada and elsewhere (see O'Faircheallaigh 1999). The premise behind ABAs is that conducting work on Indigenous land will probably have a social, environmental, or economic impact on the community in question. Thus, to minimize adverse effects and to ensure local benefits in employment and training, communities and companies enter into binding agreements. In the Sahtu, where land claim beneficiaries are landowners, companies must also acquire permission and pay for access to or across Sahtu Settlement Lands. Thus, ABA negotiations focus on payment and conditions for access, and on commitments to economic opportunities for local communities. In the Sahtu, as elsewhere in the Northwest Territories, ABAs are confidential and their terms, conditions, and commitments are known only to the company, the land corporation beneficiaries, regulators, and Indian Affairs and Northern Development Canada. ABAs are required for licensing and permitting processes, and most must be approved by the minister of Indian Affairs. Their negotiation often occurs in the early stages of regulatory processes, prior to the submission of application permits or community consultations. ABAs are typically negotiated between oil and gas companies and land corporation presidents and management boards. Sometimes, the president and board ask their beneficiaries to vote on the terms of an ABA; sometimes they do not, though the status of the project, the ABA, and other land corporation financial dealings is presented at the annual corporation meeting.

ABAs are often created relatively quickly, as companies seek to begin their extractive projects and require an ABA before they submit their permit applications. In negotiations, land corporation presidents are sometimes aided by staff and outside lawyers and consultants. All must function well in a boardroom setting and must understand how oil and gas projects work. Presidents typically attempt to maximize benefits in the form of access payments, allocation of business contracts and opportunities, joint-partnership ventures, training, and other community initiatives without jeopardizing the negotiation process. They must intuit how much a company is willing to give and under what conditions. And they must be generally familiar with how well other land corporations have fared in similar situations.[29]

ABA negotiations are conducted over the phone, via e-mail and the Internet, and to a certain extent, through face-to-face meetings. A company often holds at least one consultation meeting with community members, but most of the actual negotiation occurs in closed meetings.[30] These sometimes take place in the community, but most are conducted in urban boardrooms, particularly in Calgary.[31] All of this presents a series of complications. First, a closed meeting necessarily means that most beneficiaries are excluded from the negotiation process. Thus, the president and staff of the land corporation wield a significant amount of power to determine the terms of access and the types of benefits that the community will receive. Second, presidents and staff are often flown to Calgary for ABA meetings, where they are housed at very expensive hotels, courtesy of the oil and gas company. Company executives and negotiation teams often host dinners and have even established open-bar tabs at some of the hottest Calgary nightclubs for their Sahtu guests – all gestures of goodwill, perhaps, but ones that can significantly sway the results of the negotiation. In one community, the chief asked oil and gas companies to stop providing land corporation delegates with open tabs at Calgary nightclubs and bars.

The exclusion of beneficiaries, either because a meeting is held remotely or because it is closed, is in direct opposition to conventional decision-making processes in the Sahtu. Typically, when a major decision must be made, or when important information must be shared or moral instruction given, the entire community is invited to a gathering where elders present long oratories and instruction through stories. Elders are seen as vast stores of primary knowledge, and their words and advice are highly regarded. As a local man said, "Prophets and elders always talked about how we should live our lives in the future ... what to protect. We have to use this knowledge to make us stronger."[32] However, ABA meetings often exclude elders in their conventional role as advisors. One elder commented,

> Today, it is really different. We have young leaders so they have hardly been on the land. The young leaders don't ask the elders or involve them in the decision-making process. The young leaders just go out and make the deci-sion right there. I went out on the land just recently across the lake, and all of the lodges are closed but there were some big-game hunters at [a nearby] bay and I didn't know anything about it.[33]

In many ways, the exclusion of elders and other beneficiaries from ABA negotiations results from the use of the non-local discursive fields of the oil and gas industry and perhaps from unfamiliarity with corporate politics and norms. Many land corporation presidents are young men who have had some formal education outside the community. Elders, on the other hand, often speak very little English, and though they may not frame their questions in oil and gas linguistic register, they have tremendous repertoires of knowledge regarding the environment, the history of their people, and the values and norms of their community. Ironically, those who know the most about the land are often excluded from ABA decisions, either because they are not at the meeting or because the corporate community does not readily understand the ways in which they speak about it. Several people in the Sahtu argue that the elders must play a more direct role in the early stages of these decision-making processes. As one person put it, "The elders are smart people, and what are they doing, they are just sitting there ... They are doing nothing. We need to bring them back. They have things to say."[34] The gaps in generation and in discursive fields used in decision-making processes have led to a widening chasm between older and younger generations in Sahtu communities.

The ABA process can have other significant consequences for Sahtu communities. First and foremost, an ABA essentially permits the company to conduct the work in question. Because title to the land rests with the land corporations, signing an ABA fulfills the requirement that companies must obtain "permission" from the landowner, even if the beneficiaries of the land corporation, the local people themselves, know nothing about the proposed project. And because subsequent stages of the regulatory approval process cannot proceed without an ABA, it is often in place before community consultation occurs. Thus, local people commonly find themselves in information or consultation meetings where the "permission of the landholders" is a fait accompli. As one local woman stated, "Nobody reports to the community about what was said in meetings. They are really secret about it. People don't know what is going on. Even us, when we ask for information, we are told it is confidential."[35]

The closed-door nature of ABA meetings can also evoke widespread rumours or suspicions that the negotiators are somehow profiting from private business contracts or business dealings. One morning, I was sitting at my kitchen table when a local man came to visit. He told me that he had worked as a slasher and an environmental monitor on some of the oil and gas projects near his community, and that the companies did not listen to him when he voiced his concerns. As he explained, they "take water out of the good fishlakes and the beaver lakes. And the companies don't report it when they spill water or oil on the land. At one lake, they use the ice surface as an airfield, and they store drums of fuel on the lake."[36] He added that he was very worried because oil spilt from a drum would go straight into the lake. He said that he and another man from the community were "the first ones to raise concerns about all of the oil companies, but that the leadership did not listen. All the leadership was getting rich off of all of the development. Maybe they were getting paid by the companies, and they were making money only for themselves and their families."[37]

There is a general apprehension that those who negotiate ABAs are focused on money and business contracts rather than on the needs of the community or appropriate human relationships with the land. In part, this is because the prophets have warned about Dene dependence on money and the effects that this might bring. As one elder said, "Old Andre [a prophet], he told them what to watch out for in the future, which is true. One of these things that we should watch out for is money. In the future, money would be controlling Dene people, so that young people would say yes to things right away without thinking about the results. The land is alive."[38] Now, some people say, the words of the prophets are being fulfilled. As one person put it, "People want money so badly they just sign the contract just to make money, but they don't know what they are doing. Contractors will make money but not the people here."[39]

In general, as a result of the corporate nature of the land claim, and because oil and gas companies that secure subsurface rights on Crown land do have a right of access across SSA lands, provided that compensation is paid, land corporation representatives *are* highly motivated to secure the most profitable ABA.[40] After all, under the terms of the land claim agreement, simply owning the land, as the district land corporations do, does not confer a veto right when access to land with subsurface potential is involved. Thus, in many ways, a profitable ABA ensures that local communities will receive at least some benefits from a development project, even if they are ridiculously smaller than the project's total revenues.

And community leaders are not alone in seeing the benefits of industry. On several occasions, I was surprised to hear that people who were adamant about maintaining Dene law could also approve of development projects. One family with whom I stayed was very careful to uphold Dene law: family members observed proper relations with other-than-human persons and relied to a large extent on country food. Most meals included some form of Dene food, and dry-meat or dry-fish often hung from racks outside the house or in their laundry room or kitchen. So when we were invited to a nearby house to have dinner with some engineers who had flown in on their private jet to assess the possibility of building a turbine dam on the Great Bear River, I was startled to hear them say that a dam might be a good idea because their electricity bills would go down. Running a diesel generator in a remote location with limited road access is very costly, and people seem to look for ways of minimizing their expenses. These seemingly conflicting pressures – between upholding Dene law and reducing costs – are a reality for many Sahtu residents.

People in the Sahtu are likewise engaged in quests for power and prestige, and are therefore neither simply the agents nor the victims of large development projects. Access to resources, both political and economic, differs from person to person, as do motives, visions for the future, and constraints and opportunities to manoeuvre. People who work in the land corporations tend to possess the skills and complex fields of knowledge that are required for work in oil and gas projects, and they can often afford the equipment and supplies necessary to procure business contracts. Thus, some businesses owned or operated by current or former land corporation presidents have benefitted from oil and gas contracts and business opportunities. This is not necessarily due to nepotism or corruption on their part (though it may sometimes be the case). Instead, it can arise because their work with the land corporation enables them to establish strategic business networks with companies, because they possess competency in procurement and business processes, because they are familiar with the rules of the game, and because they need fallback employment should they lose their seat in the land corporation during the next election. Thus, though certain people do benefit more than others from oil and gas development, this is because many who negotiate ABAs are in the best position to operate independent businesses.

The idea that a handful of people would benefit at the expense of everyone else, or that they would make unilateral decisions about land use, contradicts what many elders say about proper social relations in the Sahtu. Still, perhaps because of the emphasis on non-interference and social cohesion, these conflicts do not seem to jeopardize relationships between people, at least not in public. One day, after a long focus group meeting, I asked an elder if he would like to speak into the tape recorder so that future generations could hear him. This is what he said:

> From today on, I hope that the youth work together. It can't be just one person who has a good job and makes good money. Everyone should be the same. No more than the other. It is the only way it will work. The important thing is that I hope that they love one another and support one another and know that there is a Creator out there who can help them. I hope that they never let go of that. To love one another and support one another and not to let go of the stories, and the hand games, and the drum dances, and the songs ... the traditional way of life.[41]

The Role of Sahtu Economies

There are tensions between Sahtu Dene who seek to maintain traditional lifeways and those who see a sustainable hydrocarbon-based economy as a key to the future for their youth. However, these tensions clearly exist within people themselves: those who seek oil and gas development as a way forward display a cautious optimism and a concern over both ecological and socio-cultural impacts and the loss of Dene lifeways. Those who seek to maintain land-based lifestyles increasingly realize that young people both want and need to participate in a cash economy alongside subsistence pursuits. Local leaders, especially those with the authority to approve industrial permits on Sahtu lands, are often caught in the middle. These tensions between protecting a valued way of life and looking toward a future of sustainable hydrocarbon exploration and production are very much a reflection of changing Sahtu economies.

Most Sahtu elders were born and raised in the bush. They grew up on the land and know the ways of the earth, the animals, the water, and the weather; they know how to locate animals, how to set traps, how to prepare furs, how to find moss for diaper bags, how to build shelters and keep warm, how to make fire, how to obtain medicine. Their lives depended on the seasonal rounds and the ability to cultivate the sustenance of the land. They are comfortable on the land and spend time there whenever possible. One couple with whom I stayed in Colville Lake spent the fall months trapping on the land, though both were well into their eighties.

It is important to note that the transition to a sedentary life in communities occurred relatively recently in the Sahtu, during the last fifty years or so. A Tulit'a leader, for example, talked about his experiences with this change. As we sat in his office overlooking the Mackenzie River, he said that, as a child, he lived in the bush for most of the year, but he loved to come to town and as soon as he saw the smoke rising above Fort Norman (now Tulit'a), he knew that town was not far away. When his family first moved into town, they lived in a small log house near the river and constantly returned to the bush, "hunting all over." As long as the dog team was the norm, he said, people often went into the bush, but they became somewhat fearful when they got skidoos because the skidoos could break down and leave them stranded far from town. "One thing is for sure," he said, "a dog team does not break, and you don't need to fix it." But people gradually learned how to work with skidoos. They went out in pairs, so that if one skidoo broke down, no one would be stranded. And they tied skidoos together when hauling packed moose or caribou meat. During a recent hunting trip to Drum Lake, he and his companions had shot fourteen woodland caribou and had tied all the skidoos together to carry them home. "It was a lot of work," he said, "but also a lot of fun."

These days, spending time on the land typically requires a cash outlay. Very few people in the Sahtu continue to raise or use dog teams, and most people travel by skidoo in the winter and ATV or motorized boat in the summer. This equipment is expensive (particularly because one must pay freight costs or make the long trip to Yellowknife or Edmonton to pick it up). Fuel is expensive as well; its cost is the focus of frequent and fervent dialogue in the Sahtu, and the local price is often three or more times higher than in the South. As my discussions with hunters revealed, the high cost of fuel was by far the most significant barrier to spending time on the land. Hunters must also buy equipment such as guns and ammunition, traps, fishnets, and other essential supplies, all of which are costly. Consequently, going out on the land is not cheap and can be prohibitively expensive for those who lack access to cash. Increasingly in the Sahtu, anyone who wishes to hunt and trap must also participate in a cash economy. Yet, this has the immediate consequence of limiting the time spent in land-based activities and the distances that people can travel, simply because they must remain at home to work.

According to the Northwest Territories Bureau of Statistics Selected Socio-Economic Indicators, 15.1 percent of Sahtu residents were unemployed in 2006 (GNWT 2008). Most people who had jobs worked in government, health, or social service sectors; a very high percentage of residents were engaged in rotational or seasonal employment. Government, health, or social service positions often require some formal schooling, though not necessarily post-secondary education. For most young people, school enrolment requires that they reside full-time in the community.[42] However, though attending school provides necessary training for employment and participation in cash economies, it simultaneously limits both the time that youth spend in the bush and their ability to acquire land-based skills. Though the school system does offer formal on-the-land programs, time spent on the land is often limited to after school, weekends, and the summer months.[43] Again, this shapes the seasons and directions of travel, and the amount of time allocated to acquiring land-based skills. This is not to say that young people in the Sahtu are not learning such skills; they are remarkably interested in doing so and can be exceptionally proficient in obtaining sustenance in the bush. Many say that being on the land and protecting traditional lifeways are vitally important to them. However, they are often less comfortable than previous generations with spending extended time in the bush and tend to focus on gaining meaningful employment after graduation.

In two of the three communities where I conducted my research, land corporation presidents hunted, trapped, fished, and gathered berries after work and on the weekends, though their demanding jobs did tend to diminish their time in the bush. Land corporation presidents commonly feel that living permanently on the land is no longer possible for Sahtu Dene, and thus their view of the future emphasizes job creation, especially for youth. Of course, people who view oil and gas exploration as a means of increasing employment do not see the land as an insignificant aspect of community life. Their ideal future involves a balance, in which sustainable employment complements hunting and trapping, and cash and subsistence economies exist side by side. Younger leaders typically assume that local people will hunt close to home, thus leaving more inaccessible places, or places farther from town, open for development. Sitting in his office, discussing the intent of two large oil companies to conduct exploratory work, a land corporation president said to me,

> The elders used the land in one way, and the younger generations use it in the same, but also different ways. Young people often go out on weekends and use snowmobiles. There are fishlakes that were really important when people were using dog teams, but these lakes are not as important to younger generations, because they have snowmobiles. Both elders and young people have really important knowledge, and that knowledge is equal and valuable. But it is different, and the use of the land is different as well. When we look at the land, we see it differently than our elders did.

Accordingly, land corporation leaders often concentrate on controlling the pace and location of development, and on ensuring that meaningful benefits flow to their communities in the form of money and jobs. Indeed, the corporatization of land and decision making in the Sahtu, and the lack of a veto power where subsurface rights belong to the Crown, influences this form of prioritizing in a very significant way.

Yet, for others, the creation of jobs, the procurement of business contracts, and the generation of wealth are not worth the risk of disrupting vital relationships with the land. As one person stated in the Joint Review Panel (JRP) hearings,

> Without the animals on the land, as Aboriginal people, it's not worth living. That's how it is. That's how I feel. Even for me, I think about it, it's not worth living without animals. Even though you gave us lots of money, but if there's no animal what's the use? Even though there's no money, but if there's – if there's an animal on the land, I can survive by that.[44]

For Sahtu residents, the increased interest in large development projects evokes two essential questions. First, is it possible to balance subsistence and hydrocarbon-based economies? And second, can and will local communities actually benefit from development projects? The answers to these questions lie in the future. As mentioned above, hydrocarbon exploration has been relatively minimal in the Sahtu because, as yet, gas cannot be transported to southern markets.[45] And except for the line from Norman Wells to Zama, Alberta, no pipelines have been built in the Sahtu. If the Mackenzie Gas Project proceeds, interest in producing gas in the Colville Hills and Stewart Lake area would probably increase, as would exploration. Should this occur, will Sahtu Dene communities eventually reach a tipping point, both in terms of ecological sustainability and their capacity to choose whether to participate in a cash or a subsistence economy?

CONCLUSION

The Sahtu Dene originally hoped that resolving their land claim would enhance their control of their own territory, that their authority would outweigh coercive state power to unilaterally make decisions about Sahtu lands and resources. However, many are growing increasingly frustrated with the resulting institutions, which are formulated on non-local lines of authority and decision making. Yes, Sahtu Dene people now sit on the corporate and co-management boards that issue land use permits, conduct environmental assessments, and negotiate terms of access. Nonetheless, the rules of engagement still come from elsewhere: the boards must adhere to the terms of the land claim agreement and must follow rules that are at odds with local ideas about appropriate uses of the land and the way in which decisions ought to be made. In the end, what the claim actually did achieve was to put Sahtu representatives on corporate and co-management boards in the position of upholding and applying federal laws concerning land management and development.

Some people maintain that the complications of the land claim are internal – that they arise from the ways in which community leaders communicate and consider the voices and concerns of locals. To some degree, they may be right. However, the internal fissures, miscommunications, and strategies for social and economic profits are also manipulated and exploited by outside agencies. Oil and gas companies *do* wine-and-dine Sahtu Dene leaders during their meetings in Calgary, and Ottawa *does* exploit community divisions to achieve its ends. Not long after returning from a trip to the Sahtu, I received a very unusual phone call from a federal government employee. While in Tulit'a, I had done some work for the community and had spoken to its leaders, the employees of various organizations, land claim institution leaders, and local residents, after which

I wrote a report on diverse community perspectives regarding consultation processes. The report was given to Tulit'a leaders, who were at liberty to share and use it as they wished. No one else received copies. The government employee told me that her department had a copy, and she asked me to reveal the names of everyone with whom I had spoken regarding consultation. She said that her department was preparing to meet with Tulit'a on consultation, that my report "was not reliable" without the names of the interview participants, and that they were essential in determining its "validity." Having promised to protect the identities of my interviewees, and knowing that Tulit'a had a history of political fracture, I refused to comply for fear that the government would use the names in the upcoming meeting. I politely suggested that if she wanted to confirm whether my report reflected community opinion, she should discover how her department had received its copy. I then called Tulit'a and confirmed what I had suspected: that its leadership had sent the report to government agencies as an example of community views concerning appropriate consultation, and that it was possible that the federal employee was really fishing for names of "allies" and "troublemakers" rather than trying to determine the "validity" of the report. This is but one instance of the ways in which outside interests can and have manipulated local politics and decision-making processes in the Sahtu.

The use of a corporate model to settle land claims and establish jurisdiction over Indigenous territories has been criticized for other areas of the Canadian North and Alaska. In *From Talking Chiefs to a Native Corporate Elite,* Marybelle Mitchell (1996) traces the transformation of Inuit economic and political systems and their attendant social relations from early contact to the creation of Nunavut. She shows that rather than being instruments of economic development and increased authority for the Inuit population, Inuit development corporations have created a rigid class structure in which an Inuit elite serves the interests of the state and of non-Inuit private enterprise. Mitchell (ibid., 397-98) writes,

> The development corporations are the vehicles that perpetuate an Inuit ruling class, one without a power source of its own. The original capital comes from the state. We can say, therefore, that the state created a ruling class that facilitated industrial development of the north. This dependent 'ruling class' is helping state/industry to dispossess all Inuit of their land, and it controls the capital paid by the state to all Inuit (indirectly) as compensation for dispossession.

Her words strongly resemble the aftermath of corporatization in the Sahtu.

In *Village Journey*, the report of the Alaska Native Review Commission, Thomas Berger (1985) offers a telling critique of the Alaska Native Claims Settlement Act (ANCSA), which was passed in 1971. Following general dissatisfaction with the act, the threat of alienation and the "selling" of tribal lands, the widening gap between rich and poor development corporations, and the disjuncture between the goals of village corporations and those of local people, the Inuit Circumpolar Conference commissioned Justice Berger to review ANCSA. In hearings throughout the state, Berger listened as Alaska Natives spoke about their experiences under the act; some wished to retribalize their lands by removing them from the jurisdiction of ANCSA corporations and returning them to tribal governments.[46] In recommending that this should indeed be done, Berger (ibid., 159) explains,

> A corporation cannot take from the rich and give to the poor without facing a shareholder's suit; but a tribal government can implement measures designed to achieve social justice. A corporation can claim no immunity to state laws – it is a creature of state laws – but a tribal government can assert immunity from them. A profit-making corporation is comprised of stockholders who own shares but a tribal government is comprised of members identified by who they are, not what they own. A corporation's existence depends upon statements of its profits and loss, but a tribe's existence is endlessly renewed with each generation.

Berger also recognizes the inherent contradiction between the needs and visions of Alaska Natives and those of their village corporations. He (ibid., 9) states that "the village corporations are legally constituted to make profits, to pursue economic purposes. Yet, the villagers themselves are chiefly concerned with subsistence activities. This can place the corporations at cross purposes with their village shareholders."

Writing some twenty years later, Kirk Dombrowski (2001) also shows that ANCSA has provided for some benefits to Alaska Native shareholders but that if these benefits are to be realized, they must come through the development of natural resources by ANCSA corporations. He essentially argues that ANCSA was designed to achieve two goals for the American government: to open Alaskan land and offshore waters for development and to relieve the federal and state governments from costly support programs for remote Native villages. Dombrowski (ibid., 69-70) suggests that

ANCSA was assimilationist, creating "business firms" that would "use the money and land awarded by the state to produce income for themselves and their stockholders." However, when ANCSA corporations failed to produce profits, Congress passed a 1988 amendment to ANCSA that "allowed timber corporations to count any losses in the value of their standing timber between the time of purchase and the time of harvest as operating losses" (Dombrowski 2002, 1065). Subsequently, these "paper losses" could serve as tax shelters, or if the ANCSA corporation had not made a profit, could be sold to third-party corporations. In his analysis of the effects of net operating loss legislation on southeast Alaska Natives, Dombrowski shows a number of consequences. First, because the timber had to be logged to calculate the loss, ANCSA corporations agreed to the clear cutting of large areas. Second, many village corporations were controlled by non-resident shareholders, who were unlikely to invest much of the capital gained as a result of the legislation into village job creation or other village-level programs. Finally, non-shareholder village residents, who according to Dombrowski (ibid.), were "most dependent on hunting and gathering for daily subsistence," received none of the money that was issued as dividends to shareholders, but bore the brunt of the effects of ecological damage as a result of clear cutting. The impact wrought by ANCSA and its subsequent amendment may foreshadow long-term consequences in the Sahtu.

Although the organizing structures of the Sahtu land claim agreement and those of ANCSA are not synonymous, the critique of the corporatization of lands and land use decision making is remarkably unified. In both cases, Aboriginal people believed that their claim would protect their territories. Yet many feel that, in the end, the claims and the "development corporations" that administer them have become the very tools of dispossession and transformation.

The Sahtu land claim agreement does have its local detractors, but openly voicing a critique can be difficult. The people who negotiated and ratified it are often vital members of Sahtu communities: they are fathers, brothers, uncles, and friends. Thus, criticizing the agreement can amount to criticizing the actions of relatives and friends. In getting to know many of these people, I came to understand that they believed that the land claim would better the lives of their people, and though it did not bring the hoped-for independence, there is evidence that comprehensive land claims in general have contributed to improvements in local economic development (Saku and Bone 2000a, 2000b; Saku 2002). Second, several components of the agreement were implemented many years after its ratification; a notable example is the Sahtu Land Use Plan, which was not approved until 2013.[47] During the MGP assessment, Sahtu residents feared that the project would be approved before a ratified land use plan was in place and that development would quickly monopolize areas that might be considered for protection. Third, an overwhelming number of Sahtu Dene people voted to ratify the agreement, and many more have enrolled as beneficiaries. In fact, except for a few Tulit'a residents who refuse to participate in the claim, most people who are eligible to enrol have done so, with 3,173 enrolled as of 2008 (Sahtu Secretariat Incorporated 2008, 15). In a very real way, the Sahtu Dene are and always have been participants in their comprehensive land claim, though not without constraints imposed by outside forces. Involvement has not always been on their own terms, and in many ways it has undermined local practices. Still, choosing not to participate would have resulted in a lack of security for Sahtu Dene rights, no involvement in resource decision making, and virtually no economic benefit from development projects in the region. In the next chapter, I will examine the politics of participation and the ways in which local involvement in non-local land use decision making and environmental assessments is used to legitimize and naturalize non-Dene institutional apparatuses and models of development.

4

Consultation and Other Legitimating Practices

In our culture, it would be shameful for someone to go to another community and determine its future.

– Colville Lake resident at a consultation meeting

IN THE SAHTU region, community participation in decisions about non-renewable resources comes in several forms. Local people can attend public hearings as general stakeholders in environmental assessment processes, they can negotiate access and benefits agreements (ABAs) as is required by their land claim, they can involve themselves in distinct consultation processes with the Crown, and they can participate through "traditional knowledge" gathering and documentation as mandated by regulatory boards and the Mackenzie Valley Resource Management Act. Whereas previous chapters have examined Sahtu Dene participation in public hearings, environmental assessment, governance, and ABA negotiations, this chapter focuses on the legal category of consultation and the use of traditional knowledge studies as an aspect of regulatory compliance.

In Canada, companies and governments increasingly emphasize consultation with Aboriginal peoples as a formal component of resource decision making, a development that stems from two interrelated corporate and institutional realities. First, working alongside local communities to streamline permit applications and avoid unnecessary delays and costs resulting from community grievances simply makes good business and policy sense. Second, due to recent court decisions, the Crown has a legal duty to consult with Aboriginal peoples in decisions that could affect their rights or lands. Under this new dispensation, Aboriginal rights to participate in decisions related to lands and resources have been supported in law, and in the case of the Sahtu, by the Sahtu Dene and Metis Comprehensive Land Claim Agreement. Thus, for governments and proponents, failing to consult could result in costly delays, denials of regulatory permits, lengthy litigation, and the eventual derailing of the project in question. Not surprisingly, then, government and industry take the duty to consult quite seriously.[1]

A cursory examination of recent judicial considerations of Aboriginal rights in resource management decisions suggests that courts *are* increasingly invoking higher standards in how industry and governments ought to interact with Aboriginal peoples. The entrenchment of "existing" Aboriginal rights in section 35(1) of the Constitution, ongoing land claim and self-governance processes, and the recognition of the Crown's fiduciary duty to consult with Aboriginal groups on projects that could infringe on their rights and lands have provided a legal framework whereby Aboriginal rights might at last be taken seriously by project proponents and the Canadian state. In the Northwest Territories, several avenues for participation in development and land management decisions have been embedded in law as a result of comprehensive land claim agreements; these include the cooperative management boards that issue land and water permits, and the requirement that traditional knowledge be included in land and water permit applications.

Yet, complications regarding the nature and extent of consultation, and indeed the very essence of the consultative relationship, persist. Michael Asch (1997b, i), a prominent anthropologist who has written extensively on law and its relation to Aboriginal peoples in Canada, states that

> the law has two contrasting faces ... Since Confederation, Canadian law has represented a fundamental means whereby the values and institutions derived from the culture of settlers, immigrants, colonists, and their descendants were to be imposed upon Indigenous peoples. At the same time, there have been moments when these institutions and values have been successfully challenged through the application of the rule of law.

Indeed, several scholars have shown that the norms of the Canadian judicial system, and associated forms of discourse and fact-finding processes, may not coincide with Aboriginal views about the world. For example, anthropologist Andie Palmer (2000) reveals that the courts have treated oral history as a lesser standard of proof in establishing evidence for land claims. Paul Nadasdy (2003, 5) suggests that legal discourses of property and ownership reflect long-standing Euro-Canadian beliefs about human and societal development, and that the participation of Aboriginal groups in legal processes may, in fact, "serve to reinforce the symbolic power of the dominant classes." And Catherine Bell and Michael Asch

(1997, 74) argue that the principle of *stare decisis* (observing precedent) limits the ability of the courts to discard outdated rulings and create an instrument through which they can determine legal rights fairly.

This chapter examines the consultative processes in the Sahtu, with particular attention to Sahtu Dene claims that they have not significantly enhanced community influence in decisions about non-renewable resources or necessarily improved relations between local communities and the proponents of development projects. It seems important, then, to explore the contexts, associations, and ultimately the power relations involved in consultation, and to ask: What can consultation, as a state-sanctioned mechanism for eliciting Aboriginal input into resource management decisions, tell us about the relationships between Aboriginal people and Ottawa?

LEGAL REQUIREMENTS FOR ABORIGINAL CONSULTATION

Canadian jurisprudence and recent case law have addressed the Crown's duty to consult with and (where appropriate) accommodate Aboriginal people in decisions concerning their rights and lands. The duty to consult originates in the fiduciary duty of the Crown under its responsibility to Aboriginal peoples. Thomas Isaac and Anthony Knox (2003, 58) note that the Supreme Court of Canada began its serious discussion of the Crown's duty to consult in *Delgamuukw v. British Columbia* (1997) by observing that "the fiduciary relationship between the Crown and Aboriginal people may be satisfied by the involvement of Aboriginal peoples in decisions taken with respect to their lands." However, the consultation requirement was first established some years earlier, in *R. v. Sparrow*, which the court heard in 1990. In this case, the court ruled that laws interfering with the exercise of constitutionally protected Aboriginal rights must conform to constitutional standards of justification. In other words, the court found that though Aboriginal rights under section 35(1) of the Constitution must be taken seriously, they are not absolute. Nonetheless, their infringement must pass what is known as the Sparrow test: setting the rights aside must serve a legitimate purpose and must be consistent with the honour of the Crown (Culhane 1998). Consultation plays an essential role in the Sparrow test.

Prior to 2004, judicial references to the Crown's duty to consult focused solely on Aboriginal rights that were entrenched in the Constitution. Therefore, the duty to consult came into play only in situations where

Aboriginal rights already existed, and it did not apply to potential rights or future rights. However, in 2004, the Supreme Court of Canada issued rulings in two cases involving BC First Nations – *Haida Nation v. British Columbia* and *Taku River Tlingit First Nation v. British Columbia.* Both dealt with the Crown's duty to consult. The court found that the duty to consult applied in situations where Aboriginal rights could *potentially* be infringed and where land claims could potentially be adversely affected before they were settled. This extension of the duty to consult can be seen as a step forward, but *Haida Nation* and *Taku River* left open both the nature of consultation and the degree to which third parties were obliged to engage in it. Effectively, *Haida Nation* stipulated that the honour of the Crown, and thus the *duty* to consult, did not extend to third parties, though they could be held liable if they did not engage in meaningful consultation. In addition, both *Haida Nation* and *Taku River* established that though the Crown had a duty to consult, it did not have a duty to reach an agreement with Aboriginal groups. Finally, both rulings also maintained that the level of consultation could vary with the circumstances. This established a wide spectrum, which ranged from "minimal consultation" (such as notifying Aboriginal groups of decisions that could potentially affect their lands or rights) to "deep consultation" (aimed at finding a mutually satisfactory solution and possible accommodation of community requirements).

The duty to consult is intended to give Aboriginal groups an increased role in the decisions that affected their lives, and perhaps more importantly, to aid in reconciling relationships between Aboriginal peoples and the Crown. However, questions remain as to the effectiveness of a consultation dialogue and the extent to which it enables Aboriginal groups to influence decisions. The reasons for this, I believe, are twofold: First, neither "consultation" nor the point at which the duty to consult and accommodate is triggered are clearly defined (though the former was addressed to some degree in the 2005 case *Mikisew Cree First Nation v. Canada* and *Dene Tha' First Nation v. Canada* in 2006). Second, proponents, governments, and Aboriginal groups have differing approaches to consultation.

Generally speaking, the courts have been vague in defining Aboriginal consultation. As Justice Lamer explained in *Delgamuukw* (1997 at para. 168),

The nature and scope of the duty of consultation will vary with the circumstances. In occasional cases, when the breach is less serious or relatively minor, it will be no more than a duty to discuss important decisions ... Of course, even in these rare cases when the minimum acceptable standard is consultation, this consultation must be in good faith, and with the intention of substantially addressing the concerns of the Aboriginal peoples whose lands are at issue. In most cases, it will be significantly deeper than mere consultation. Some cases may even require the full consent of an Aboriginal nation.

In *Halfway River First Nation v. British Columbia* (1999 at para. 160), the court elaborated on the nature of the duty to consult:

The Crown's duty to consult imposes on it a positive obligation to reasonably ensure that Aboriginal peoples are provided with all necessary information in a timely way so that they have an opportunity to express their interests and concerns, and to ensure that their representations are seriously considered, and wherever possible, demonstrably integrated into the proposed plan of action.

And in *Mikisew Cree First Nation v. Canada* (2005 at para. 64), the Supreme Court found that the Crown had breached its duty to properly consult with the Mikisew:

The Crown is required to provide notice to the Mikisew and to engage directly with them. This engagement should include the provision of information about the project, addressing what the Crown knew to be the Mikisew's interests and what the Crown anticipated might be the potential adverse impact on those interests. The Crown must also solicit and listen carefully to the Mikisew's concerns, and attempt to minimize adverse effects on its treaty rights ... It [the Crown] failed to demonstrate an intention of substantially addressing aboriginal concerns through a meaningful process of consultation.

As these rulings reveal, the Supreme Court has been reluctant to define minimal consultation, preferring instead to establish a framework in which the duty to consult (and, where appropriate, to accommodate) is laid out in general – but not universally binding – terms. On the one hand, this approach allows for flexibility: Aboriginal people, industry, and government can tailor consultation as they see fit. On the other hand, many Aboriginal groups are reluctant to enter into consultation specifically *because* it is not clearly defined. For example, several groups, including the Deh Cho in the Northwest Territories and the Dene Tha' in Alberta, have expressed reservations about "jumping into consultation" regarding the Mackenzie Gas Project (MGP) without fully understanding what that might entail. They suggest that the responsibilities of each party should be clearly outlined, to ensure a formal consultation process, to give Aboriginal groups sufficient time to secure funding for technical expertise and analysis, and to avoid situations in which, though failing to participate meaningfully, industry nonetheless asserts that it has consulted with First Nations.

Concerns about the legitimation of authority in participatory environmental management are also relevant here. Part of the legitimation for infringement includes consulting with the Aboriginal groups that will be affected by the abrogation of the right. In the extreme, proponents and governments could see consultation as a means to justify the abrogation of potential or existing Aboriginal rights through legal means. After all, as established by the Supreme Court, consultation does not amount to a veto right for Aboriginal groups. Thus, though the requirement to consult does seek to establish a legal framework whereby the values and needs of local communities must be considered, the actual process of consultation tends to limit the ability of managers and proponents to fully and accurately do so. Once Aboriginal groups have been consulted, infringing the right could be seen as justified. Here again, it is through participating in consultation that Indigenous people have so much to lose.

The question of third-party or industry consultation with Aboriginal groups remains even more ambiguous. Both *Haida Nation* and *Taku River* indicate that third parties are not legally required to consult with Aboriginal groups, but risk potential liability if meaningful consultation is not undertaken. Aware of this risk, third-party and industry sectors have begun to develop their own Aboriginal engagement processes and have implemented strategies to facilitate consultation. Although this step significantly acknowledges Aboriginal rights and corporate responsibility to Aboriginal communities, it can also create complex organizational bureaucracies and failed partnerships, as the goals of communities and the timelines of industry do not always coincide.

Generally, the goals of industry are market-driven and outcome-oriented. They do not entail cementing long-term relationships with Aboriginal groups or addressing their wider cultural, spiritual, economic, or social needs. Corporations often declare that they are not in the business of providing social programs or reconciling Aboriginal peoples and the Crown – these, they rightly assert, are the responsibility of government. However, for some Aboriginal communities, consultation does encompass a relationship-building process that includes historical, spiritual, and cultural understandings in addition to specific economic goals. After all, development projects can have very serious social consequences for northern Aboriginal groups, which typically have much more than an economic bottom-line at stake. For them, consultation is not limited to a single meeting, project, or outcome: it involves a range of long-term commitments and the establishment of sustainable relationships (McLafferty and Dokis 2004).

Recently, government departments and agencies, and various industry sectors, have begun to offer seminars to staff and managers that are intended to increase their knowledge and understanding of Aboriginal cultures, histories, economies, and perspectives on legal frameworks. The hope is that seminar participants will become more effective "consulters." These one-day seminars often explore Indigenous worldviews and relationships to the land, as well as so-called best practices in Aboriginal community consultation. In 2004, a regulatory institution asked me and some colleagues to develop a training seminar on good practices for "Aboriginal engagement" and to deliver it to its management and staff. The *Haida Nation* and *Taku River* rulings had just come down from the Supreme Court, and the organization was particularly focused on undertaking consultation with Aboriginal stakeholders and doing so effectively, even though its legal team had determined that because it was not part of the federal government, it was not legally required to consult. The purpose of the training was to increase management and staff awareness of diverse Aboriginal cultures and to help them facilitate communication and understanding between their organization and Aboriginal stakeholders. Thus, during a four-hour class, participants were exposed to various Aboriginal cultures from across Canada and listened to facilitators talk about building relationships with Aboriginal communities. Many reported that they came away with a greater understanding and appreciation of Aboriginal cultures and communities but were not sure how to apply this knowledge to actual consultation meetings. In part, this was because they saw the meetings not as cultural events but as just another aspect of doing business. In other words, though they were well intentioned, they approached consultation as a business meeting – most people who took our training engaged in consultation as part of their jobs and returned to their homes and families and lives once it had ended.

In the Sahtu, the requirement for consultation rests not only in Canadian jurisprudence, but also in the licence and permitting processes of the Sahtu Land and Water Board, and in the Sahtu Dene and Metis Comprehensive

Land Claim Agreement. Under the terms of the agreement, the government must consult with the Sahtu Tribal Council in matters ranging from wildlife harvesting regulations to the creation of national or territorial parks or protected areas and the tendering of calls for nomination for oil or gas subsurface licences. The agreement also stipulates that any "person" who wishes to explore for oil and gas must consult with the Sahtu Tribal Council before doing so. By contrast, "persons" who wish to explore for minerals other than oil and gas must consult with the tribal council only if their activity requires a land use or water licence, or if they wish to develop or produce the material.

These differences in requirements for oil and gas and mining sectors have had several consequences. First, because oil and gas companies are always obliged to consult, they tend to have a great deal of experience with the process. Second, because consultation must predate exploration in the case of oil and gas, local people often assume that the same is true for other minerals. Thus, they can be confused and distressed when mining prospectors suddenly enter their lands and begin work without notice. In fact, the differing regulations have generated much confusion among local people about who should be consulting and when.

Just prior to my first trip to Colville Lake, in March 2006, I had heard that its long-time resident and former missionary, Bern Will Brown, rented out bunks to visitors. When I called him regarding their cost and availability, he told me that $120 a night would pay for a bunk, a pail of fresh water every morning, and some wood for the stove. On learning that I would be travelling alone, he suggested that his bunks were not appropriate for me. "These are shared bunks," he explained, "twelve bunks to a room, and right now I have eleven diamond prospectors staying with me. You might want to find something else." Incidentally, during the following month, elders in Colville Lake emphatically remarked at the Joint Review Panel hearings that they did not want the diamond prospectors "poking around" their lands without their knowledge or consent.

During my time in the Sahtu, I heard many people say that they had a right to be consulted regarding any projects on or near their lands. They correctly pointed out that this is enshrined in the land claim agreement, section 2.1.1 of which defines consultation as follows:

(a) the provision, to the party to be consulted, of notice of a matter to be decided in sufficient form and detail to allow that party to prepare its views on the matter;

(b) the provision of a reasonable period of time in which the party to be consulted may prepare its views on the matter, and provision of an opportunity to present such views to the party obliged to consult; and

(c) full and fair consideration by the party obliged to consult of any views presented.

Like Canadian jurisprudence, the land claim agreement provides only a general outline of consultation; it describes neither the process itself nor how it is to be carried out. For example, though notice must be given in "sufficient form and detail," the agreement does not indicate what that form might be or who determines whether it is sufficient. Similarly, the time allotted to consultation must be "reasonable," but standards of reasonableness are variable, particularly when communities and governments have diverse pressures and objectives. Finally, though a proponent must fully and fairly consider community views, the agreement does not stipulate how the effectiveness of its consideration is to be evaluated. In other words, it does not specify what constitutes fairness and who gets to decide whether community views have been fully considered. The haziness of this definition has had significant implications for relationships between Sahtu communities and proponents in three different areas: the format of community consultations, the constitution of fairness and reasonableness in the consultative relationship, and the timing of consultation in the overall project planning and permitting process.

The Community Consultation Process in the Sahtu

Despite the lack of clarity in the land claim agreement, consultation in the Sahtu typically follows a certain pattern. In contrast to an ABA negotiation, which is usually conducted behind closed doors with land corporation representatives, consultation takes place in public meetings. Regardless of where the meetings are held, their structure and format are virtually identical: the company representatives introduce themselves and ask people to sign a "list of attendees," which records who was at the meeting.[2] They present their project and then provide time for people to ask questions. To encourage attendance, they often have the event catered and either bring in Chinese food from Norman Wells or hire local cooks to provide moose, fish, turkey, potatoes, salads, bannock, and other food.[3] Without exception, they fly into the community a few hours before the public meeting to attend private meetings with land corporations or other government leaders, and they fly out as soon as the meeting ends. Afterward, the company prepares a short report of the meeting, including the names of those who attended, and submits this with its permit applications to the Sahtu Land and Water Board.

I have attended several consultation meetings in the Sahtu for both mining and oil and gas sectors. The following describes one of them, and though the meeting was generally representative, it was also an especially powerful example of how poorly the process serves to develop relationships between proponents and communities. For this particular meeting, the company representatives flew into the community at about four o'clock one Tuesday afternoon in April. The meeting began at seven that evening, but as usual, it was slow getting started. Before long, several local people came in and began to enjoy the incredible feast prepared by several local women who were hired to cook for the occasion. As the crowd chatted, a company representative walked around the room and shook everyone's hand. After a while, a company employee stood up and said that the meeting should begin.

The company reps gave a very technical PowerPoint presentation that described both the mineral deposits in the area of interest and the plan for their extraction. They mentioned how many local jobs the project was expected to create and what its environmental impact would be. Then the floor was opened for questions.

The president of one of the two local land corporations asked the first question: Why had his corporation not been consulted regarding the project? The company representatives replied that they had consulted with the other land corporation and the hamlet, and had thought this sufficient. They had not been aware that consultation with the other corporation (and with chief and council) was required as well. After further prodding, it was revealed that the company had already submitted its licence application to the Sahtu Land and Water Board and had not yet negotiated the terms of an access and benefits agreement (ABA). Locals pointed out that it "would be hearing from the Sahtu Land and Water Board soon," as consultation and the negotiation of an ABA were necessary for licensing approval.[4] The land corporation president then suggested that perhaps while the representatives were in town, they could meet to discuss the development of an ABA. The reps replied that they would be leaving immediately after the meeting, and that even if they could stay, none of them had the authority to negotiate an ABA.

After the event ended, I spoke briefly with the land corporation president. He was obviously frustrated by both the meeting itself and the company's lack of consideration for his corporation. He kept saying, "No matter what, they are going to have to come back and consult." He added, "I don't know why companies won't consult. It is like they think that we are anti-development, that consultation will lead to us either saying no or asking for a million dollars. We are not anti-development, we just want to participate."

As the above example shows, the use of public meetings as the primary forum for community consultation presents several barriers. First, though meetings are often prefaced by an informal period during which people can mingle as they share a feast, this is often very brief and does not give locals enough time to get to know company representatives – something that is often vital in the development of a trust relationship with outsiders. Since the late nineteenth century, fur traders, mining prospectors, military personnel, researchers, and oil and gas developers have all come to the Sahtu, often leaving disastrous consequences in their wake. Very few of their endeavours have ever benefitted Sahtu communities, and local people were rarely asked for their views on the projects. This history of outside exploitation plays a significant role in local perceptions of proponents and consultation processes. When company representatives come and go quickly (as most do), and do not spend time developing a rapport with community leaders, elders, and members, they are often deeply distrusted, as are their projects and promises of jobs.

The impersonal nature of consultation meetings does little to ease local concerns about the accountability of proponents or whether community voices are being heard in development plans. In the Sahtu, most people exchange information in informal settings: through visiting homes, sharing tea, or at church, hand games, or other celebrations. And, at least in my experience, the exchange is just that: an *exchange*. By flying in and out within hours of consultation meetings, proponents send the clear message that they are not interested in an exchange, in learning about or getting to know a community. Instead, they are interested in winning project approval in the quickest, most cost-effective way possible. For them, consultation is largely the key that turns the lock.

By way of contrast to this, I offer an account of my first meeting with Frank, a Colville Lake elder, to juxtapose the differing approaches to relationship building.[5] As I mentioned in Chapter 1, several people in Colville Lake suggested that I make of point of visiting Frank because he was a person who "knew things." He was known for his bush skills, and though he was well into his seventies, he spent most of his time on the land. He spoke little English, so I went with a translator to visit him late one October evening. When we reached his log house in the centre of town, he was at his kitchen counter, listening to the evening broadcast on the bush radio. When Colville Lake residents are in the bush, they rely on the radio to communicate with each other. Everyone listens to the radio at 10:00 a.m., 1:00 p.m., 4:00 p.m., and 10:00 p.m. to ensure that everyone is okay and to learn whether anyone needs supplies.

Heated by a woodstove, Frank's sparsely furnished house was warm. A table and three chairs were pushed against the wall next to the kitchen, and all manner of trapping supplies and equipment was spread across the large room. The translator greeted Frank cordially and shook his hand. He introduced me, told him about my project, and said that I had wanted to meet him. I had brought a can of Tim Hortons coffee as a token of thanks, and Frank politely took it and told me, through the translator, that he would like us to sit down and have a coffee. So we did.

My time in other Sahtu communities had taught me that letting the host guide the conversation was often best. For many people, small talk, such as idle and obvious remarks about the weather, is often met with disfavour. This is also true for abrupt and direct questions, such as "What do you think about the pipeline?" Likewise, boisterous or loud behaviour is often seen as humorous or, more likely, as impolite. So, in very many cases, building relationships of trust involves a great deal of silence.

In writing about the role of silence among the Western Apache, anthropologist Keith Basso suggests that his findings might be more widely applicable. He rightly points out that knowing any given language system also involves developing communicative competence (see also Hymes 1964) and understanding when to employ extra-linguistic factors in face-to-face encounters. With respect to silence, Basso (1970, 215, emphasis in original) reminds us that "knowledge of when *not* to speak may be as basic to the production of culturally acceptable behavior as a knowledge of what to say." As he observes, Western Apache who meet a stranger for the first time will refrain from speaking, which is perfectly acceptable and even expected. In fact, "strangers who are quick to launch into conversation are frequently eyed with undisguised suspicion" (ibid., 218).

In the Sahtu, silence is similarly valued, so during my first visit with Frank, I decided to wait for him to speak when he felt comfortable. For some time, we sat at his kitchen table drinking coffee, and he did not utter a word to the translator or myself. I became very aware of how uncomfortable *I* was with silence and had to make a real effort not to speak (and especially not to chat about the weather). After about thirty minutes, Frank finally said something in Slavey to the translator, which turned out to be

"This is good coffee." After another half hour of silence, Frank stood up, thanked us for coming, and invited us to come again. I did visit him again, and he was very generous in sharing his knowledge and experiences with me.

In contrast to the example provided above, consultation meetings consist largely of a formal presentation made by the proponent to community members. This usually includes PowerPoint presentations, very detailed Cartesian maps, engineering designs, and specialized geophysical graphs and data that are often very difficult to understand, particularly in a short time. As in environmental assessment hearings, these highly technical data can be extremely intimidating for local residents, especially if they are not familiar with industry vernacular. They often told me that they felt very intimidated asking questions in the formal meetings. A local land corporation employee told me that the meetings can present a barrier to effective engagement with elders and that the process is highly flawed:

> Elders are often not consulted, and they are sometimes too shy to participate in public hearings. There is one elder in particular who is Tulit'a's best trapper. He is very knowledgeable and he has told me that he has a lot to say about this development as it is going on all along his trapline. But he will not go to the public meetings, because no one will listen to him anyway, and it is just a waste of his time. There are a lot of people that do not know what is going on with the projects, and they are often confused about what is happening. People in the community have a lot to say about this.[6]

Proponents often spend months preparing detailed studies of a project's anticipated impacts and design features. By contrast, community members often know nothing about the project until it is unveiled at the public meeting. At that point, they must digest the difficult information in the company's brief presentation, which often lasts about thirty minutes, and must immediately formulate their questions, a challenging task even for people who are familiar with the industry. This approach, with its short timelines and question-and-answer framework, differs markedly from Sahtu Dene norms. In the Sahtu, information exchange and decision making can consume a much longer period. People often talk about sitting down and "really thinking about" what is under consideration. This holds true for personal dilemmas but is especially applicable when a "big decision" is to be made – and for Sahtu people, development projects are certainly big decisions. Like the knowledge gained via stories or land-based experience, important information acquired through meetings is not time-specific and must be fully considered before any decision can be made. For example, the knowledge transference of stories is not immediate but rests on both the preparedness of listeners to understand the story and the work that they put into its comprehension. Similarly, it is generally understood that important decisions cannot be rushed but can be made only when they have revealed themselves through a great deal of "thinking about" them. As one elder stated at the Joint Review Panel hearings, "For now, we don't say 'yes' and [we don't say] 'no.' We have to really think about it, and if we say 'yes,' it's just like we put a rock over there, and then we have to work together."[7]

In situations where a company wishes to extend previous work in an area, local people may be more familiar with the project plans and can thus speak to certain impacts that they themselves have witnessed. However, their observations are often countered by highly technical reports prepared by the proponent. This occurred in 2005, in connection with the Summit Creek/Keele River area, which lies about sixty kilometres southwest of Tulit'a in the foothills and eastern slopes of the Mackenzie Mountains. Several extended families in Tulit'a have used this region since time immemorial, and its traditional trails connect important harvesting locations and fishlakes such as Stewart Lake. People hunt, fish, trap, and have cabins there. In fact, most of the food provided for the Tulit'a Hand Game Tournament came from around Stewart Lake.

Husky Oil, which had already conducted seismic exploration nearby, wanted to expand its Summit/Keele operations and planned to conduct more seismic work, drill three wells, and develop a 180-person camp as a staging location for its activities. When it submitted its regulatory applications, it had scouted two locations for wells that it wanted to drill in 2006 and a third well that it wished to drill at a later time. A 60-person camp was anticipated at each well location, and an additional 60-person camp was planned for the road construction and maintenance crew.

After reaching an ABA with the Tulit'a District Land Corporation, Husky held a consultation meeting in Tulit'a on 27 July 2005. The meeting lasted from 6:30 p.m. to 8:30 p.m. and was attended by representatives from the Tulit'a Land Corporation and the Fort Norman Metis Land Corporation, as well as the Tulit'a Dene Band, the Tulit'a Renewable Resource Council, and members of the public. According to Husky, thirty-eight people signed the register, others refused to sign, and some came and went as the meeting progressed. The event included a meal, during which Ken

Hansen, Husky's team lead for the territories, gave a presentation on a trip that recent Tulit'a High School graduates had taken to Husky's Moose Mountain operations in Alberta to see a development that was similar to the one being proposed for Summit/Keele. After the meal, the Husky reps presented the proposed drilling program and opened the floor for questions.

Although the local people at the meeting did indicate their general support for the project and the jobs that it would bring, some expressed concerns, particularly about the proximity of the access route to an important fishing location, Stewart Lake. As Husky's meeting report states,

> Discussions during the question and answer period surrounded the proximity of the program access route to Stewart Lake. The concern has since been reviewed, and an attempt was made to identify an alternate route. During the July reconnaissance, no reasonable alternative route was identified. During the presentation, and in the side discussion following the formal presentation, Husky representatives explained that with proper barriers, spill kits, signage and speed control, the road can be safely navigated and the potential for spills to enter Stewart Lake can be mitigated.[8]

At the request of the Tulit'a Dene Band, a second consultation meeting was held in Tulit'a on 9 August. This occurred as part of the regular band meeting, and a Husky employee delivered the same presentation that had been given on 27 July. Prior to the band meeting, Husky staff also attended a Tulit'a elders' meeting that had been organized by the Sahtu MLA Norman Yakeleya, where they spoke with elders about the company's plans for the area and the potential benefits and impacts that would accompany the discovery of a commercially viable field. In its report regarding the elders' meeting, Husky notes that

> several elders identified a need to re-evaluate the existing access at Stewart Lake. Participants voiced their concern that vehicular traffic through the area could threaten important fish stocks in the lake, and in the event of a disaster, could irreparably damage an area of significant traditional value. The community stated that regardless of any mitigation measures imposed, some risk to Stewart Lake will remain.[9]

Although Husky had already evaluated other options for the access road, it "recognized the strong expression of concern" from local people and agreed to organize a scouting trip for elders. The trip would "endeavour to find an alternative access route that is safe for project personnel and low in environmental impact."[10]

A helicopter scouting trip was conducted in late August, with representatives from Husky, Northern EnviroSearch (who had undertaken the environmental assessment on Husky's behalf), and three Tulit'a elders. A potentially viable route – called Alternate Route B – was identified from the air and examined from the ground the next day. In assessing it, the Husky report states that "the alternative route slopes would require cattows, but would be navigable." Nonetheless, it ultimately concludes,

> Husky project management team examined the Stewart Lake and Alternate Route B options from the perspective of safety, environment, cultural values, long term planning, and regulatory compliance. Once all of the pertinent information was balanced, the team elected to use the existing Stewart Lake access route for the 2005/2006 drilling season.[11]

The report summed up the situation with the following claim:

> A review of the available information indicates that those consulted have no significant concerns in the areas proposed for development. Areas of traditional and historical significance can be protected by taking a progressive and consultative approach to land and water use in the planning and execution phases of the proposed drilling program.[12]

Husky received a land use permit from the Sahtu Land and Water Board on 16 September 2005.

The Summit/Keele example illustrates three fundamental aspects of the consultative relationship between proponents and Sahtu communities. First, as in environmental assessments, the consultation process is proponent-driven, and information commonly flows in just one direction – from proponents to communities – rather than as part of an exchange. When companies come to the Sahtu to "consult," their development plans are usually in place, so consultation typically entails explaining their plans to locals. In the case of Summit/Keele, Husky was open to discussing and exploring alternative access routes but ultimately chose to retain its original design.

Second, even when local people do give their opinions or suggestions, or voice their reservations, there is no guarantee that they will be accommodated. Providing a space in which concerns can be expressed is entirely different from appropriately listening to those concerns. In choosing its access route, Husky Oil applied its own criteria for "safety," environmental impact, and "long-term planning." Thus, though it took community concerns into consideration, other factors overruled them. Ironically, in suggesting that the project could decrease fish stocks in the lake, local people were also talking about safety, the environment, and long-term planning, but from their own positionality.

Third, proponents – not communities – submit reports of consultation meetings and processes to regulatory boards for permit applications. For the most part, these reports feature items such as the date of the meeting and how many people attended (including their names). Only occasionally do they provide an overview of what was said. Every consultation report that I read concluded on the same general theme: "A review of the available information indicates that those consulted have no significant concerns in the areas proposed for development." This holds true even when community concerns *are* voiced in consultation meetings, as they were regarding the Summit/Keele project. The key word here is "significant." The fact that the company defines what matters (or not) can severely undermine the views of local people and subverts their position as equal players in consultation processes. Not surprisingly, locals have begun to see consultation as the tool through which proponents obtain regulatory permits, rather than a process of meaningful relationship building, and in some cases, they have chosen to opt out of the exercise.

The perceived lack of consideration in consultation meetings speaks to diverse Sahtu Dene conceptions of what a consultative relationship ought to be. Locals are correct when they say that proponents must consult with them: the land claim agreement requires them to do so. However, neither the interpretation of consultation as laid out in the agreement nor how it operates in practice are what Sahtu Dene people intended. The chief of a Sahtu community said to me,

> When the land claim was created, the people thought that consultation would mean building relationships and having a real say in what happens on the land. But now, companies can come in and shake your hand and say that they have consulted. And if the person that they talk to says no, then they can just go and talk to someone else who says yes – then they will say that they have consulted and the community says yes.[13]

What constitutes consultation, then, has become a question of voice, of who speaks for a community and of what consultation means for the people whom it most affects.

The Consultative Relationship:
Exchange, Reconciliation, and Sustainable Partnerships

When I first arrived in the Sahtu, I asked a man who worked for a local Sahtu Designated Organization for a definition of consultation. "A meeting," he smiled in return. His reply reflects the general experience of Sahtu people: very often, consultation is just another checkmark on the list of corporations that want access to their lands. Sahtu Dene people have said that public meetings can be useful but should not be the sole form of consultation. When I rephrased my question and asked what he thought consultation ought to be, I received a very different answer. He explained that consultation should be a process whereby local people and proponents can begin to feel comfortable enough with each other to start talking about a project and a permit application.

This contradiction between the real and the ideal explains why so many people in the Sahtu have become disenchanted with engagement in participatory processes. As they see it, the current form of consultation has little in common with what a consultative relationship ought to be. Many people told me that most companies view consultation as a way of fulfilling regulatory requirements, rather than engaging communities in a meaningful dialogue. Their favoured tool – the public meeting – is commonly grounded in the old paternalistic idiom of telling local people what will be done with their lands. In some instances, depending on the nature of the project, consultation can consist of no more than contacting selected Sahtu Designated Organizations by telephone. Proponents document all forms of communication with community representatives as "consultation," recording the number and nature of their phone calls and the names of people who attend their public meetings. This information is included in consultation reports to regulators as evidence of community consultation for permitting purposes. One February evening in 2007, as I was having dinner with a local land corporation president, our conversation ultimately turned to consultation. The president said,

> You know, companies use any communication with the community as an example of consultation. They call up here and they say that they have consulted. That is not consultation; it is just to set up meetings. People at the public meetings are forced to sign their names. But I tell my people not to sign their names, because this means that the meetings are consultation and that they have agreed to participate. It can be used against them.

In part, the complications arise from the vagueness of the word "consultation." In English, "consultation" can range from getting a doctor's opinion, to seeking the advice of a lawyer, to asking a spouse for his opinion about a new job. Politicians often "consult" with their constituents. The Oxford English Dictionary defines the verb consult as "to seek information or advice from," and consultation usually does entail some measure of taking counsel, of seeking another's opinion, and perhaps even asking for guidance. However, to consult carries no obligation to abide by the resulting advice; people are not obliged to act on the words of their doctors or lawyers, and indeed, the degree to which politicians heed the advice of their constituents is always a matter for debate. Hence, the consultative relationship is ultimately unilateral; even when one party has sought the counsel of others, it retains the power to choose its own course.

Canadian jurisprudence is equally vague regarding "consultation." As discussed above, *Delgamuukw v. British Columbia* (1997) ruled that consultation depended on the circumstances. It also specified that the duty to consult was proportionate to the strength of the case supporting the existence of the right or title and the seriousness of the potentially adverse effect on the right. Yet, though *Delgamuukw* did stipulate that consultation must be done with the intent of substantially addressing Aboriginal concerns, it did not specify how this was to be accomplished. The *Halfway River* (1999 at para. 160) ruling did go slightly farther in providing concrete outcomes for consultation processes and suggested that, when voiced, Aboriginal concerns must "wherever possible, be demonstrably integrated into the proposed plan of action." Nevertheless, though recent decisions such as *Halfway River, Mikisew Cree First Nation v. Canada* (2005), and *Dene Tha' First Nation v. Canada* (2006) demonstrate that the Crown's duty to consult is indeed taken very seriously by the courts, its precise nature continues to be determined on a case-by-case basis. This can leave Aboriginal groups vulnerable to diverse interpretations regarding the strength of their claims to land title and rights, and to the possibility that judges and proponents may not appropriately hear their concerns about potential development projects. And though *Mikisew Cree First Nation* described consultation as a means of reconciliation between Aboriginal peoples and the Crown, it is important to remember that the first mentions of the Crown's duty to consult revolved around the infringement of constitutionally protected Aboriginal rights. In other words, according to *R. v. Sparrow* (1990 at para. 13), consultation (along with other components of the Sparrow test) can enable the regulation of a constitutional right in the interest of conservation, public safety, or the public interest. That is, consultation, at least as the courts originally envisioned it, was a means through which governments could legitimately restrict Aboriginal rights.

However, in the Sahtu, specific Sahtu Dene rights are protected both constitutionally and through the land claim agreement. Thus, the nature of consultative relationships, in the Sahtu at least, should be clear and obvious. Proponents are required to consult with Aboriginal communities before exploring for oil and gas, and prior to "developing" any mineral claim, and though the communities do not hold veto rights, mechanisms such as regulatory and permitting processes and the requirement for proponents to obtain access to Sahtu lands from district land corporations could be seen as providing them with substantial power in resource management. Thus, in the Sahtu, questions about consultation do not focus on whether it should occur, but rather, on what it ought to look like.

The Slavey language has no word that equates with "consult." When I asked Sahtu Dene people if there was a Dene word to describe something like "consultation," they replied that in Dene the essence of a consultative relationship is "a very long concept." Throughout the Sahtu, people told me very directly that consultation was not a one-time event, but a process of building and maintaining long-term relationships so that companies and communities can work together to ensure that everyone benefits. In consultation, the two sides get to know each other, with the result that proponents will understand what people mean when they say that the land is important to them and how much they depend on it for physical, social, and spiritual sustenance. Companies will also be familiar with community priorities for future economic development. It is a matter of learning how to listen appropriately.

Perhaps more recent Canadian court rulings on consultation have come closer to Sahtu Dene ideas about consultation – that it hinges on exchange and partnership. In *Mikisew* (2005 at para. 1), Justice Ian Binnie writes,

The fundamental objective of the modern law of aboriginal and treaty rights is the reconciliation of aboriginal peoples and non-aboriginal peoples and their respective claims, interests and ambitions ... The multitude of smaller grievances created by the indifference of some government officials to aboriginal people's concerns, and the lack of respect inherent in that indifference has been as destructive of the process of reconciliation as some of the larger and more explosive controversies.

Binnie (ibid. at para. 54) added that

consultation that excludes from the outset any form of accommodation would be meaningless. The contemplated process is not simply one of giving the Mikisew an opportunity to blow off steam before the Minister proceeds to do what she intended to do all along.

In other words, consultation ought to be grounded in reconciliation and in building positive connections. It should not be a unilateral transference of knowledge or an exercise in one-sided decision making, but a genuine and appropriate consideration of the needs, rights, and visions of Aboriginal people. Thus, consultation is not to be undertaken for consultation's sake or to necessarily justify an abrogation of Aboriginal rights, but rather to mend relationships between Aboriginal and non-Aboriginal Canadians and to establish them anew.

The Timing of Consultation in the Sahtu

A complicating factor in the establishment of a reconciliatory consultative process in the Sahtu is when the community consultation actually occurs in the course of project planning. Because proponents require permission from the landowners, now embodied in the land corporation, the local corporation is the first point of contact for many. Its support is required to ensure the feasibility of the project and as a first course of action in securing regulatory permits. This support is formalized in an access and benefits agreement (ABA), which, as mentioned above, is negotiated in closed meetings between land corporation presidents, selected staff, and the proponent. Although the content of an ABA is not made public, the beneficiaries of the land corporation can obtain it at the corporation office. This rarely occurs, however, because beneficiaries are often unaware of the negotiations until the ABA is signed. Only once during my fieldwork was a proposed ABA put to the community for a vote prior to its execution by a land corporation. The failure of corporations to consult with their beneficiaries is not necessarily an attempt to exclude them, but more often reflects both the overwhelming number of companies seeking to negotiate ABAs and the "consultation fatigue" of community leaders and members at large.

As a consequence, however, when proponents hold consultation meetings, their presentations tend to imply that the project has already been approved by community authorities, and if an ABA has been signed, this is often the case. Thus, though they may modify project plans to accommodate what local people say during consultation meetings, the essential approval of the project has already been obtained through the ABA. As a result, locals often feel that what they say in consultation processes does not really count. As one community member said to me, "What is the point of doing consultation if an access and benefits agreement has already been signed?"[14]

Technically speaking, local people can influence the permitting approval of any development project on their lands, even when an ABA has been signed. The regulatory process, as established in the Mackenzie Valley Resource Management Act, does provide a means for their concerns to be heard outside of consultation meetings and ABA negotiations. The Sahtu Land and Water Board (SLWB) regulates all land use permits and water licences in the Sahtu, including on Crown lands, Sahtu lands, and private lands. Once the SLWB receives a complete application from a proponent (including, in the case of oil and gas development, an ABA and evidence of consultation and the use of traditional knowledge in its environmental impact statement), it can either issue a permit subject to certain conditions, hold public hearings on the proposed project, or refer it to the Mackenzie Valley Environmental Impact Review Board (MVEIRB) for an environmental assessment. One criterion for referring a permit application to the MVEIRB is evidence of significant public reservations, as occurred in 2003, when Northrock Resources applied for a permit for its Summit Creek drilling program, and in 2004, when the same company applied for a land use permit for a winter airstrip near the Peele River staging area.[15] However, the degree of concern is open to the interpretation of third parties. For example, when a company applied for a land use permit to conduct mineral exploration on the McTavish Arm of Great Bear Lake, several Sahtu agencies, including the Sahtu Renewable Resources Board and the Déline Renewable Resources Board, expressed significant concerns, both informally and in writing to the SLWB. Nevertheless, the SLWB concluded that the project would have no adverse environmental impact and had not prompted public concern, and thus it recommended that the land use permit be issued. Not until the MVEIRB conducted its own preliminary screening and found that, indeed, the community was alarmed about caribou migration and a potential conservation zone, did the project receive further review. Exercising its authority under the Mackenzie Valley Resource Management Act, the MVEIRB ordered in September 2007 that the project be subject to an environmental assessment. Thus, whereas public concern expressed outside consultation meetings can potentially influence project approval, this rarely occurs, partly because it is dependent on regulatory boards such as the SLWB and the MVEIRB.

The negotiation of ABAs, rather than engaging local people in a reconciliatory process of consultation, is often seen as the only substantial means for communities to benefit from a proposed development. Proponents acquire the right of access when they obtain a land parcel from Indian and Northern Affairs Canada, so there is a general perception that ABAs are the best way of securing financial and other benefits from them. Although projects can be forwarded to environmental assessments, the outcomes of these depend on third-party interpretations, which leaves communities vulnerable to outside decision-making authorities. In contrast, when a community enters into an ABA negotiation before the permitting process begins, its land corporations are in a position of relative power: no proponent wants its project to undergo environmental assessments or be obliged to satisfy other supplementary regulatory requirements, as this is very costly and can result in substantial delays. Thus, companies are commonly quite eager to engage community interests as long as doing so produces an ABA, and they are often willing to provide additional incentives to gain favour. For example, proponent monies have funded several fairly significant local events, such as community hunts and hand game tournaments, and companies often pay travel and accommodation expenses for select locals to attend conferences and trade shows in southern Canada.

Still, using ABAs to negotiate project approval has been critiqued in both the Sahtu and elsewhere. One cold February afternoon, while I was on the way to the Northern Store, I stopped to talk with a local police officer, and perhaps because yet another consultation meeting was scheduled for that night, our conversation eventually turned to the topic of consultation. As the officer saw it, "Companies come in and they have already purchased the land parcels that were put up for sale by Indian and Northern Affairs Canada. The companies already have their drilling, or mining, or exploration plans, and they come to buy off the community with access and benefits agreements." For him, consultation processes were not consultation at all, in the sense that people had a real say: they "have become a negotiation – a negotiation for money, for an access and benefits agreement, for jobs."[16]

Some communities have capitalized on ABAs and have established subsidiary corporations and business development branches of their land corporations. Again, there is no doubt that ABAs have provided training and employment opportunities to some community workers and some contracts for local businesses. However, local people point out that direct capital gained through ABAs does not trickle down to those who use the land, most specifically not to hunters and trappers who want to maintain a land-based economy.[17] Many land users with whom I spoke were very uncomfortable with the process of "selling the land," as ABAs are often thought to do, and felt that project impacts on the land received very little attention in the negotiation process and proponent consultation, which concentrated instead on money and jobs. And generally speaking, they felt that their priority of maintaining a sustainable land-based economy was subsumed under the rubric of corporate aspirations, by both proponents and local business elites.

PARTICIPATION AS CO-OPTATION: TRADITIONAL KNOWLEDGE AND LEGITIMATION

One way in which local land users do participate in the negotiation of ABAs is through what has been termed the traditional knowledge study. According to the SLWB permitting process, proponents are required to collect "current, practical and site-specific" traditional/local ecological knowledge from "elders and others who have an intimate knowledge of the proposed project area" (Sahtu Land and Water Board 2004, 5); these data are assembled in a traditional knowledge study. The costs of the study are negotiated between proponents and the relevant land corporations, often as part of ABA bargaining, and include items such as the budget and timing of the study. How the studies are produced depends on the community. For example, the MacKay Range Development Corporation has assumed responsibility for conducting traditional knowledge studies for the Tulit'a Dene; it has employed a very competent local person who undertakes the study in conjunction with Dene land users and who retains the information in an internal database for community use. MacKay Range then prepares a traditional knowledge study report for proponents, but it maintains proprietary rights over the information. Tulit'a uses the knowledge in schools and for other initiatives, and it has remained under community control. Other communities have no formal process for conducting studies, so they are often produced on short notice by various community researchers whom the land corporation hires on short-term contracts, or when they are not available, by outside researchers or environmental consulting firms.

In the Sahtu, the traditional knowledge study is submitted with the application for a land use permit and is expected to contain certain information, as indicated in the SLWB's 2004 application checklist. Thus, the studies tend to follow a similar format. The SLWB suggests that a study may discuss spatial elements, topography, soils, geology, climate, vegetation, water use, stream flow, wildlife considerations, annual and seasonal trends, transportation, burial sites or other sites of archaeological significance, and concepts. It also recommends that the study address why the land is important to the Sahtu Dene and include specific local beliefs associated with the site and its use (Sahtu Land and Water Board 2004, 6). The studies amass their information through interviews or focus groups with local land users and also via secondary sources such as books, government reports, and data collected in an ongoing Sahtu GIS project.

Anthropologists and others working in the Canadian North have criticized the use of what has been termed traditional or local ecological knowledge in environmental management. Stephen Ellis (2005) and Paul Nadasdy (2003) both convincingly argue that traditional knowledge is seen as legitimate only when it is incorporated into "the specialized narrative of science" (Ellis 2005, 72), thus serving to discount the ways in which traditional knowledge holders see the world. Indeed, Mark Stevenson (1996, 282) points out that Aboriginal people who participate in traditional knowledge gathering are often required to "communicate their concepts and understanding of the environment and their place in it in the language of the dominant ideology" of wildlife management. This, Stevenson suggests, has prompted some Aboriginal people to view traditional knowledge gathering as theft and appropriation, and has made them reluctant to involve themselves in it. Derek Armitage (2005) notes that in the context of the Mackenzie Valley Resource Management Act, the institutionalization of collaborative approaches to knowledge integration for assessment and permitting processes does show evidence of the gradual transformation of power relationships and continued local challenges to the non-local worldviews and values embedded in resource management. However, Armitage (ibid., 252) adds that as a result of economic development goals, the absence of land use plans, and the proponent-driven nature of traditional knowledge gathering, "proponents are able to sidestep much of the responsibility" for seriously examining the politics of knowledge integration in the assessment of development projects. Given this, local people can be reluctant to involve themselves in knowledge integration practices. Even the definition of "traditional" is problematic: Who decides what forms of knowledge are traditional, especially as much of this knowledge is used in the present?

In analyzing traditional land use studies in the Alberta tar sands, Clinton Westman (2013, 138) criticizes their methodological and analytical rigour. None of the reports that Westman examined were written by consultants who had advanced training in the social sciences, and, largely due to their "shortcomings in methodology, data analysis, literature reviews, and other problems," none were successful. Westman (ibid., 140) concludes that in many traditional land use studies, the narratives of affected Indigenous trappers are backgrounded rather than highlighted, and their remarks are presented as "data in grids, point form, or tables." Likewise, in the Sahtu, the politics of knowledge integration is exemplified by the ways in which knowledge represented in environmental management traditions and those of local peoples collide in the context of traditional knowledge gathering. Although local researchers are often hired to conduct the interviews or facilitate focus groups, the design and execution of traditional knowledge studies reflect distinctly non-local interests and conceptions of the land.

In the Sahtu, the quality of traditional knowledge studies is quite varied, ranging from highly detailed reports to very brief summaries. In part, this discrepancy arises from the time constraints and demands of proponents. Because a company cannot apply for licences and permits until the study is concluded, it is often eager to have it completed. In addition, work in the oil and gas sector is often extremely time sensitive, as companies must bring in equipment at certain times of the year when travel is easiest, particularly in the fall, before winter freeze-up. This can result in enormous demands on proponents to obtain timely project approval and permits, and in turn places immense pressure on land corporations, who consequently have a very short time to negotiate ABAs before the proponent declares that the planned annual activities are no longer feasible. Thus, some traditional knowledge studies in the Sahtu have been produced in just a few weeks. Husky Oil's Summit/Keele study was allotted just eight days, from 9 to 17 May 2005.

The content of traditional knowledge studies maximizes proponents' ability to document and address areas of potential ecological and political sensitivity, and to identify local community members who might be adversely affected and thus might require additional consultation or compensation. Rather than attempting to document Sahtu Dene relationships with the land, the studies create a kind of ecological inventory and a list of who is using the land and for what purposes. For example, one study asked the following interview questions:

- What types of animals, birds, or fish are found in the area?
- How did people from (community X) use the area in the past?
- Which families or individuals used the area?
- How do people from (community X) use the area now?
- Which families or individuals use the area?
- How will people from (community X) use the area in the future?
- How will the planned activities affect the way that people from (community X) use the area now and in the future?

In the traditional knowledge study for Husky Oil's Summit/Keele program, which was directed by MacKay Range and facilitated by Greenpipe Industries, interviews focused on similar topics: Who uses the areas? What are the traditional boundaries? What are the topography, water bodies, and vegetation? What are the transportation routes, land uses, and burial sites?

In answering most of these interview questions, respondents are required to describe just one aspect of the environment at a time. For example, they list the wildlife species in the area, then the birds, and finally the fish. This approach, which categorizes and compartmentalizes, resembles that of the environmental impact statement.[18] Most Sahtu Dene people emphatically state that the landscape cannot be broken into categories: all its parts are intimately bound together on various ecological, social, and moral planes.

As I reviewed the traditional knowledge studies that were done for Sahtu licensing and permitting processes for a community agency, a person with whom I was working explained how he asked his grandfather for information about places. If his grandfather were telling a story, he would simply listen. Or, if he wanted to know about a certain place, he would ask just one question about it, and his grandfather would tell him everything he knew. The grandfather would start by pointing out the similarities between where they currently were and the area under discussion. Then he told stories about it, which would contain all the pertinent information. In fact, it was rude to ask about the place again, because that would be like asking the same question twice – as if the listener had not heard the answer. "Someone only needs to ask the right question once," he said.

The data acquired during the traditional knowledge study form the basis for the final reports that are forwarded to the SLWB as part of licensing applications. Predictably, given the nature of the knowledge study, they too present the landscape as inanimate and detached. Except for the reports submitted by MacKay Range in Tulit'a, the proponent submits most study reports to the SLWB. Thus, community participants in the studies have very little say in the composition or accuracy of the final report, and, indeed, often do not see it prior to or even after its submission. This, of course, has serious implications for their ability to verify the accuracy of both the content and relevance of knowledge collected.

Most study reports are very short, often consisting of fewer than three pages (the one filed for the Husky Summit/Keele drilling program was only two pages long). They detail the ecological features or the wildlife of the area under consideration and often discuss its importance as a travel route, a heritage site, or a traditional use location. In most cases, they list the people or families who have used the land or continue to do so, they present hunting and fishing as important economic activities, and they indicate how potential impacts on wildlife (especially caribou and fur-bearing animals) might influence hunting or trapping. Occasionally, they identify potential burial sites or other important landscape features such as old camps. Thus, most focus on ecological, archaeological, and economic factors in explaining why the land is important. Proponents often use this information to offer mitigation aimed at reducing potential adverse impacts of the project or to offer compensation to affected land users. Yet, the final reports do not typically address the cultural or moral relationships between many Sahtu Dene and their land. They include very few, if any, stories about local relationships with the land and very rarely address the ways in which the land and land-based activities are essential to the physical, social, and moral well-being of the Sahtu Dene. Thus, they offer a categorical inventory of certain items or activities rather than genuinely incorporating Sahtu Dene perspectives on and knowledge of the land.

Many proponents have stated that they wish to generate just one traditional knowledge study for several different projects, despite the SLWB requirement that every permit application must have its own study. For example, when one local land corporation was engaged in intense access and benefits bargaining, the proponent requested that it pay for just one traditional knowledge study, which would cover proposed work that was expected to span several years. Husky Oil's Summit/Keele study relied on traditional knowledge that had been collected in previous years (for previous permits). However, the idea that traditional knowledge is neither site-specific nor fluid runs contrary to local views. People who acquire knowledge of the land see it as dynamic: both it and the ways in which the land is used change over time. Producing just one traditional knowledge study for a large area or a range of projects limits the effective inclusion of local knowledge in project planning, design, and assessment.

In part, the fact that the final study reports pay so little attention to cultural and moral relationships between Sahtu Dene and the land reflects the ways in which the study data have become codified and reworked to fit into the twin narratives of Western environmental science and economic development. Indeed, a proponent's environmental impact statement has very little room for old-timer stories or Sahtu Dene connections with the land. Traditional knowledge studies focus on quantifiably measuring baseline environmental and economic data for the purposes of predicting project impacts and establishing mitigation measures to avoid adverse effects, or when this is not possible, to identify means of compensation. However, for local people, relationships with the land do not fit with the typical cost-benefit analysis that proponents and regulators often employ to assess the harms and benefits of potential projects. After all, compensating a trapper when a project diminishes an animal population and thus decreases his income is relatively straightforward, but compensating someone who perceives a seismic line or road as a literal tearing apart of his or her physical and social body is impossible.[19]

However, there is another potential reason for the absence of stories of cultural or moral significance – people's apprehension regarding how the stories will be used and who will "take care" of them. Stevenson's (1996) argument that northern peoples often hesitate to participate in traditional knowledge gathering due to concerns over appropriation also applies to many in the Sahtu. Proponents and those who conduct traditional knowledge studies often emphasize that their purpose is to forestall the disruption of sensitive ecological and cultural sites. However, study participants often find that proponents translate the mere fact of their involvement into acceptance of project approval. In consultation summaries submitted to the SLWB along with traditional knowledge study reports, proponents assert that they have consulted with the appropriate land users through the study, often name the participants, and state that they identified no significant concerns. This, however, is misleading as the studies do not solicit information about concerns. Instead, they ask for other types of data such as the location of camps or traplines, or which species live in the area. Thus, participation in a traditional knowledge study is indeed a form of co-optation, an appropriation not only of knowledge, but also of consent.

The reliance on traditional knowledge studies places local land users in a difficult situation. On the one hand, if they do not contribute to the study, their ties to a particular area will go undocumented, which means that influencing project planning or claiming compensation for loss of income in the future will be very difficult. A land corporation president who was in the midst of negotiating an ABA that included a traditional knowledge study said to me,

> The traditional knowledge study must be thorough, because it forms a part of consultation. The intent is to inform the proponent about any areas of possible cultural, biological, spiritual, or harvesting sensitivity, and to help them avoid those areas. If the information is not contained in the traditional knowledge study, if the First Nation has complaints later, the company will say, "Well, you should have addressed that in the traditional knowledge study."[20]

However, if local land users do take part in the studies, they run the risk that proponents will mistake their involvement for consent. Proponents see traditional knowledge gathering as a form of consultation, and many Sahtu residents also see it as one of several avenues for consultation. As a community leader told me, "Because meetings are sometimes poorly attended, much of the consultation process comes through the traditional knowledge studies." However, even she agreed that the studies were "often short and do not always identify community needs."[21]

Clearly, participating in traditional knowledge gathering can have negative consequences for local people. There is no guarantee that their knowledge will be heard, recorded, or interpreted with accuracy, and though they are never asked for their views of the project, the simple fact of their involvement can be taken for consent.

Beyond the Margins

In their analysis of participatory environmental management, Thomas Webler, Hans Kastenholz, and Ortwin Renn (1995, 444) write that "public participation is deemed to represent the proper conduct of democratic government, and the legitimacy of decision-making is enhanced through open and fair processes and the accountability of institutions." Yet, as this chapter demonstrates, consultation in the Sahtu does not necessarily improve the transparency, standards of fairness, or accountability of proponents or regulators. Nor does it automatically enhance the capacity of governments or proponents to appropriately hear or address community concerns. On the contrary, it can be used to legitimate non-renewable resource decisions even when local land users have significant reservations, if not outright objections. This is particularly true when consultation occurs in an intercultural context, where visions of appropriate economic development, relationships with the land, and the definition of consultation itself are not shared between parties.

Although commentators have strongly criticized the use of consultation processes in resource development projects, there is hope for improvement. Community members often emphatically state that they "have a right to be consulted," indicating a trust that consultation could increase local influence in resource decision making. During my time in the Sahtu, several local people expressed a keen interest in working with proponents to establish a consultative process that satisfied legal and regulatory requirements but also met the needs of their communities. Ultimately, however, consultation will be successful only if it is grounded in a reconciliatory approach and if local perceptions are taken seriously. Until greater parity exists between First Nations, proponents, and governments in connection with land use decisions, and until the economic benefits of non-renewable resource extraction are distributed fairly, consultation will remain coercive.

The current environmental management regimes are essentially a political compromise between Aboriginal organizations that wanted to maximize Aboriginal control over lands, resources, and governance, and a federal government that, as Graham White (2002, 97) notes, was "equally adamant that public interests required public government" and was reluctant to forfeit its regulatory and land use powers. Indeed, the Crown ultimately retains jurisdiction over the land because Sahtu Dene rights can be abrogated if doing so meets tests for justification, including engaging in consultation. And though Sahtu land corporations do receive a share of resource royalties, their portion is by no means equal; Sahtu communities shoulder most of the impacts of development projects and receive a disproportionately tiny share of the economic benefits. As one Sahtu Dene person stated to proponents during a Colville Lake consultation meeting, "We cannot survive on bones alone."[22] If the Sahtu Dene are to truly participate in decisions about land use, proponents must amend their view that Sahtu communities are impediments to development projects and must see them as equal partners. Yet this can occur only if genuine power sharing is in place and if Sahtu communities themselves are able to determine their own futures.

v

CONCLUSION

The Politics of Participation

We can protect this land until hell freezes over, but if we do not have an economic base our people will perish.

— Fred Carmichael, chair of the Aboriginal Pipeline Group

ANTHROPOLOGIST CAROLE BLACKBURN (2005) writes that for modern states, attempts to manage multiple social, political, economic, and ecological domains are increasingly threatened by escalating dimensions of risk and uncertainty. In her compelling discussion of diverse interests in the negotiation of Aboriginal rights in British Columbia, Blackburn demonstrates that the primary goal for governments in the negotiation of modern-day treaties is certainty. She argues that a central role of the state is to optimize the economic conditions of production – a task made all the more complicated in a time of globalization and mobile capital. Ambiguity surrounding Aboriginal rights is risky because it threatens to interfere in economic growth. In other words, outstanding questions about Aboriginal rights and title can lead to a lack of confidence for investors, who may choose to move their capital elsewhere. It is the job of the state, then, to secure certainty and to ensure that resource extraction can proceed unburdened.

Through an examination of the Nisga'a Treaty negotiations, Blackburn shows how the Canadian state is duly disciplined by mobile capital and the reproduction of the conditions of production, and by Canadian jurisprudence that has, in some cases, required it to take Aboriginal rights seriously. In the face of this tension, certainty is achieved by new processes of governmentality in which the state codifies Aboriginal rights through complex technical and legal discourse and practice that ultimately aims to provide economic and political security. Where Aboriginal rights are undefined or ambiguous, as in much of British Columbia, the state seeks to transform or modify what Native people see as inherent rights into property law so that by some magical process, they can legally exist.

Matthew Coon Come (2004, 159-60), former national chief of the Assembly of First Nations and former grand chief of Quebec's Grand Council of the Crees, makes a similar observation about the James Bay and Northern Quebec Agreement of 1975:

> Our treaty is often referred to as the first modern land-claims agreement in Canada. It is very long and very detailed, but we are learning that it is actually not very new. It is true that since we entered into our agreement with Canada and Quebec, things have improved socially for the James Bay Crees. We have obtained schools, clinics, local administrations, and certain programmes and services. But these are things that all other peoples in Canada take for granted. The reality is that our treaty is built on the same structure as all the treaties that went before it. Its foundation is the extinguishing of our Aboriginal rights. Consider this: on the one hand, Aboriginal rights are now guaranteed and affirmed in the Constitution of Canada. At the same time, the federal government still insists, as a condition of reaching agreements with Aboriginal peoples, that these rights be extinguished or given up.

Although the Nisga'a Treaty and the James Bay and Northern Quebec Agreement differ in some substantial ways from the Sahtu Dene and Metis Comprehensive Land Claim Agreement, their goals and outcomes are remarkably similar.[1] All three transform diverse metaphysical relationships to the land into the language of property law and craft capitalist subjects who are compelled to treat their land as a commodity.[2]

In cases such as the Sahtu, where the issue of Aboriginal rights and title has largely been resolved, the desire for certainty and the preservation of the central economic role of the state remains. A 2008 report commissioned by the federal government and prepared by Neil McCrank, former head of the Alberta Energy and Utilities Board, made a series of recommendations to streamline the Northwest Territories regulatory process (McCrank 2008). Citing industry complaints about long regulatory delays, the report calls for "greater efficiency" in the licensing and permitting process, even if this means modifying existing land claim agreements. Consultation, McCrank writes, is burdensome, though he suggests that it could be improved if Ottawa were to better define the principles and standards associated with consultation and to "streamline" the process. McCrank also points out that, though proponents cannot legally be denied access to lands where they hold Crown subsurface leases, they can encounter "protracted" or "failed" access and benefits negotiations with land corporations, which sometimes result in long delays and the abandonment of projects. To address this, McCrank (ibid., 29) recommends that Ottawa "consider some legislative solution to resolve the current difficulty of surface access to land." Yet, though the report calls for greater efficiency, clarity, and legislative action to remedy uncertainty, it also states that Ottawa's role is problematic, particularly because the government controls regulatory board appointments and, even with co-management structures in place, the development decisions themselves.

In writing on legitimation, Jürgen Habermas makes clear that government involvement in the economy shifts responsibility from the market to the state and that this generates crises of legitimation. Habermas (1975, 3) distinguishes between essential and non-essential structures, arguing that the former are important for the continued existence of the social system, whereas the latter "can change without the system's losing its identity." I have suggested in this book that changes to non-essential structures – increasing Aboriginal participation through land claims and in regulatory processes and establishing legal requirements for consultation – do not seriously threaten the state's economic role. In other words, the legitimation crisis envisioned by Habermas has been addressed through participatory processes without significantly altering the central role of the state in determining development decisions. Importantly, as Habermas (ibid., 36, emphasis added) notes, this is achieved despite the motivations of individuals in the system: "The arrangement of formal democratic institutions and procedures permits administrative decisions to be made largely independently of specific motives of the citizens. This takes place through a legitimation process that elicits general motives – that is diffuse mass loyalty – *but avoids participation.*"

In examining the use of social impact assessment (SIA) to evaluate the impacts of the Alberta tar sands, anthropologist Clinton Westman offers insight into how mass loyalty is won through environmental assessment processes. Westman (2013, 135) states that the production of SIA documents is essentially a creative undertaking that has the power to "not only describe, but inscribe the future." Westman shows how SIA documents capture fears of what Alfred Gell (1992) calls opportunity costs, or the risks of actions not taken. As an exercise in predicting and engineering possible futures, SIA envisions and enacts a specific kind of future, one that carries the lowest perceived risk and is embedded in a particular orientation toward nature, progress, and development. The promise and claims of expertise embedded in SIA are in "preventing disastrous futures" (Westman 2013,

137) – uncertain futures and futures where opportunities have been lost – which is achieved via the technocratization of everyday experience and the assumption of the authority to tell one kind of story in preference to another. In this way, SIA specifically envisions (and consequently creates) scenarios in which energy-based economies are the only possible future.

This valorization of certain futures (and ways of predicting and knowing them) and the correlated association of foraging peoples with the past are based in constructions of modernity that have their roots in the European Enlightenment; they include the development of objective science, rational forms of management, and the control of nature. In particular, as George Stetson (2012, 81) notes, "Modernity reorients the idea of history and progress around the logic of development, where 'perpetual betterment' is always possible."[3] In this sense, those who envision an unimaginable (or impossible) future, or who are otherwise characterized as unmodern or underdeveloped, can be saved from this future through the promise of modernity and all its accompaniments. Stetson rightly notes in his examination of oil politics in the Peruvian Amazon that not only does modernity offer certain forms of "salvation" for Indigenous peoples, but more importantly, it imposes and strengthens a logical structure that he terms "coloniality." Unlike colonialism, which is rooted in particular historical places and times, coloniality includes a logical structure of domination that is based on the imposition of a Eurocentric representation of knowledge and progress that undermines and sometimes violently represses alternative means of knowing and being. Thus, the Peruvian Amazon is presented as an idle space that is undercapitalized and poor, but that given the right capital investments, technology, and privatization of land, could realize the benefits of development. Stetson's argument strongly resembles that of Stephanie Irlbacher-Fox (2009), raised earlier, that the Canadian state likewise sees itself as the harbinger of prosperity and justifies its intervention in the lives of Aboriginal people by characterizing the injustices that they suffer not as a result of colonialism or coloniality, but as rooted in underdevelopment and pathology.

Yet, as Carole Blackburn reminds us, capitalism itself is inherently unstable, and the later decades of the twentieth century – what some might call post- or late modernity – have been marked by increased uncertainty as globalization and deregulation erode our faith in a knowable future. Still, the quest for alternative possible futures is not sincerely considered, as Blackburn (2005, 594) writes: "Significantly, nobody is describing uncertainty as something intrinsic to capitalism itself." This is particularly true of extractive industries in the present global economy, where the allocation of resources by large multinational firms is based on a maximization of capital investment and where conducting work in rural or remote locations can be costly. Indeed, rural or remote resource-based towns are most vulnerable to fluctuations in global commodities or changes in global markets (see O'Faircheallaigh 2013), but likewise are seen as more vulnerable to the "risk" of missed opportunities, which the advent of development would assuage. As Westman notes (2013) about the assessment of the Alberta tar sands, SIA documents convey a sense of dread and loss for those who are engaged in foraging economies and offer energy-based futures as their one best hope.

There are reasons to believe that this assessment of participatory practices in the Sahtu has wider relevance, and that the legitimation crisis faced by the Canadian state is mitigated in a similar fashion in other jurisdictions as well. Increasingly pressured by international forums to legally recognize Indigenous rights, some countries have done so, and international financial institutions such as the International Finance Corporation and the Inter-American Development Bank have also begun to address the impacts of development on Indigenous people. In particular, the principle of free prior informed consent, or the idea that Indigenous people have rights to participate in decisions that might affect their lands, livelihoods, and cultures, has been enshrined in the International Labour Organization's 1989 *Convention on Indigenous and Tribal Peoples* and in subsequent international instruments, including the United Nations 2007 *Declaration on the Rights of Indigenous Peoples,* to which Canada is now a signatory. Although the meaning and constitution of free prior informed consent differ in diverse political jurisdictions, it is generally seen to encourage a more involved role for Indigenous peoples in the planning and management of development projects. Yet, a review of recent literature on their involvement in oil and gas project management and planning suggests that though they are participating in greater numbers, this has not substantially increased their control over project outcomes. In an analysis of the construction of the Eastern Siberia–Pacific Ocean pipeline, Natalia Yakovleva (2011) demonstrates that its assessment did not significantly address the concerns of the Indigenous Evenki communities of Yakutia in central Russia, despite legislation that called for the inclusion of ethnocultural impacts in the assessment. Although Russian legislation provides certain protections for Indigenous peoples – under a 1999 federal law, they have a right of free possession and use of land in their traditional territories – Yakovleva (ibid., 716) concludes that federal legislation "fails to secure their rights in relation to the extractive sector." Citing ambiguity and complications around land tenure, complexities in legislation, poorly planned public meetings and consultation sessions held away from traditional territories, lack of access to project details, and the Russian state's central economic role in the extractive sector, Yakovleva (ibid.) writes,

> The legislation gives indigenous minorities an opportunity to be involved in consultation on projects proposed in the areas of traditional economic activities. However, it does not give them the right to object to any development projects, initiated by the state, municipality, or industry. Indigenous minorities in Russia do not have the right to say 'no' to a proposed development, if it does not conform to their needs and aspirations. Instead, indigenous minorities can be offered relocation ... as well as reimbursement for losses caused by such removal.

Importantly, she points out that the Evenki did not really expect that participating in the pipeline assessment would influence the project; nor did they necessarily oppose it outright. As Yakovleva (ibid., 717) notes, the Evenki "did not pretend to oppose the pipeline project altogether, but wished the industry and government would consider their opinions concerning impact."

Even in cases where Indigenous involvement in oil and gas project planning and assessment has been lauded as a remarkable achievement, the fact that Indigenous people are often unable to say no to these projects restricts their capacity to influence the outcomes of participatory processes. Ciaran O'Faircheallaigh (2013) documents how Indigenous people in the Kimberly region of Australia's northwest coast were involved in developing culturally appropriate consultation structures for the consideration of a liquid natural gas processing facility's impacts, the sharing of any benefits, and ultimately the selection of potential sites. In O'Faircheallaigh's view, a consultation process, established in large part by a traditional owners taskforce, represented a significant departure from previous extractive projects in which Indigenous cultural views were omitted from project assessment and approval. Yet after a change of government, the premier discontinued the collaborative site-selection process because "it was unacceptable for government to give a right of veto to local Aboriginal people" (ibid., 26). In fact, the government gave Indigenous people three months to reach an agreement with it regarding the location of the processing facilities and announced that it would enact compulsory acquisition powers if this did not occur. Under this immense pressure, Indigenous organizations were forced to negotiate because non-participation (and thus lack of agreement) could result in the appropriation of their lands. As O'Faircheallaigh (ibid., 26) explains, they were "very strongly opposed in principle to the State's use of the threat of compulsory acquisition ... However, they decided that the agreement they negotiated was the best that could be achieved under the circumstances, and that it was preferable to the outcomes likely to eventuate if the State proceeded with compulsory acquisition."

Yet, despite this intense pressure, Indigenous communities have continued to pursue what Blaser, Feit, and McRae (2004, 5) call their own life projects, even if these projects must be furthered through "the cracks left open." Harvey Feit (2004) documents why Cree leaders continue to engage in participatory processes, though logging and hydroelectric development have had detrimental impacts on Cree lands, lives, and communities. Their involvement does not spring from their contradictory or opportunistic positions, or the pursuit of economic and social benefits through agreements that provide monetary compensation. Rather, participation is important for them even when – perhaps especially when – relationships are at stake. The goal was not to oppose hydroelectric development or logging but to establish respectful relationships that offer mutual recognition for diverse life projects. As an example of this, Feit discusses the interconnections between Cree knowledge and understanding of life-supporting relationships, and how this grounds their participatory practices. Using affidavits given by Cree hunters at a meeting of the Waswanipi Cree Trappers Association, Feit demonstrates that they were reminding us that though some moose choose to leave areas affected by logging or hydroelectric projects, some opt to stay, showing their generosity, their love, and their ability to teach us how to survive and strive to establish relationships of respect even in the face of great suffering and difference. In other words, they remind us of the continued importance of "sitting down and talking about it." For Cree people, the effort to establish respectful, life-sustaining relationships is not about acquiescence to external control: it is essential to the maintenance of Cree life projects. For the Dene, as I have suggested here, it is essential to being a good human being.

Participatory Practices in the Sahtu

Throughout this book, I have argued that current participatory resource management practices in the Sahtu have legitimated and entrenched non-local forms of land tenure, decision making, governance, and economies.

I have suggested that they are a form of co-optation in which the voices and general metaphysics of Sahtu Dene people are reduced to "stories" that may appear as evidence in transcripts but are not taken seriously in decision-making processes.[4] Instead of being heard appropriately, or on their own terms, Sahtu Dene people are often made complicit in resource development decisions through the very act of participation. This situation arises in part because there is an underlying assumption among corporations, government, and regulatory institutions of the inevitability of the expansion of market economies, that wage labour will always overtake other ways of making a living, and that money is more valuable than anything else.

When Sahtu Dene people do take part in environmental management and assessment, their views are often extracted from their cultural framing and translated into the discourse of techno-science. Epistemological foundations via which environmental impacts are determined and assessed remain viewed through the cultural lens of Western scientific rationality. Thus, environmental managers and assessment practitioners do not seriously consider the idea that moose may choose to absent themselves in response to human activity on the land (see Feit 2004; Nadasdy 2007). Instead, they apply the so-called scientific model, relying on statistics and wildlife surveys to predict moose behaviour, and the information they solicit from Sahtu Dene participants is confined to items such as the number of species in a certain area and whether they are increasing or decreasing. Consequently, the relationships between the Sahtu Dene people and the land are considered for their economic and ecological significance, not for reasons of kinship, morality, or intertwined subjectivities. As Paul Nadasdy (2005, 2007) points out, not only are Aboriginal concepts and experiences of environmental impacts evaluated by Euro-Canadian frameworks, but the frameworks themselves are seen as rigidly objective and culture-free, whereas Aboriginal conceptions of the land (and their associated concerns over environmental impacts) are viewed as distinctly cultural.

An additional, and perhaps more serious, consequence of current participatory processes in the Sahtu is that fundamentally political issues are transformed into anti-political problems to be solved, mitigated, or managed by bureaucrats. During the Berger Inquiry, Dene people in the Sahtu and elsewhere vehemently objected to the Mackenzie Valley pipeline. They pointed out that the Government of Canada had never acknowledged Dene jurisdiction over Denendeh, and they voiced the strong apprehension that their nation and lifestyle were threatened by the interference of governments, market economies, and multinational corporations. These days, Sahtu Dene people often talk about how people had more power to talk at the time of the Berger Inquiry. As a Dene woman said to me, "When Berger was talking in the region, he said that there would be no pipeline for ten years, but then they opened it up again, and I don't know why. Those days, people had a lot of power to talk and listen to people, but it is not true today."[5]

On 6 August 1975, Steven Kakfwi, then a young Sahtu Dene activist, told the Berger Inquiry hearing in Fort Good Hope,

> Our reality is that the pipeline is just a poorly masked attempt to overwhelm our land and our people with a way of life that will destroy us. Our reality is that all of the "help" your nation has sent us has only made us poor, humiliated and confused. Our reality is that we are in great danger of being destroyed.[6]

Almost thirty years later, Kakfwi has become one of the pipeline's biggest supporters. During the 1980s, as president of the Dene Nation, he was involved in developing a framework for comprehensive land claims. He entered public politics in 1987 and was premier of the Northwest Territories from 2000 to 2003. His changed stance on the Mackenzie pipeline has caught the attention of journalists and northerners alike. Interviewed in 2002 by the *Far North Oil and Gas Review,* Kakfwi stated,

> Once you have [an idea of the type of political institutions that you need] it also becomes apparent that you don't want to live on a handout and that free housing and free education and free government does not exist anywhere in the world. It does not lead to independent, self-reliant individuals and families and communities. So I mean a government by itself, an agreement [for self-government] by itself doesn't do anything ... Governments need to be financed, they have to be economically affordable and they have to be workable. (quoted in Abele 2005, 223)

Since the time of the Berger Inquiry, some Sahtu Dene people have moved from their resounding "no" to compliance with the pipeline proposal. How did this happen? In part, it reflects the broad changes and challenges in Sahtu Dene life, including Western-style education, the influx of television and other aspects of popular culture, and participation in a cash economy. Yet, most of these changes were accompanied by some degree of reluctance and skepticism as Sahtu Dene people worked to maintain what they saw as core elements of their culture. However, Sahtu Dene compliance with the pipeline rests not so much in their belief that they will profit from a pipeline running through the heart of their territories, or that it will make their lives better: instead, after years of involvement in "participatory" practices, they have become disenchanted, frustrated, and ultimately resigned to the unequal power relations that are still very much present concerning lands and resources in the Sahtu. As a Sahtu grandmother told me, "Once a tourist asked why the people were not doing anything about the pipeline. My husband said that they have to go by the law in the land claims; people like the federal government said that they are going ahead with the pipeline and we are upset about that."[7]

In many ways, it is the land claim that has restructured decision-making forums, lines of authority, and forms of governance in the Sahtu such that decisions about the land are often made in boardrooms and corporate offices rather than according to local practice. The story of the Tulit'a Hand Game Tournament, recounted above, is instructive because it reveals the contradictions between decision making as formalized through environmental assessments, management, and consultation, and that embedded in cultural practice. The tournament is essentially political because it closely resembles continued forms of distinctly local decision making and consensus building, and because the social bonds that are established there spill into other aspects of community life. The rules of institutionalized decision making do not extend to the tournament, and thus it reveals how community members reach decisions according to local practice and how this contrasts with its counterparts, such as the negotiation of access and benefits agreements.

In addition to altering governance structures in the Sahtu, the land claim agreement formulated participatory avenues along lines of non-local practice. Some Sahtu residents feel that the agreement and its associated decision-making processes emphasize the acquisition of money and jobs at the expense of the land. As I have argued here, many see the establishment of Sahtu Dene entitlements to the land in the form of private property rights that are managed by corporate entities designed to generate profits from the exploitation of land as fundamentally at odds with how the land ought to be treated. From the outset, governments saw comprehensive land claims as instruments for the integration of northern Aboriginal communities into market economies and the reduction of economic uncertainty (Saku 2002; Blackburn 2005). Through the corporatization of land, Sahtu Dene beneficiaries find themselves participating in institutions that are ostensibly intended to protect their rights but that simultaneously endorse the commodification of land and land-based activities. This dilemma is exacerbated by the fact that a final land use plan has yet to be established in the Sahtu.

Yet, because the Sahtu Dene are implicated in a global market economy, local leaders must seek to maximize community benefits from extractive industries. Life in the Sahtu now requires access to cash, and though many young people state that they wish to engage in a land-based economy, they also look to a future that includes at least some employment in a cash economy. Given the interest by oil and gas companies in the region, and the opportunities and capital available through ABAs (and to a lesser extent resource-royalty-sharing arrangements), it is not surprising that some Sahtu Dene see the oil and gas industry as central to community and regional economic development. Some local leaders have repeatedly stated that they welcome controlled oil and gas development, as long as communities can participate as equal players in both its regulation and the benefits and profits that it would generate. Should the pipeline and various spin-off projects actually proceed, it remains to be seen whether Sahtu communities will truly benefit.

THE FATE OF THE MACKENZIE GAS PROJECT

After years of delay, the Joint Review Panel (JRP) submitted its final report, titled *Foundation for a Sustainable Northern Future*, on 30 December 2009. The report stated that "the adverse impacts of the MGP [Mackenzie Gas Project] and the Northwest Alberta Facilities would not likely be significant and that the Project and those Facilities would likely make a positive contribution towards a sustainable northern future" (JRP 2009, 2:615). It also made 176 recommendations aimed at mitigating potential adverse effects of the pipeline, all of which involved implementing management or monitoring strategies to track or offset ecological or socio-economic impacts. In other words, none of the recommendations acknowledged the moral or metaphysical effects of such a large industrial project on Dene lands or communities.

One of the more notable sections of the JRP report is Chapter 12, which is titled "Harvesting." It is illustrative of how Sahtu Dene comments about what is meaningful were transformed into quantifiable measurements of costs and benefits associated with a commodity market. In summarizing participant views about harvesting – as the JRP heard them – the chapter states,

Some harvester organizations stressed the need to ensure that the ability to harvest not be impaired by restrictions on access, as did a number of participants who spoke at Community Hearings. None suggested that the Proponents' proposed mitigations were inappropriate or insufficient, or that Project activities, if implemented, would constitute a significant disruption to harvesting activities. (ibid., 2:367)

Clearly, this passage fails to consider the numerous times that Sahtu Dene participants spoke about the effects of the pipeline on all inhabitants of the landscape, including wildlife. As a case in point, recall Charlie Neyelle's comments at the Déline hearing: he stated that moose would not return to specific areas, because they could sense that the universal law had been broken, and he went on to say that any disruption to the landscape was like a physical tearing of his own body. Hearing participants may not have used the language of environmental management, but they repeatedly said that they were concerned about the pipeline's effect on their ability to hunt and otherwise use the land. Their remarks were not simply about wildlife numbers, but were characterized by the burden of breaking Dene law and therefore not behaving like proper human beings.

Furthermore, as the panel heard many times, the breaking of Dene law could not be resolved through monetary measures – people stated clearly that they could not buy back lost relationships with the land. This, too, was not reflected in the JRP report, as its recommended mitigation measures for impacts on harvesting make clear:

> The Proponents propose to take measures to minimize the disruption potentially caused to harvesters, which the Panel finds appropriate and reasonable. The Panel considers that these measures, if applied to the Project as Filed, would result in minimal and negligible disruption, with no significant adverse impacts on harvesting. Any exceptions experienced by individual harvesters could and should be addressed by the harvesting compensation measures set out elsewhere in this chapter. (JRP 2009, 2:367)

The JRP hearing process clearly demonstrated that, for Sahtu Dene people, questions surrounding the effects of industrial development are not solely of economic, environmental, and political concern, but are also moral in nature and are founded on conceptions of respect, integrity, and what it means to be human. Their words revealed a perception of industrial impacts that differed substantially from those presented by Imperial Oil.

People expressed their desire to maintain a way of life that they saw as both valuable and jeopardized by industrial projects. For them, the damage wrought by extractive industry could not be measured by technocratic instruments; nor could it be mitigated by altering the project design or providing monetary compensation.

Upon receiving the JRP final report and recommendations, and engaging in one more round of hearings, the National Energy Board (NEB) issued its final report and reasons for decision on 16 December 2010. The National Energy Board (2010, 216) approved the project, stating, "We are satisfied that the proposed Mackenzie Valley Pipeline is, and will be, required by the present and future public convenience and necessity." After receiving federal cabinet approval in March 2010, the NEB issued a certificate of public convenience and necessity for the pipeline. Ultimately, the fate of the pipeline will rest in the economic conditions of the future. Currently, the natural gas market is flooded due to an abundance of shale gas, and gas prices are not expected to rise in the near future. The present economic climate and low price of gas makes building an economically viable $16.2 billion pipeline something of a long shot. Perhaps reporter Dina O'Meara (2010, C1) summed up the situation perfectly when she said in a *Calgary Herald* article that "money, more than any regulatory process, will have the final say on whether a proposed Mackenzie natural gas pipeline goes ahead."

For Our Public Convenience

The final JRP hearings were held in Inuvik in late November 2007. They generated much less fanfare than the opening hearings held there some twenty-one months earlier. My very limited budget forced me to choose between attending the hearings or spending more time in Colville Lake; my prior experience with JRP hearings told me that I would be more productive in Colville, and besides, no one from the three Sahtu communities in which I had worked was going either, though Colville Lake was sending a lawyer to submit concluding remarks on its behalf. Thus, I decided to conduct additional fieldwork in Colville Lake and to listen to the hearings on the radio. Indeed, as I listened to the familiar voices of the panel, and the unfamiliar ones of the lawyers, bureaucrats, and consultants, the shuffling of paper, and the speakers breathing into the microphone, I noticed that, except for Nellie Cournoyea representing the Inuvialuit Regional Corporation, Fred Carmichael representing the

Gwich'in Tribal Council, and the Deh Gah Got'ine Dene Council lawyer, no community members spoke to the panel. Twenty-one months of hearings, numerous intervenors, and one of the largest environmental assessments in Canadian history, and, at least for Colville Lake, the final JRP hearings passed with relatively little reference.

Late one February night in 2007, I was driving around Tulit'a with a local RCMP officer. A Dene man from Tulit'a, he had worked as a Yellowknife RCMP officer for the last few years and was now replacing the Tulit'a officer for a few weeks while the latter vacationed in the South. The night was brutally cold, and the town was quiet at the late hour. We drove onto the winter road on the Mackenzie and looked back at the scattered lights of Tulit'a. "Remember this place as it is now," he said of the small town of 550 people, "because if the pipeline goes ahead in four or five years, it will be really, really different."[8] He did not say whether the change would be bad or good for Tulit'a, only that if the pipeline were to come, change was certain as well. As a four-hundred-person work camp is planned for just four miles out of town if the pipeline goes ahead, I imagine that he might well be right.

Notes

FOREWORD: THE PARADOXICAL POLITICS OF PARTICIPATORY PRAXIS

1 *The Report of the Royal Commission (Canada) on the* Ocean Ranger *Marine Disaster* (Ottawa: Canadian Government Publishing Centre, 1984); Susan Dodd, *The Ocean Ranger: Remaking the Promise of Oil* (Halifax: Fernwood, 2012).

2 Royal Society of Canada, Expert Panel Report, *Environmental and Health Impacts of Canada's Oil Sands Industry* (Ottawa: Royal Society of Canada, 2010), https://rsc-src.ca/en/expert-panels/rsc-reports/environmental-and-health-impacts-canadas-oil-sands-industry.

3 Northern Oil and Gas Directorate, Indian and Northern Affairs Canada, *Petroleum Exploration in Northern Canada: A Guide to Oil and Gas Exploration and Potential* (Ottawa: Minister of Public Works and Government Services Canada, 1995), http://www.aadnc-aandc.gc.ca/DAM/DAM-INTER-HQ/STAGING/texte-text/nog_pubs_penc_ch1_1324576128970_eng.pdf.

4 When the *Exxon Valdez* ran aground on Bligh Reef, Prince William Sound, Alaska, and spilled between 11 million and 38 million gallons of Alaska crude oil, it was en route from Valdez to Long Beach, California. John Keeble, *Out of the Channel: The Exxon Valdez Oil Spill in Prince William Sound* (New York: HarperCollins, 1991); J. Stephen Picou, D.A. Gill, and M.J. Cohen, eds., *The Exxon Valdez Disaster: Readings on a Modern Social Problem* (Dubuque, IA: Kendall/Hunt, 1999).

5 These developments are well treated in Stephen Haycox, *Alaska: An American Colony* (Seattle: University of Washington Press, 2006); and Stephen Haycox, *Frigid Embrace: Politics, Economics, and Environment in Alaska* (Corvallis: Oregon University Press, 2002).

6 Recent discussions about the development of an LNG facility to export gas from Alaska envisage a liquefaction plant on the Arctic slope, a pipeline to the southern coast, and storage and docking facilities there; expected costs for this "Alaska South Central LNG" project are between $45 and $65 billion. See Stan Jones, "Liquefaction Plant Single Largest Cost for Alaska LNG Project," 4 June 2013, http://www.arcticgas.gov/liquefaction-plant-single-largest-cost-alaska-lng-project.

7 Robert Page, *Northern Development: The Canadian Dilemma* (Toronto: McClelland and Stewart, 1986), 1.

8 On rising environmentalism in Canada, see Ryan O'Connor, *The First Green Wave: Pollution Probe and the Origins of Environmental Activism in Ontario* (Vancouver: UBC Press, 2015); Stephen Dale, *McLuhan's Children: The Greenpeace Message and the Media* (Toronto: Between the Lines, 1996); Frank S. Zelko, *Make It a Greenpeace! The Rise of Countercultural Environmentalism* (New York: Oxford University Press, 2013); Judith I. McKenzie, *Environmental Politics in Canada: Managing the Commons into the Twenty-First Century* (Toronto: Oxford University Press, 2002); quotation from Page, *Northern Development,* 83.

9 Quoted in Page, *Northern Development,* 101-2.

10 Berger, "Synopsis of Volume Two," of *Northern Frontier, Northern Homeland,* 11, 3, 2, 4, 27, https://docs.neb-one.gc.ca/ll-eng/llisapi.dll?func=ll&objId=234849&objAction=browse&viewType=1.

11 Claude Lévi-Strauss, *La pensée sauvage* (Paris: Plon, 1962), Chapter 1, as suggested in Fikret Berkes, "Traditional Ecological Knowledge in Perspective," in *Traditional Ecological Knowledge: Concepts and Cases,* ed. Julian T. Inglis (Ottawa: Canadian Museum of Nature, 1993), 3.

12 Fikret Berkes, "Co-Management: Bridging the Two Solitudes," *Northern Perspectives* 22, 2-3 (1994): 18-20.

13 David A. Lertzman and Harrie Vredenburg, "Indigenous Peoples, Resource Extraction and Sustainable Development: An Ethical Approach," *Journal of Business Ethics* 56 (2005): 239–54, quote on 245; David A. Lertzman, "Caveat on Consilience: Barriers and Bridges for Traditional Knowledge and Conservation Science," in *Experiments in Consilience: Integrating Social and Scientific Responses to Save Endangered Species,* ed. Frances Westley and P.S. Miller (Washington, DC: Island Press, 2003): 284-97.

14 Berkes, "Traditional Ecological Knowledge," 3.

15 G.H. Brundtland, *Our Common Future* (New York: Oxford University Press, 1987), 114-15.

16 Ibid., 115-16.

17 "Frequently Asked Questions: Declaration on the Rights of Indigenous Peoples," http://www.un.org/esa/socdev/unpfii/documents/FAQsindigenousdeclaration.pdf. Australia, Canada, New Zealand, and the United States initially voted against the declaration, but in 2010 Canada endorsed it as an "aspirational" document.

18 See Timothy W. Luke, "Developing Planetarian Accountancy: Fabricating Nature as Stock, Service, and System for Green Governmentality," in *Nature, Knowledge and Negation,* ed. H.F. Dahms (Bingley, UK: Emerald Group, 2009), 129-60.

19 Timothy Luke, "Eco-Managerialism – Environmental Studies as a Power/Knowledge Formation," Aurora Online, 2003, http://aurora.ic.aap.org/index.php/aurora/article/view/79.

20 Dean Bavington, *Managed Annihilation: An Unnatural History of the Newfoundland Cod Collapse* (Vancouver: UBC Press, 2010).

21 See for one introduction, Ullica Christina Olofsdotter, ed., *Beyond the Science Wars: The Missing Discourse about Science and Society* (Albany: State University of New York Press, 2000).

22 Alexis Schulman, "Bridging the Divide: Incorporating Local Ecological Knowledge into U.S. Natural Resource Management" (Master's thesis, Massachusetts Institute of Technology, Department of Urban Studies and Planning, 2007).

23 Bavington, *Managed Annihilation,* especially Conclusion. For examples of the ways in which these ideas are being touted as a basis for policy formation, see the review of *Managed Annihilation* by G. Peterson in *Ecological Sociology,* http://ecologicalsociology.blogspot.com/2010/07/review-managed-annihilation-unnatural.html; and J. Yard, "Review of *The Aquaculture Controversy in Canada: Activism, Policy, and Contested Science* by Nathan Young and Ralph Matthews," *BC Studies* 169 (2010): 148-52. Also "Irish Scientists to Listen to Fishermen," 7 January 2010, http://www.fishsec.org/2010/01/07/irish-scientists-to-listen-to-fishermen/.

24 T. Lynam, W. De Jong, D. Sheil, T. Kusumanto, and K. Evans, "A Review of Tools for Incorporating Community Knowledge, Preferences, and Values into Decision Making in Natural Resources Management," *Ecology and Society* 12, 1, (2007), http://www.ecologyandsociety.org/vol12/iss1/art5/.

25 Caroline Desbiens, *Power from the North: Territory, Identity, and the Culture of Hydroelectricity in Quebec* (Vancouver: UBC Press, 2013); Hans M. Carlson, *Home Is the Hunter: The James Bay Cree and Their Land* (Vancouver: UBC Press, 2008).

26 Matthew Coon Come, quoted in Graeme Wynn, *Canada and Arctic North America: An Environmental History* (Santa Barbara: ABC Clio, 2007), 313.

27 Claudia Notzke, *The Barrière Lake Trilateral Agreement* (Barrière Lake, QC: Barrière Lake Indian Government, 1993), quoted in David C. Natcher, "Co-Management: An Aboriginal Response to Frontier Development," *Northern Review* 23 (Summer 2001): 146-63. For more on co-management approaches, see Berkes, "Co-Management: Bridging the Two Solitudes"; Fikret Berkes, "New and Not-So-New Directions in the Use of the Commons: Co-Management," *Common Property Resource Digest* 42 (1997): 5–7; Fikret Berkes, P.J. George, and R.J. Preston, "The Evolution of Theory and Practice of the Joint Administration of Living Resources," *Alternatives* 18 (1991): 12–18; Claudia Notzke, "A New Perspective in Aboriginal Natural Resource Management: Co-Management," *Geoforum* 26 (1995): 187–209; and Ryan Plummer and J. Fitzgibbon, "Co-Management of Natural Resources: A Proposed Framework," *Environmental Management* 33, 6 (2004): 876–85.

28 Tracy Campbell, "Aboriginal Co-Management of Natural Resources: Is It Working?" in *Sustainable Forestry Partnerships: Forging a Network of Excellence, Conference Summaries* (Edmonton: Sustainable Forest Management Network, University of Alberta, 1996), 129-31.

29 Tracy Campbell, "Co-Management of Aboriginal Resources," *Information North* 22, 1 (March 1996), http://arcticcircle.uconn.edu/NatResources/comanagement.html; and Berkes, "Co-Management: Bridging the Two Solitudes."

30 Campbell, "Co-Management of Aboriginal Resources."

31 Canadian Council of Forest Ministers, *Sustainable Forests: A Canadian Commitment,* National Forest Strategy, Canadian Council of Forest Ministers (Hull, QC: Canadian Council of Forest Ministers, 1992), 39. For more on this, see Deborah McGregor, "From Exclusion to Coexistence: Aboriginal Participation in Ontario Forest Management Planning" (PhD diss., Forestry, University of Toronto, 2000).

32 Indian and Northern Affairs Canada, *Report of the Royal Commission on Aboriginal Peoples* (Ottawa, 1996),Vol.2 *Restructuring the Relationship,* Part 2 Ch 4, section 7:3. Available at: https://qspace.library.queensu.ca/bitstream/1974/6874/4/RRCAP2_combined.pdf.

33 Stan Stevens, ed., *Indigenous Peoples, National Parks, and Protected Areas: A New Paradigm Linking Conservation, Culture, and Rights* (Tucson: University of Arizona Press, 2014).

34 John Sandlos, "National Parks in the Canadian North: Comanagement or Colonialism Revisited?" in ibid., 132-49.

35 Ibid., 144.
36 Blue Ribbon Panel, National Forest Strategy, *Sustainable Forests: A Canadian Commitment,* Final Evaluation Report, National Forest Strategy Coalition (Ottawa, 1997), quoted in McGregor, "From Exclusion to Coexistence," 6.
37 Paul Nadasdy, *Hunters and Bureaucrats: Power, Knowledge, and Aboriginal-State Relations in the Southwest Yukon* (Vancouver: UBC Press, 2003); Paul Nadasdy, "The Politics of TEK: Power and the 'Integration' of Knowledge," *Arctic Anthropology* 36, 1-2 (1999): 1-18; Paul Nadasdy, "Re-Evaluating the Co-Management Success Story," *Arctic* 56, 4 (December 2003): 367-80; Julie Cruikshank, "Legend and Landscape: Convergence of Oral and Scientific Traditions in the Yukon Territory," *Arctic Anthropology* 18, 2 (1981): 67-93; Julie Cruikshank, "Uses and Abuses of 'Traditional Knowledge': Perspectives from the Yukon Territory," in *Cultivating Arctic Landscapes: Knowing and Managing Animals in the Circumpolar North,* ed. David G. Anderson and Mark Nuttall (Oxford: Berghahn Books, 2003), 17-32.
38 R. Kuptana, "Indigenous Peoples' Rights to Self Determination and Development: Issues of Equality and Decolonization" (Keynote address to "International Seminar on Development and Self-Determination among the Indigenous Peoples of the North," University of Alaska Fairbanks, 5 October 1996), quoted in Marc G. Stevenson, "Review of Paul Nadasdy, *Hunters and Bureaucrats,*" *Arctic* 57, 1 (March 2004): 101-4, quote on 102.
39 The National Energy Board approved the project in 2011, and Imperial Oil was required to give an updated cost estimate by the end of 2013. This filing placed the cost of the pipeline and gas-gathering system at $16.1 billion, and that of the entire development, including three natural gas fields in the Mackenzie Delta on the Beaufort Sea coast, at $20 billion or more. Jeffrey Jones, "Mackenzie Valley's New Price Tag: $20-Billion (and Rising)," *Toronto Globe and Mail,* 23 December 2013. Available at: http://www.theglobe andmail.com/report-on-business/international-business/us-business/mackenzie-valleys -new-price-tag-20-billion-and-rising/article16095114/. According to the TransCanada website, "The project proponents continue to monitor ways to move the project forward but, to date, natural gas market conditions do not signal a commercially viable opportunity." TransCanada, "Mackenzie Gas Project," http://www.transcanada.com/mackenzie -valley.html.
40 "Canadians' Future 'Hangs in the Balance' in Pipeline Debate: Prentice," *Maclean's,* 1 December 2014, http://www.macleans.ca/economy/business/canadians-future-hangs-in -the-balance-in-pipeline-debate-prentice/.
41 Stephanie Irlbacher-Fox, *Finding Dahshaa: Self-Government, Social Suffering and Aboriginal People in Canada* (Vancouver: UBC Press, 2009), 7; Jürgen Habermas, *Legitimation Crisis* (Boston: Beacon Press, 1975).
42 Habermas, *Legitimation Crisis,* 36; Clint Westman, "Social Impact Assessment and the Anthropology of the Future in Canada's Tar Sands," *Human Organization* 72, 2 (2013): 135-44.
43 George Stetson, "Oil Politics and Indigenous Resistance in the Peruvian Amazon: The Rhetoric of Modernity against the Reality of Coloniality," *Journal of Environment and Development* 21, 1 (2012): 76-97.
44 John Ralston Saul, *The Comeback: How Aboriginals Are Reclaiming Power and Influence* (Toronto: Penguin Canada, 2014), Ch. IV.
45 Michael Asch, *On Being Here to Stay: Treaties and Aboriginal Rights in Canada* (Toronto: University of Toronto Press, 2014), 11.

46 Glen Coulthard, *Red Skin, White Masks: Rejecting the Colonial Politics of Recognition* (Minneapolis: University of Minnesota Press, 2014).

47 Hayden King and Shiri Pasternak, "Don't Call It a Comeback: While Indigenous People Keep Resisting Assimilation, It's Canada That Needs to Catch Up," *Literary Review of Canada* 23, 1 (January-February 2015): 22-23. The discussion in the preceding paragraph draws heavily from this essay, a review/reflection on Saul, *The Comeback*.

PREFACE

1 Recent literature by scholars such as Taiaiake Alfred (2011) argues that "Aboriginal" is an assimilative government term imposed on diverse peoples who have varied experiences, languages, histories, and cultures; it suggests that "Indigenous" might be more appropriate in referring to the first peoples of Canada. A 2014 press release by the Anishinabek Nation: Union of Ontario Indians makes a similar point, and the chiefs from the forty-two member communities endorsed a resolution at their 2014 Grand Council Assembly to discontinue use of the word. Yet, the Sahtu Dene commonly self-identify as Aboriginal. Therefore, though recognizing the problematics of such terminology, I employ it throughout this book.

2 A few exceptions to this include the Norman Wells oil field in the Sahtu (operated by Imperial Oil), the Bent Horn oil field on Cameron Island (run by Panarctic Oils from 1985 to 1986), and the Ikhil field/Inuvik Gas Project (owned equally by the Inuvialuit Petroleum Corporation, AltaGas, and Enbridge).

3 For example, the Arctic Council (an intergovernmental forum that promotes cooperation among the eight member Arctic states) recommended in 2002 that the Arctic Monitoring and Assessment Programme should assess oil and gas activities in the Arctic; this culmin- ated in the Arctic Council Oil and Gas Assessment, released in 2007.

INTRODUCTION: PEOPLE, LAND, AND PIPELINES

1 Mackenzie Valley Pipeline Inquiry Transcripts, 24 June 1975, vol. 7, 595-96. The Berger Inquiry transcripts are available at Prince of Wales Northern Heritage Centre, http://www. pwnhc.ca/exhibitions/berger/documentation/.

2 In July 1981, despite the suggestions of the Berger Report and the overwhelming opposition to the pipeline, the National Energy Board granted Interprovincial Pipeline (now Enbridge) permission to construct an 866-kilometre buried pipeline to carry oil from Norman Wells to Zama, Alberta. This was the first major hydrocarbon transportation project in the Northwest Territories (Jennifer Wilson 1992). Its approval and construction, coming only a few years after the Berger Report, had long-standing effects on how the people of the Sahtu view industrial approval processes and the extent to which their voices are heard with respect to industrial activity on their lands.

3 James Ferguson (1990) suggests that the conceptual apparatus of development has specific effects, including producing particular fields of power and governmentality. In his case study of the development industry in Lesotho, Ferguson shows how the effects of develop- ment have served to transform political concerns about resource allocation into the expan- sion of bureaucratic and state power.

4 Similarly, the governor-in-council, rather than the Joint Review Panel mandated to conduct public hearings, will decide whether the Enbridge Northern Gateway Pipeline will be constructed.

5 The figures are from Statistics Canada (2006), which typically does not distinguish between Dene and Metis. In the communities where I worked, unlike in other parts of Canada, I did not see large cultural differences between Dene and Metis who enrolled in the land claim agreement. As Chapter 3 explains, the requirement that beneficiaries of the agreement must identify as either Dene or Metis is not consistent with the way in which people see themselves. It also creates political discord in Sahtu communities. In applying "Dene" to everyone of Dene descent, I do not negate that some people have enrolled in the land claim as Metis; my intent is to avoid divisive structuring practices. For the same reason, I have refrained from giving the names of interviewees unless I was explicitly asked to include them.

6 The Northern Store is a chain that sells groceries, supplies, and household items throughout northern Canada. Except for Colville Lake, every Sahtu community has a Northern Store.

7 Author interview, 22 August 2006.

8 An access and benefits agreement is a contract negotiated and signed between development corporations and Indigenous communities in Canada and elsewhere. It outlines the terms of the corporation's access to the land in question and the benefits that it will provide to the community in exchange for the access, including compensation for any environmental, social, or cultural impacts.

9 Author interview, 8 October 2007. Dene apply the word "mola" to people of European descent; it means "ringed finger," a reference to the wedding rings commonly worn by early fur traders.

10 This is, of course, with the exception of the Norman Wells field and associated Enbridge pipeline.

11 "Thomas" is a pseudonym, used to protect the participant's identity.

12 Sahtu people sometimes view Greenpeace negatively because of its association with the anti-fur movement of the 1970s, which had detrimental consequences for the fur-based economy of the North.

13 Personal conversation, 3 September 2006.

14 Fieldnotes, 7 September 2006.

15 Author interview, 16 September 2006.

16 Fieldnotes, 3 September 2006.

17 Ibid.

CHAPTER 1: "VERY NICE TALK IN A VERY BEAUTIFUL WAY"

1 Imperial Oil originally estimated that the project would cost approximately $7.2 billion. On 12 March 2007, the company filed a revised cost estimate of $16.2 billion.

2 The "pipeline to the future" appeared in MGP advertisements published in *Up Here Magazine* in 2006-07. Bob Reid, president of the Aboriginal Pipeline Group, referred to the "basin-opening pipeline" during a newspaper interview (*Calgary Herald* 2006).

3 As the EIS points out, though Ottawa will accrue significant tax revenue, such is not the case for the Government of the Northwest Territories (GNWT), because the tax revenue will reduce the formula financing grant issued by the federal government (see Mackenzie Gas Project 2004a, 1:section 6, 9).

4 The Aboriginal Pipeline Group advertises ownership in the MGP in *Above and Beyond: Canada's Arctic Journal*, January-February 2006, 45, and in presentations to the Sahtu Secretariat Incorporated General Assembly, held in Déline on 7-9 September 2006.

5   APG ownership and benefits grow with pipeline volumes. For example, a 33.33 percent
    ownership would be realized *only* if the shipment of gas through the pipeline increases in
    volume to +400 million cubic feet per day. If the volume does not increase, the APG would
    own only a 3 percent share. Additionally, it has negotiated a loan in excess of $100 million
    from TransCanada Corporation to cover its share of project costs during the pipeline pre-
    development period and would seek bank loans to cover its portion of construction costs
    should the MGP receive regulatory approval. Thus, any profits initially generated by the
    APG from pipeline tolls will be used to repay loans and will not be transferred to share-
    holders. Data taken from an APG presentation to the Sahtu Secretariat Incorporated
    General Assembly held in Déline on 7-9 September 2006.

6   An environmental impact assessment (EIA) is the general process of reviewing the effects
    of a proposed industrial project or its components. The Mackenzie Valley Environmental
    Impact Review Board uses the term "environmental assessment" (EA) to refer to the second
    level of environmental impact assessment. An environmental impact review (EIR) is the
    board's highest level of environmental impact assessment, as outlined in the Mackenzie
    Valley Resource Management Act (see Northern Pipeline Environmental Impact Assessment
    and Regulatory Chairs' Committee 2002, 1).

7   "Jamie" is a pseudonym.

8   The Sahtu has a robust prophet tradition in which people with strong powers receive vi-
    sions that enable them to help others and foretell future events. Anthropologists working
    among northern Athabaskan peoples have documented their prophecy traditions (see
    Brody 1981; Mills 1982, 1986; Ridington 1988, 1990; Goulet 1996, 1998). Missionary and
    ethnographer Émile Petitot reported that, in the 1860s, "seers" at Fort Good Hope proph-
    esied that a flood would destroy its mission, trading post, and "white man's buildings"
    (quoted in Abel 1993, 129).

9   Fieldnotes, 2 April 2006.

10 Fieldnotes, 31 March 2006.

11 Bobby Clement, JRP Hearing Transcripts (JRPHT), 4 April 2006, vol. 17, 1745, 28-31.

12 Gordon Yakeleya, JRPHT, 4 April 2006, vol. 17, 1723, 6-14.

13 The "In Brief" document, which summarizes the environmental impact statement
    (Mackenzie Gas Project 2004a), was designed to allow easier interpretation of the MGP
    EIS.

14 Bobby Clement, JRPHT, 4 April 2006, vol. 17, 1745, 33-42.

15 Alvin Orlias, JRPHT, 10 April 2006, vol. 21, 1976, 29-31, 34.

16 Maurice Mendo, JRPHT, 4 April 2006, vol. 17, 1761, 1-6.

17 Dolphus Baton, JRPHT, 3 April 2006, vol. 16, 1683, 7-9.

18 Author interview, 3 October 2007.

19 Maurice Mendo, JRPHT, 5 April 2006, vol. 17, 1763, 23-26.

20 Michael Neyelle, JRPHT, 3 April 2006, vol. 16, 1626, 26-35.

21 Charlie Neyelle, JRPHT, 3 April 2006, vol. 16, 1642, 29-33.

22 Fieldnotes, 5 September 2006.

23 "Frank" is a pseudonym.

24 Personal communication, 1 April 2006.

25 Conflicting sources place his birth between 1850 and 1858 (see Blondin 1990, 239; Auld
    and Kershaw 2005, 23; Déline First Nation 2005, 6).

26 Leo Modeste, JRPHT, 3 April 2006, vol. 16, 1647, 8-14.

27 Both names are pseudonyms.

28 Author interview, 5 October 2007.
29 Alfred Taniton, JRPHT, 3 April 2006, vol. 16, 1649, 1-4.
30 Dora Vital, JRPHT, 3 April 2006, vol. 16, 1671, 33-39.
31 Men's focus group, Déline, 13 September 2006.
32 Ibid.
33 Fieldnotes, 22 February 2007.
34 Charlie Kochon, JRPHT, 10 April 2006, vol. 21, 2000, 11-12.
35 According to Imperial Oil, two rounds of community meetings and a regional workshop were held in the Sahtu. The first round of meetings (identification and scope of community issues) was held in Déline on 11 March 2003, in Tulit'a on 12 and 13 March 2003, and in Colville Lake on 15 April 2003. The second round of meetings (to share potential effects of the MGP and mitigation measures) was in Colville Lake on 17 February 2004, Tulit'a on 19 February 2004, and Déline on 20 February 2004. The first round of workshops was on 4 and 5 June 2003, and the second round was on 3 and 4 December 2003 and again on 11 and 12 May 2004.
36 Fieldnotes, 21 September 2006.
37 Fieldnotes, 30 August 2006.
38 Personal communication, MVEIRB member, 7 September 2006.
39 Joe Martin Oudzi, JRPHT, 10 April 2006, vol. 20, 2006, 35-36.
40 Leo Modeste, JRPHT, 3 April 2006, vol. 16, 1648, 3-4.
41 Frank Andrew, JRPHT, 4 April 2006, vol. 17, 1738, 35-41.
42 Maurice Mendo, JRPHT, 4 April 2006, vol. 17, 1762-63, 39-2.

Chapter 2: "A Billion Dollars Cannot Create a Moose"

1 Fieldnotes, 29 August 2006.
2 For an excellent discussion of the connection between health and narratives of country foods, see Adelson (1998).
3 Personal communication, 25 August 2006.
4 Hyacinth Kochon, JRP Hearing Transcripts, 10 April 2006, vol. 21, 1995, 8-10.
5 Isadore Cuzon, Mackenzie Valley Pipeline Inquiry Transcripts, 21 August 1976, vol. 75, 8308-9.
6 Sometimes called Dene law, the universal law is a complex moral code that governs how to be a good human being. It typically consists of between seven and nine laws. According to George Blondin (1997), Yamoria brought the universal law to the Dene, creating peace and order among them, though various groups have slightly different versions of how they received it. The Sahtu Dene word for this law is Dene ʔeʔah, but the English terms "Dene law" and "universal law" are also used and may reflect the syncretic nature of Dene and Catholic belief systems. As Dene groups commonly use the English names, I have followed suit.
7 Fieldnotes, 10 September 2006.
8 Sahtu Dene elder Raymond Taniton makes a similar point in a story he shared in Taniton and Willett (2011).
9 Fieldnotes, 2 April 2006.
10 Men's focus group, Déline, 18 September 2006.
11 Randy Ottenbreit, JRP Hearing Transcripts (JRPHT), 3 April 2006, vol. 16, 1666, 25-29.
12 Ibid., 3 April 2006, vol. 16, 1614-15, 30-31.

13　In creating its EIS, Imperial Oil conducted surveys of local hunters and harvesters (both Aboriginal and non-Aboriginal) to gain insights into wildlife distribution and population levels for baseline data.

14　Charlie Neyelle, JRPHT, 3 April 2006, vol. 16, 1643-45, 21-14.

15　Men's focus group, Déline, 18 September 2006.

16　Fieldnotes, Déline, 7 September 2006.

17　Joe Naedzo, Mackenzie Valley Pipeline Inquiry Transcripts, 24 June 1975, vol. 7, 604.

18　Paul Macaulay, ibid., 27 June 1975, vol. 8, 898.

19　Pierre Blancho, ibid., 21 August 1976, vol. 75, 8310-11.

20　Victor Dolphus, ibid., 26 June 1975, vol. 9, 817.

21　Alfred Taniton, JRPHT, 3 April 2006, vol. 16, 1651-52, 40-5.

22　Morris Neyelle, JRPHT, vol. 16, 1636, 29-32.

23　John B. Gully, JRPHT, 10 April 2006, vol. 21, 1996, 37-42.

24　Ibid., 23-25.

25　Leroy Andre, JRPHT, 3 April 2006, vol. 16, 1618, 19-39.

26　"Angus" is a pseudonym.

27　See, for example, Dee Brandes (community relations, Imperial Oil), JRPHT, 4 April 2006, vol. 17, 1709, 29-34.

28　Charlie Neyelle, JRPHT, 3 April 2006, vol. 16, 1645, 15-17.

29　Women's focus group, Déline, 14 September 2008.

Chapter 3: Life under the Comprehensive Claim Agreement

1　People in the Sahtu tell their own story of how the oil was found. Elder John Blondin stated, "There is a thing I would like to say about the oil in Lególi (Norman Wells). What was the name of the man who found that oil? It was our own father, Francis Nineye. When he found the oil, he took a sample of it, put it in a lard pail and brought it out into Tulit'a. That same summer, he had an accident and died. Now the white people turn around and claim they found the oil. My dad was the first guy to find that oil ... He gave it to Gene Gaudet, the Hudson's Bay Manager and he sent it out on the boat ... We never heard of that oil again and we never got the lard kettle back" (quoted in Auld and Kershaw 2005, 21).

2　Exceptions to this include the Hay River reserve, established on the east bank of the Hay River in 1974, and the Salt River First Nation Indian Reserve, established as part of a treaty land entitlement agreement in 2008 at several locations in and around Fort Smith and Wood Buffalo National Park.

3　Michael Asch and Norman Zlotkin (1997, 212) rightly note that in Ottawa's view, questions of underlying title included not only land ownership, but also jurisdiction to govern the land in question.

4　The caveat filed by the Indian Brotherhood of the Northwest Territories included lands in the southern part of the Northwest Territories covered under Treaty 8. Treaty 8 was negotiated in the summer of 1899, with subsequent adhesions made between 1900 and 1914, and included Slavey, Dogrib, Chipewyan, and Yellowknives south of Great Slave Lake. Much like Treaty 11, Treaty 8 was never fully implemented in the Northwest Territories, and the Dene argued that they did not surrender jurisdiction to the land in treaty negotiations.

5　The first appeal was heard by the Supreme Court of Alberta, which was then the court of appeal for cases heard by the territorial Supreme Court.

6 Although the Sahtu Settlement Lands are privately owned, title is held in the collective interest of Sahtu Dene and Metis beneficiaries. Their sale or transference to non-beneficiaries of the land claim agreement is restricted. In this they are unlike the lands governed by the Alaska Native Claims Settlement Act (ANCSA), which has been criticized because shares in village and regional corporations can be alienated.

7 In 1930, the Natural Resources Transfer Agreement (NRTA) shifted jurisdiction over Crown lands and resources in Manitoba, Saskatchewan, Alberta, and British Columbia from the federal government to the provinces themselves. Aboriginal groups were not consulted regarding this process, but Ottawa did require the provinces to provide sufficient unoccupied Crown land to fulfill outstanding treaty obligations to First Nations. The NRTA also limited the ability of the provinces to pass legislation concerning Aboriginal hunting, trapping, and fishing on unoccupied Crown lands. In many of these provinces, Crown lands are still the subject of treaty land entitlement settlement negotiations.

8 For example, MacKay Range Development Corporation created MacKay Range Oilfield Services specifically for oil- and gas-related opportunities; it provides oil field transportation and services in the Tulit'a District. Partners in MacKay Range Oilfield Services include various drilling, transportation, and oil field service companies. The Déline Land Corporation has shares in the Grey Goose Lodge, NorthWright Airways, and Techi?q Limited.

9 Requirements for enrolment in the claim, listed in section 4.2.1. of the land claim agreement, include descent, residence, enrolment in other claims, adoption by a Sahtu Dene or Metis person, and Canadian citizenship.

10 The land claim agreement does have provisions for the separate negotiation of self-government agreements but does not include the substance of self-government institutions and powers. Self-government must be negotiated by individual communities as part of a separate process. Tulit'a, Déline, and Fort Good Hope are currently engaged in self-government negotiations with the federal and territorial governments.

11 Of the 283,171 square kilometres of the Sahtu Settlement Area, only 41,437 are retained by the Sahtu Dene in fee simple title.

12 Approximately 250 kilometres south of Tulit'a, Wrigley lies outside the Sahtu Settlement Area on lands currently under negotiation as part of the Deh Cho comprehensive land claim process.

13 Because it is shallow, Willow Lake thaws rapidly in the spring and attracts some of the earliest northward migrations of ducks and geese.

14 Personal communication, 15 February 2006.

15 As K'asho Got'ine people recall, their ancestors used stone corrals to hunt caribou at Horton Lake. The corrals were arranged in a triangle, and caribou were driven into them to be killed. Remnants of these corrals are still visible.

16 Fieldnotes, 3 October 2007.

17 Fieldnotes, 2 October 2007.

18 "David" is a pseudonym.

19 Author interview, 4 October 2007.

20 Indeed, as per the land claim agreement, beneficiaries who intend to build a cabin that will be used primarily for harvesting do not need a permit.

21 In fact, the agreement must also be accepted by yet a third land corporation – the Ernie MacDonald Land Corporation in Norman Wells – which is involved because Norman Wells is part of the Tulit'a District.

22 Fieldnotes, 9 February 2007.

23 Fieldnotes, 17 February 2007.
24 Steven Kakfwi, presentation at the Tulit'a Unity Accord, 17 February 2007.
25 Angus Lennie, Protected Areas Strategy presentation at the Tulit'a Unity Accord, 17 February 2007.
26 Kakfwi, presentation at the Tulit'a Unity Accord, 17 February 2007.
27 Author interview, 3 October 2007.
28 Ibid.
29 Because presidents and boards are not normally aware of the terms of other ABAs, they cannot use them as leverage in their own negotiations.
30 Consultation and general community participation will be addressed in more detail in the following chapter.
31 Oil and gas ABA negotiations are often held in Calgary because most companies are headquartered there. Negotiations for mining ABAs often take place in Vancouver, for the same reason.
32 Men's focus group, Déline, 13 September 2006.
33 Women's focus group, Déline, 14 September 2006.
34 Public comment, Tulit'a Unity Accord, 17 February 2007.
35 Author interview, 9 September 2006.
36 Author interview, 7 October 2007.
37 Ibid.
38 Men's focus group, Déline, 13 September 2006.
39 Women's focus group, Déline, 14 September 2006.
40 Where the subsurface rights rest with the Crown (as is the case in 281,904 square kilometres of the Sahtu Settlement Area, which consists of 283,171 square kilometres), companies that are issued a subsurface lease have the right to access the land, subject to negotiating the terms of access with the local land corporation. If the negotiations fail, the matter can be referred to the surface rights board. The board can review disputes and determine compensation for access or environmental impacts, but it cannot revoke a company's access. Companies must also consult with the local land corporation on issues such as environmental impacts and employment.
41 Men's focus group, Déline, 18 September 2006.
42 In Colville Lake, children commonly spend several autumn months trapping in the bush with parents or elders. To my knowledge, Colville Lake is the only community in which they are excused from school during this time.
43 The schools offered a trapping skills program in 2004 whereby students learned how to trap, survive in the bush, and prepare and market hides.
44 Morris Neyelle, JRP Hearing Transcripts, 3 April 2006, vol. 16, 1635, 12-17.
45 The Norman Wells oil field is an exception here, but it is fairly small.
46 Berger recognizes the rich cultural heritage of Alaskan Indigenous groups, such as the Yup'ik, Inupiat, and Athabaskan people. However, he refers to them collectively as "Alaskan Natives."
47 The Sahtu Land Use Planning Board was created in 1998 to develop a Sahtu Land Use Plan as required by the claim. The board released a Preliminary Draft Land Use Plan in 2004 (Sahtu Land Use Planning Board 2004). Between 2004 and 2010, the plan underwent three further drafts. The delay in its ratification stemmed in part because its compilation required so much research and because stakeholders sometimes disagreed on what ought to be designated as protected areas. At the Tulit'a Unity Accord, Steven Kakfwi stated that

community leaders could be reluctant to "sign off" on the protection of certain areas because doing so could jeopardize development opportunities. Additionally, some community members criticized the idea of establishing bounded units as "protected areas," arguing that the practice did not represent Sahtu Dene views of the land. For a similar discussion of the consequences of mapping traditional territories, see Thom (2009) and Nadasdy (2012).

Chapter 4: Consultation and Other Legitimating Practices

1 There are exceptions to this rule: in *Dene Tha' First Nation v. Canada* (2006), the Federal Court found that Ottawa had breached its duty to consult the Dene Tha' on the creation and environmental review processes for the Mackenzie Gas Project as early as the planning of the regulatory process, and had persisted in its course until a remedy to Dene Tha' participation in the regulatory process could be reached at a "remedies hearing."
2 The list is appended to the proponent's licence and permit application to demonstrate that it has consulted with the affected community.
3 Norman Wells has the only Chinese restaurant in the Sahtu, whose food is considered a special treat among locals.
4 Fieldnotes, 10 April 2007.
5 "Frank" is a pseudonym.
6 Author interview, 12 February 2007.
7 JRP Hearing Transcripts, 3 April 2006, vol. 16, 1648, 26-27.
8 Husky Oil Operations Ltd., Land Use Permit and Water Licence Application (Summit/Keele 2006 Drilling Program).
9 Ibid.
10 Ibid.
11 Ibid.
12 Ibid.
13 Author interview, 5 April 2007.
14 Author interview, 9 April 2007.
15 The land use permits and water licences issued to Northrock were transferred to Husky Oil in 2005 for its Summit/Keele drilling and seismic program.
16 Author interview, 9 February 2007.
17 For a detailed discussion of the tension between hydrocarbon- and land-based economies in the Sahtu, see Chapter 3.
18 For more on the ways in which environmental impacts are considered in environmental impact statements, see Chapter 2.
19 For more on the ways in which local people perceive development impacts as a disruption in the social and physical body, see Chapter 2.
20 Author interview, 19 September 2006.
21 Author interview, 24 August 2006.
22 Fieldnotes, 12 October 2007.

Conclusion: The Politics of Participation

1 Executed in 2000, the Nisga'a Final Agreement resembles the Sahtu land claim agreement in that it provides for the transfer of land in fee simple title, along with fishing and hunting rights and a role in the management of fisheries and other wildlife, and the transfer of

capital payments to the newly created Nisga'a government. An important difference between the Nisga'a Treaty and the Sahtu agreement is that the former includes self-government provisions and therefore established a government (rather than a corporate structure) to manage the lands, resources (financial and natural), and other community services.

2 This is not unique to the Sahtu land claim agreement or the Nisga'a Treaty. For a discussion of its application in the Nunavut land claim, see Marybelle Mitchell (1996).

3 An interesting example of this appears in the diverse views regarding land that has been reclaimed after industrial use. In its environmental impact statement for the Mackenzie Gas Project, and in its presentation to Déline, Imperial Oil claimed that the pipeline right-of-way would increase moose habitat and could thus benefit moose populations. In other words, technological intervention would make the landscape even better, even more fruitful. Déline residents disagreed, suggesting that changes to the land would break Dene law and that moose would choose to stay away as a result. Clinton Westman (2013, 138) makes a similar observation for Cree people affected by the Alberta tar sands: A report prepared for the Syncrude Aurora Mine claimed that the creation of pit-lakes as fish habitat would lead to increased fishing and that medicinal and spiritual plant gathering locations would be improved after reclamation because the numbers of hills and lakes had been increased. Again, Westman (ibid., 139) shows how this contrasts with Cree beliefs that, because the mine has damaged the spirit of the place, such plants will not thrive there.

4 Clinton Westman (2013) makes a similar point about the consideration of interviews given by Cree hunters, trappers, and gatherers in the production of environmental assessment documents for the Alberta tar sands.

5 Women's focus group, Déline, 14 September 2006.

6 Mackenzie Valley Pipeline Inquiry Transcripts, 6 August 1975, vol. 19, 1843.

7 Women's focus group, Déline, 14 September 2006.

8 Fieldnotes, 12 February 2007.

References

Abel, Kerry. 1993. *Drum Songs: Glimpses of Dene History*. Montreal and Kingston: McGill-Queen's University Press.

Abele, Frances. 2005. "The Smartest Steward? Indigenous People and Petroleum-Based Economic Development in Canada's North." In *Energy Policy and the Struggle for Sustainable Development*, ed. Bruce Doern, 223-45. Toronto: University of Toronto Press.

Adelson, Naomi. 1998. "Health Beliefs and the Politics of Cree Well-Being." *Health* 2, 1: 5-22. http://dx.doi.org/10.1177/136345939800200101.

–. 2000. *'Being Alive Well': Health and the Politics of Cree Well-Being*. Toronto: University of Toronto Press.

Alfred, Taiaiake. 2011. "Colonial Stains on Our Existence." In *Racism, Colonialism, and Indigeneity in Canada*, ed. Martin Cannon and Lisa Suseri, 3-11. Don Mills: Oxford University Press.

Armitage, Derek R. 2005. "Collaborative Environmental Assessment in the Northwest Territories, Canada." *Environmental Impact Assessment Review* 25, 3: 239-58. http://dx.doi.org/10.1016/j.eiar.2004.06.012.

Asch, Michael. 1977. "The Dene Economy." In *Dene Nation: The Colony Within*, ed. Mel Watkins, 47-61. Toronto: University of Toronto Press.

–. 1984. *Home and Native Land: Aboriginal Rights and the Canadian Constitution*. Vancouver: UBC Press.

–, ed. 1997a. *Aboriginal and Treaty Rights in Canada: Essays on Law, Equality, and Respect for Difference*. Vancouver: UBC Press.

–. 1997b. "Introduction." In *Aboriginal and Treaty Rights in Canada: Essays on Law, Equality, and Respect for Difference*, ed. Michael Asch, ix-xv. Vancouver: UBC Press.

Asch, Michael, and Catherine Bell. 1997. "Challenging Assumptions: The Impact of Precedent in Aboriginal Rights Litigation." In *Aboriginal and Treaty Rights in Canada: Essays on Law, Equality, and Respect for Difference*, ed. Michael Asch, 38-74. Vancouver: UBC Press.

Asch, Michael, and Norman Zlotkin. 1997. "Affirming Aboriginal Title: A New Basis for Comprehensive Claims Negotiations." In *Aboriginal and Treaty Rights in Canada: Essays on Law, Equality, and Respect for Difference,* ed. Michael Asch, 208-30. Vancouver: UBC Press.

Auld, James, and Robert Kershaw. 2005. *The Sahtu Atlas.* Norman Wells: Sahtu GIS Project.

Basso, Ellen. 1978. "The Enemy of Every Tribe: 'Bushman' Images in Northern Athapaskan Narratives." *American Ethnologist* 5, 4: 690-709. http://dx.doi.org/10.1525/ae.1978.5.4. 02a00040.

Basso, Keith. 1970. "To Give Up on Words: Silence in Western Apache Culture." *Southwestern Journal of Anthropology* 26, 3: 213-30.

–. 1996. "Wisdom Sits in Places: Notes of a Western Apache Landscape." In *Senses of Place,* ed. Steven Field and Keith Basso, 53-90. Santa Fe: School of American Research Press.

Berger, Thomas. 1977. *Northern Frontier, Northern Homeland: The Report of the Mackenzie Valley Pipeline Inquiry.* Vol. 1. Ottawa: Minister of Supply and Services Canada.

–. 1985. *Village Journey: The Report of the Alaska Native Review Commission.* New York: Hill and Wang.

Berkes, F., P.J. George, R.J. Preston, A. Hughes, J. Turner, and B.D. Cummins. 1994. "Wildlife Harvesting and Sustainable Regional Native Economy in the Hudson and James Bay Lowland, Ontario." *Arctic* 47, 4: 350-60. http://dx.doi.org/10.14430/arctic1308.

Blackburn, Carole. 2005. "Searching for Guarantees in the Midst of Uncertainty: Negotiating Aboriginal Rights and Title in British Columbia." *American Anthropologist* 107, 4: 586-96. http://dx.doi.org/10.1525/aa.2005.107.4.586.

Blaser, Mario, Harvey Feit, and Glenn McRae. 2004. "Indigenous Peoples and Development Processes: New Terrains of Struggle." In *In the Way of Development: Indigenous Peoples, Life Projects and Globalization,* ed. Mario Baser, Harvey A. Feit, and Glenn McRae, 1-25. London and Ottawa: Zed Books and the Canadian International Development Research Centre.

Blondin, George. 1990. *When the World Was New: Stories of the Sahtu Dene.* Yellowknife: Outcrop.

–. 1997. *Yamoria the Lawmaker: Stories of the Dene.* Edmonton: NeWest.

Brightman, Robert. 1993. *Grateful Prey: Rock Cree Human-Animal Relationships.* Berkeley: University of California Press.

Brody, Hugh. 1981. *Maps and Dreams: Indians and the British Columbia Frontier.* Vancouver: Douglas and McIntyre.

Calgary Herald. 2006. "Hearings to Start on Northern Pipeline." 23 January. http://www. canada.com/story_print.html?id=c06c80c8-4991-442f-8d65-646aa9a97706&sponsor=.

Christensen, Julia, and Miriam Grant. 2007. "How Political Change Paved the Way for Indigenous Knowledge: The Mackenzie Valley Resource Management Act." *Arctic* 60, 2: 115-23.

Coates, Kenneth, and William Morrison. 1986. "Treaty Research Report, Treaty No. 11 (1921)." Ottawa, Treaties and Historical Research Centre, Indian and Northern Affairs Canada. https://www.aadnc-aandc.gc.ca/DAM/DAM-INTER-HQ/STAGING/ texte-text/tre11_1100100028913_eng.pdf.

Coon Come, Matthew. 2004. "Survival in the Context of Mega-Resource Development: Experiences of the James Bay Crees and the First Nations of Canada." In *In the Way of Development: Indigenous Peoples, Life Projects and Globalization,* ed. Mario Baser, Harvey

A. Feit, and Glenn McRae, 153-65. London and Ottawa: Zed Books and the Canadian International Development Research Centre.

Cruikshank, Julie. 1995. "Pete's Song: Establishing Meanings through Story and Song." In *When Our Words Return: Writing, Hearing, and Remembering Oral Traditions in Alaska and the Yukon*, ed. Phyllis Morrow and William Schneider, 53-75. Logan: Utah State University Press.

—. 2005. *Do Glaciers Listen? Local Knowledge, Colonial Encounters, and Social Imagination.* Vancouver: UBC Press.

Culhane, Dara. 1998. *The Pleasure of the Crown: Anthropology, Law and First Nations.* Burnaby: Talonbooks.

Déline First Nation. 2005. *If Only We Had Known: The History of Port Radium as Told by the Sahtuot'ine.* Déline, NT: Déline Uranium Team.

Diduck, Alan, and Bruce Mitchell. 2003. "Learning, Public Involvement and Environmental Assessment: A Canadian Case Study." *Journal of Environmental Assessment Policy and Management* 5, 3: 339-64. http://dx.doi.org/10.1142/S1464333203001401.

Dombrowski, Kirk. 2001. *Against Culture: Development, Politics, and Religion in Indian Alaska.* Lincoln: University of Nebraska Press.

—. 2002. "The Praxis of Indigenism and Alaska Native Timber Politics." *American Anthropologist* 104, 4: 1062-73. http://dx.doi.org/10.1525/aa.2002.104.4.1062.

Durkheim, Émile. 1915. *The Elementary Forms of Religious Life.* London: G. Allen and Unwin.

Elias, Peter Douglas. 1995. "Northern Economies." In *Northern Aboriginal Communities: Economies and Development,* ed. Peter Douglas Elias, 3-32. North York, ON: Captus Press.

—. 1997. "Models of Aboriginal Communities in Canada's North." *International Journal of Social Economics* 24, 11: 1241-55. http://dx.doi.org/10.1108/03068299710193598.

Ellis, Stephen. 2005. "Meaningful Consideration? A Review of Traditional Knowledge in Environmental Decision-Making." *Arctic* 58, 1: 66-77.

Escobar, Arturo. 1999. "After Nature: Steps to an Antiessentialist Political Ecology." *Current Anthropology* 40, 1: 1-30. http://dx.doi.org/10.1086/515799.

—. 2001. "Culture Sits in Places: Reflections on Globalism and Subaltern Strategies of Localization." *Political Geography* 20, 2: 139-74. http://dx.doi.org/10.1016/S0962-6298(00)00064-0.

Fast, Helen, J. Mathias, and O. Banias. 2001. "Directions toward Marine Conservation in Canada's Western Arctic." *Ocean and Coastal Management* 44: 183-205.

Feit, Harvey. 2004. "James Bay Crees' Life Projects and Politics: Histories of Place, Animal Partners and Enduring Relationships." In *In the Way of Development: Indigenous Peoples, Life Projects and Globalization,* ed. Mario Baser, Harvey Feit, and Glenn McRae, 92-110. London and Ottawa: Zed Books and the Canadian International Development Research Centre.

Ferguson, James. 1990. *The Anti-Politics Machine: "Development," Depoliticization, and Bureaucratic Power in Lesotho.* Cambridge: Cambridge University Press.

Fisher, Walter. 1984. "Narration as a Human Communication Paradigm: The Case of Public Moral Argument." *Communication Monographs* 51, 1: 1-22. http://dx.doi.org/10.1080/03637758409390180.

Fumoleau, René. 1977. *As Long as This Land Shall Last: A History of Treaty 8 and Treaty 11, 1870-1939.* Toronto: McClelland and Stewart.

Gell, Alfred. 1992. *The Anthropology of Time: Cultural Constructions of Temporal Maps and Images.* Oxford: Berg.

Giles, Audrey. 2004. "Kevlar, Crisco, and Menstruation: 'Tradition' and Dene Games." *Sociology of Sport Journal* 21, 1: 18-35.

–. 2005a. "The Acculturation Matrix and the Politics of Difference: Women and Dene Hand Games." *Canadian Journal of Native Studies* 1: 355-72.

–. 2005b. "A Foucaultian Approach to Menstrual Practices in the Dehcho Region, Northwest Territories, Canada." *Arctic Anthropology* 42, 2: 9-21. http://dx.doi.org/10.1353/arc.2011.0094.

GNWT. 2008. *Summary of NWT Community Statistics.* Yellowknife: NWT Bureau of Statistics.

–. 2010a. *Colville Lake Statistical Profile.* NWT Bureau of Statistics. http://www.statsnwt.ca/community-data/Profile%20PDF/Colville%20Lake.pdf.

–. 2010b. *Déline Statistical Profile.* NWT Bureau of Statistics. http://www.statsnwt.ca/community-data/Profile%20PDF/Deline.pdf.

–. 2010c. *Tulit'a Statistical Profile.* NWT Bureau of Statistics. http://www.statsnwt.ca/community-data/Profile%20PDF/Tulita.pdf.

Goulet, Jean-Guy. 1996. "A Christian Dene Tha Shaman? Aboriginal Experiences among a Missionized Aboriginal People." In *Shamanism and Northern Ecology,* ed. Juha Pentikäinen, 349-64. Berlin: Mouton de Gruyter. http://dx.doi.org/10.1515/9783110811674.349.

–. 1998. *Ways of Knowing: Experience, Knowledge, and Power among the Dene Tha.* Lincoln: University of Nebraska Press.

Graville, F. 1985. "Traditional Games of the Dogrib and Slave Indians of the Mackenzie Region N.W.T." Master's thesis, University of Ottawa.

Habermas, Jürgen. 1975. *Legitimation Crisis.* Boston: Beacon Press.

Hallowell, Irving. 1960. "Ojibwa Ontology, Behavior, and World View." In *Culture in History,* ed. Stanley Diamond, 19-49. New York: Columbia University Press.

Heine, Michael. 1999. *Dene Games: A Culture and Resource Manual.* Yellowknife: Sport North Federation and MACA (GNWT).

Helm, June. 2000. *The People of Denendeh: Ethnohistory of the Indians of Canada's Northwest Territories.* Iowa City: University of Iowa Press.

Hunn, Eugene. 1999. "The Value of Subsistence for the Future of the World." In *Ethnoecology: Situated Knowledge/Located Lives,* ed. Virginia D. Nazarea, 23-36. Tucson: University of Arizona Press.

Hymes, Dell. 1964. "Introduction: Toward Ethnographies of Communication." *American Anthropologist* 66, 6: 1-34.

Imperial Oil. 2007. "Socio-Economic Assessment." In *Supplementary Information: Project Update 2007.* Submitted to the JRP on 15 May. JRP Exhibit J-IORVL-009530. Calgary: Imperial Oil.

Indian and Northern Affairs Canada. 1993. *Sahtu Dene and Metis Comprehensive Land Claim Agreement.* Ottawa: Minister of Government Services Canada.

–. 1994. *The Sahtu Dene and Metis Comprehensive Land Claim Agreement: Highlights.* Ottawa: Minister of Government Services Canada.

–. 2004. *Northern Oil and Gas Annual Report, 2004.* Northern Oil and Gas Branch. Ottawa: Minister of Public Works and Government Services Canada.

Ingold, Tim. 1986. *The Appropriation of Nature: Essays on Human Ecology and Social Relations.* Manchester: Manchester University Press.

–. 1993. "The Temporality of the Landscape." *World Archaeology* 25, 2: 152-74. http://dx.doi.org/10.1080/00438243.1993.9980235.

Irlbacher-Fox, Stephanie. 2009. *Finding Dahshaa: Self-Government, Social Suffering, and Aboriginal Policy in Canada.* Vancouver: UBC Press.

Isaac, Thomas, and Anthony Knox. 2003. "The Crown's Duty to Consult Aboriginal People." *Alberta Law Review* 41, 1: 49-78.

Joint Review Panel (JRP). 2009. *Foundation for a Sustainable Northern Future: Report of the Joint Review Panel for the Mackenzie Gas Project.* 2 vols. Ottawa: Minister of the Environment.

Kofinas, Gary. 2005. "Caribou Hunters and Researchers at the Co-Management Interface: Emergent Dilemmas and the Dynamics of Legitimacy in Power Sharing." *Anthropologica* 47, 2: 179-96.

Kuokkanen, Rauna. 2011. "Indigenous Economies, Theories of Subsistence, and Women: Exploring the Social Economy Model for Indigenous Governance." *American Indian Quarterly* 35, 2: 215-40. http://dx.doi.org/10.5250/amerindiquar.35.2.0215.

Long, Norman. 1989. "From Paradigm Lost to Paradigm Regained?" In *Battlefields of Knowledge: The Interlocking of Theory and Practice in Social Research and Development,* ed. Norman Long and Ann Long, 16-43. London: Routledge.

Mackenzie Gas Project. 2004a. "Environmental Impact Statement for the Mackenzie Gas Project." 8 vols. Submitted by Imperial Oil on behalf of the Mackenzie Gas Project Proponents to the National Energy Board (NEB).

–. 2004b. "Environmental Impact Statement in Brief." Prepared by Imperial Oil on behalf of the Mackenzie Gas Project Proponents.

Mahony, James. 2006. "Court Decision Should Not Slow Mackenzie Gas Project." *Daily Oil Bulletin,* 21 November.

McCrank, Neil. 2008. *Road to Improvement: The Review of the Regulatory Systems across the North.* Ottawa: Minister of Public Works and Government Services Canada.

McLafferty, Carly, and Doug Dokis. 2004. "A Guide to Dialogue and Understanding with First Nations in Canada: Tier II." Prepared for the National Energy Board Seminar Series.

Merry, Sally Engle. 1991. "Law and Colonialism." *Law and Society Review* 25, 4: 889-922. http://dx.doi.org/10.2307/3053874.

Miller, Bruce. 2011. *Oral History on Trial: Recognizing Aboriginal Narratives in the Courts.* Vancouver: UBC Press.

Mills, Antonia. 1982. "The Beaver Indian Prophet Dance and Related Movements among North American Indians." PhD diss., Harvard University.

–. 1986. "The Meaningful Universe: Intersecting Forces in Beaver Indian Cosmology and Causality." *Culture* (Canadian Ethnology Society) 6, 2: 81-91.

Mitchell, Marybelle. 1996. *From Talking Chiefs to a Native Corporate Elite: The Birth of Class and Nationalism among Canadian Inuit.* Montreal and Kingston: McGill-Queen's University Press.

Morrow, Phyllis, and Chase Hensel. 1992. "Hidden Dissentions: Minority-Majority Relationships and the Use of Contested Terminology." *Arctic Anthropology* 29, 1: 38-53.

Mulrennan, M.E., and C.H. Scott. 2005. "Co-Management – An Attainable Partnership? Two Cases from James Bay, Northern Quebec and Torres Strait, Northern Queensland." *Anthropologica* 47, 2: 197-214.

MVEIRB. 2005. *Rules of Procedure for Environmental Assessment and Environmental Impact Review Proceedings.* Yellowknife: MVEIRB.

—. 2007. *Mackenzie Valley Environmental Impact Review Board 2006-2007 Annual Report.* Yellowknife: MVEIRB.

Nadasdy, Paul. 2003. *Hunters and Bureaucrats: Power, Knowledge, and Aboriginal-State Relations in the Southwest Yukon.* Vancouver: UBC Press.

—. 2005. "The Anti-Politics of TEK: The Institutionalization of Co-Management Discourse and Practice." *Anthropologica* 47, 2: 215-32.

—. 2007. "The Gift in the Animal: The Ontology of Hunting and Human–Animal Sociality." *American Ethnologist* 34, 1: 25-43. http://dx.doi.org/10.1525/ae.2007.34.1.25.

—. 2012. "Boundaries among Kin: Sovereignty, the Modern Treaty Process, and the Rise of Ethno-Territorial Nationalism among Yukon First Nations." *Comparative Studies in Society and History* 54, 3: 499-532. http://dx.doi.org/10.1017/S0010417512000217.

National Energy Board. 2004. "Agreement for an Environmental Impact Review of the Mackenzie Gas Project." http://www.neb-one.gc.ca/bts/ctrg/mmrndm/2004mcknzgs02 -eng.html.

—. 2010. *Mackenzie Gas Project – Reasons for Decision.* 2 vols. Ottawa: National Energy Board.

Northern Pipeline Environmental Impact Assessment and Regulatory Chairs' Committee. 2002. *Cooperation Plan for the Environmental Impact Assessment and Regulatory Review of a Northern Gas Pipeline Project through the Northwest Territories.* http://www.screening committee.ca/pdf/northern_gas_coop_plan.pdf.

Notzke, Claudia. 1999. "Indigenous Tourism Development in the Arctic." *Annals of Tourism Research* 26, 1: 55-76. http://dx.doi.org/10.1016/S0160-7383(98)00047-4.

O'Faircheallaigh, Ciaran. 1999. "Making Social Impact Assessment Count: A Negotiation-Based Approach for Indigenous Peoples." *Society and Natural Resources* 12, 1: 63-80. http://dx.doi.org/10.1080/089419299279894.

—. 2013. "Extractive Industries and Indigenous Peoples: A Changing Dynamic?" *Journal of Rural Studies* 30: 20-30. http://dx.doi.org/10.1016/j.jrurstud.2012.11.003.

Olivier de Sardan, Jean-Pierre. 2005. *Anthropology and Development: Understanding Contemporary Social Change.* London: Zed Books.

O'Meara, Dina. 2010. "Mackenzie Fate Hangs on Prices." *Calgary Herald,* 24 April, C1.

Palmer, Andie. 2000. "Evidence 'Not in a Form Familiar to Common Law Courts': Assessing Oral Histories in Land Claims Testimony after *Delgamuukw v. B.C.*" *Alberta Law Review* 38, 4: 1040-50.

—. 2005. *Maps of Experience: The Anchoring of Land to Story in Secwepemc Discourse.* Toronto: University of Toronto Press.

Ridington, Robin. 1988. "Knowledge, Power, and the Individual in Subarctic Hunting Societies." *American Anthropologist* 90, 1: 98-110. http://dx.doi.org/10.1525/aa.1988.90.1. 02a00070.

—. 1990. *Little Bit Know Something: Stories in a Language of Anthropology.* Vancouver: Douglas and McIntyre.

Rushforth, Scott. 1977. "Country Food." In *Dene Nation: The Colony Within,* ed. Mel Watkins, 32-46. Toronto: University of Toronto Press.

—. 1992. "Legitimation of Beliefs in a Hunter-Gatherer Society: Bearlake Athapaskan Knowledge and Authority." *American Ethnologist* 19, 3: 483-500. http://dx.doi.org/10.1525/ ae.1992.19.3.02a00040.

–. 1994. "Political Resistance in a Contemporary Hunter-Gatherer Society: More about Bearlake Athapaskan Knowledge and Authority." *American Ethnologist* 21, 2: 335-52. http://dx.doi.org/10.1525/ae.1994.21.2.02a00060.

Sahtu Land and Water Board. 2004. "Land Use Permit Process (Draft)." Fort Good Hope, SLWB.

Sahtu Land Use Planning Board. 2004. "Sahtu Preliminary Draft Land Use Plan." Norman Wells, SLUPB.

Sahtu Secretariat Incorporated. 2008. "Sahtu Newsletter: Sahtu Secretariat Incorporated and Sahtu Dene Council." 5 June.

Saku, James. 2002. "Modern Land Claim Agreements and Northern Canadian Aboriginal Communities." *World Development* 30, 1: 141-51. http://dx.doi.org/10.1016/S0305-750X(01)00095-X.

Saku, James, and Robert Bone. 2000a. "Looking for Solutions in the Canadian North: Modern Treaties as a New Strategy." *Canadian Geographer* 44, 3: 259-70. http://dx.doi.org/10.1111/j.1541-0064.2000.tb00708.x.

–. 2000b. "Modern Treaties in Canada: The Case of Northern Quebec Agreements and the Inuvialuit Final Agreement." *Canadian Journal of Native Studies* 2: 283-307.

Savishinsky, Joel. 1974. *The Trail of the Hare: Life and Stress in an Arctic Community.* New York: Gordon and Breach Science.

Scott, Colin. 1996. "Science for the West, Myth for the Rest? The Case of James Bay Cree Knowledge Construction." In *Naked Science: Anthropological Inquiries into Boundaries, Power and Knowledge,* ed. Laura Nader, 69-86. London: Routledge.

Scott, James C. 1998. *Seeing Like a State: How Certain Schemes to Improve the Human Condition Have Failed.* Binghamton, NY: Vail-Ballou Press.

Seed, Patricia. 2001. *American Pentimento: The Invention of Indians and the Pursuit of Riches.* Minneapolis: University of Minnesota Press.

Smith, David. 1998. "An Athapaskan Way of Knowing: Chipewyan Ontology." *American Ethnologist* 25, 3: 412-32. http://dx.doi.org/10.1525/ae.1998.25.3.412.

Statistics Canada. 2006. *2006 Census Community Profiles.* http://www12.statcan.ca/census -recensement/2006/dp-pd/prof/92-591/index.cfm?Lang=E.

Stetson, George. 2012. "Oil Politics and Indigenous Resistance in the Peruvian Amazon: The Rhetoric of Modernity against the Reality of Coloniality." *Journal of Environment and Development* 21, 1: 76-97. http://dx.doi.org/10.1177/1070496511433425.

Stevenson, Mark. 1996. "Indigenous Knowledge in Environmental Assessment." *Arctic* 49, 3: 278-91. http://dx.doi.org/10.14430/arctic1203.

Taniton, Raymond, and Mindy Willett. 2011. *At the Heart of It: Dene dzó t'áré.* Markham, ON: Fifth House.

Tanner, Adrian. 1979. *Bringing Home Animals: Religious Ideology and Mode of Production of the Mistassini Cree Hunters.* New York: St. Martin's Press.

Thom, Brian. 2009. "The Paradox of Boundaries in Coast Salish Territories." *Cultural Geographies* 16, 2: 179-205. http://dx.doi.org/10.1177/1474474008101516.

Thomas, David Hurst. 2000. *Skull Wars: Kennewick Man, Archaeology, and the Battle for Native American Identity.* New York: Basic Books.

Usher, Peter. 1982. "The North: One Land, Two Ways of Life." In *Heartland and Hinterland: A Geography of Canada,* ed. L.D. McCann, 231-47. Scarborough: Prentice Hall.

—. 2003. "Environment, Race, and Nation Reconsidered: Reflections on Aboriginal Land Claims in Canada." *Canadian Geographer* 47, 4: 365-82. http://dx.doi.org/10.1111/j.0008 -3658.2003.00029.x.

Venne, Sharon. 1997. "Understanding Treaty 6: An Indigenous Perspective." In *Aboriginal and Treaty Rights in Canada: Essays on Law, Equality, and Respect for Difference,* ed. Michael Asch, 173-207. Vancouver: UBC Press.

Vincent, Sylvie, and Garry Bowers. 1988. *James Bay and Northern Quebec: Ten Years After.* Montreal: Recherches Amerindiennes au Quebec.

Webler, Thomas, Hans Kastenholz, and Ortwin Renn. 1995. "Public Participation in Impact Assessment: A Social Learning Perspective." *Environmental Impact Assessment Review* 15, 5: 443-63.

Westman, Clinton. 2013. "Social Impact Assessment and the Anthropology of the Future in Canada's Tar Sands." *Human Organization* 72, 2: 135-44.

White, Graham. 2002. "Treaty Federalism in Northern Canada: Aboriginal Government Land Claim Boards." *Publius* 32, 3: 89-114. http://dx.doi.org/10.1093/oxfordjournals. pubjof.a004961.

—. 2006. "Cultures in Collision: Traditional Knowledge and Euro-Canadian Governance Processes in Northern Land Claim Boards." *Arctic* 59, 4: 401-15.

Wilson, Jennifer Sharron. 1992. "The Norman Wells Project Coordinating Committee: An Evaluation." Master's thesis, University of British Columbia, School of Community and Regional Planning.

Wilson, Roderick. 1986. "Subarctic: A Regional Overview." In *Native Peoples: The Canadian Experience,* ed. Bruce Morrison and Roderick Wilson, 237-42. Toronto: McClelland and Stewart.

Yakovleva, Natalia. 2011. "Oil Pipeline Construction in Eastern Siberia: Implications for Indigenous People." *Geoforum* 42, 6: 708-19. http://dx.doi.org/10.1016/j.geoforum.2011. 05.005.

Zavitz, J. 1997. "The Northern Economy." In *Breaking Ice with Finesse: Oil and Gas Exploration in the Canadian Arctic,* ed. K. Clark, C. Hetherington, C. O'Neil, and J. Zavitz, 164-74. Calgary: Arctic Institute of North America.

CASES CITED

Delgamuukw v. British Columbia, [1997] 3 S.C.R. 1010.

Dene Tha' First Nation v. Canada (Minister of the Environment), [2006] 4 F.C.R. D-28.

Haida Nation v. British Columbia (Minister of Forests), [2004] 3 S.C.R. 511, 2004 SCC 73.

Halfway River First Nation v. British Columbia (Ministry of Forests) (1999), 178 D.L.R. (4th) 666 (BCAA).

Mikisew Cree First Nation v. Canada (Minister of Canadian Heritage), [2005] 3 S.C.R. 388, 2005 SCC 69.

R. v. Sparrow, [1990] 1 S.C.R. 1075.

Taku River Tlingit First Nation v. British Columbia (Project Assessment Director), [2004] 3 S.C.R. 550, 2004 SCC 74.

Tsilhqot'in Nation v. British Columbia, 2014 SCC 44.

Index

Notes: "i" after a page number indicates a photograph; "m," a map; "t," a table; JRP stands for Joint Review Panel; MGP, for Mackenzie Gas Project; MVEIRB, for Mackenzie Valley Environmental Impact Review Board; SSA, for Sahtu Settlement Area

Abel, Kerry, 70

Aboriginal consultation. *See* consultation with Aboriginal peoples; consultation with Aboriginal peoples, legal requirements

Aboriginal peoples and rights: ambiguity re rights and uncertainty re economic growth, 161–62; assumption that Indigenous peoples must adapt to modern conditions, 8; Berger on their "legitimate claims," x; consultation prior to mid-1970s, 6; discussion couched in Euro-American views of property and ownership, 11, 161–62; government's transforming rights into property law, 161–62; James Bay and Northern Quebec Agreement (1975), xii–xiii, 95; land and treaty rights in jurisprudence, 5–7; politics of refusal, xx; rights can be infringed if in "national interest," 6; rights entrenched in Canadian Constitution (1982), xiii, 131–32, 148–49, 162; traditional ecological knowledge (TEK) validated, x–xi.

See also consultation with Aboriginal peoples, legal requirements

access and benefits agreements (ABAs): Aboriginal views translated into techno-science, 168; apprehension re focus of negotiators, 119–21; beneficiaries often unaware of negotiations until ABA signed, 150; criticism of, 152–53; decision making in opposition to traditional Dene norms, 118–19; Dene negotiators, 117–19; description, 180n8; motivation of Dene to increase beenfits, 120; negotiation process, 99, 116–18, 138, 150–51; opposition to industrial development not universal, 12, 85–86, 120–21; seen as only substantial means for communities to benefit, 120, 152; significance for Sahtu communities, 119; traditional knowledge studies, 153–59

AEC West, 22

Agreement for an Environmental Impact Review of the Mackenzie Gas Project, 36–37

Alaska Federation of Natives, viii
Alaska National Interest Lands Conservation Act of 1980, viii
Alaska Native Claims Settlement Act (1971), viii, 127–28
Alberta tar sands: bitumen deposits, vii; criticism of traditional land use studies, 155; decision re Northern Gateway pipeline, 8; disregarding of relationship between Cree and their lands, 80; social impact assessment and mass loyalty, 163–64
Andrew, Frank (Sahtu Dene chief), 49, 111
Apache Canada (resource developer), 22
Apache peoples, 63, 141
Arctic National Wildlife Range, viii
Armitage, Derek, 10, 46–47, 87–88
Asch, Michael: on household as basic unit of production/distribution, 16–17; on inequities in Canadian legal systems, 43; on reconciliation of Aboriginal peoples with sovereignty of Crown, xix–xx; on settler law and Indigenous peoples, 131–32
Atlantic Richfield Company, vii
Ayah, ʔehtseo (Grandfather), 52, 57–59
Ayoni Keh Land Corporation (Colville Lake): one of three local corporations in K'asho Got'ine District, 112–13; origin of name, 104; report on consultation process, 24–25; representatives on district land corporation, 97, 98i

Basso, Ellen, 46, 48
Basso, Keith, 63–64, 141
Bavington, Dean, xii
Behdzi Ahda First Nation, 21, 25
Bell, Catherine, 131–32
Beloit, Lake, 69i
Berger, Thomas: appointment to Mackenzie Valley Pipeline Inquiry, ix; critique of Alaska Native Claims Settlement Act, 127; on need to honour "legitimate claims of the native people," x. See also Mackenzie Valley Pipeline Inquiry
Berger Inquiry (Mackenzie Valley Pipeline Inquiry): Berger's approach, 4;

comparison with MGP hearings, 4–5, 39, 42, 89, 168–70; Dene remarks on relationship to the land, 70; Dene's non-support for pipeline, 4, 168–69; evidence of contamination causing sickness, 81–83; hearings in different sites, 4, 39, 42, 89; high-water mark in participatory environmental management, 87; legitimation crisis and formation of inquiry, 7; mandate and actual extent of inquiry, ix; need to honour "legitimate claims of the native people," x; recognition of Dene-land relationship, 89; recommendation against pipeline until land claims settled (1977), ix, 87, 96; report on the impact on industrial development in North, ix–x
Berkes, Fikret, x–xi, xiii–xiv
BHP Billiton Ekati diamond mine, 35
Binnie, Ian, 149–50
Blackburn, Carole, 161–62, 164–65
Blaser, Mario, 167
Bowers, Garry, 93
Brody, Hugh, 43, 65
Brown, Bern Will, 20, 21, 22, 137

Canadian Environmental Assessment Agency, 36
Canadian Natural Resources Limited (developer), 22
capitalist states: capitalist constructions of landscape vs. Aboriginal approach, 64–66, 162; disarticulation of landscapes, 75–76; globalization, deregulation, and uncertainty, 164–65; liberal capitalist states and will formation, 6–7
Carmichael, Fred, 173–74
Christensen, Julia, 10
coloniality, 164
Colville Lake (K'áhbamitué): Ayoni Keh Land Corporation, 24–25, 97, 98i, 104, 112–13; Daniel, 55–56; decision making by Dene, 56; dislike of interfering in affairs of others, 55–57; employment sectors, 21–22; founding, 20; generosity valued, 55–56; isolation and lack of services, 21, 21i, 22; knowledge of and

living off the land, 54, 104; language-
retention rate, 20; oil and gas activities,
22; population, 14, 20, 103–4; report
for Ayoni Keh Land Corporation and
Behdzi Ahda First Nation, 24–25; research beneficial for author and community, 24–25; subsurface rights, 22;
Timothy, 55; veto on all land it claims,
112; visiting, 54–55. *See also* Sahtu
Settlement Area, land corporations
Constitution Act, 1982, and Aboriginal
rights, xiii, 131–32, 148–49, 162
consultation with Aboriginal peoples: as
understood by Sahtu people *vs.* industry or government, 135–36, 146, 147–50;
Aboriginal participation taken as "consent" for proposal, xvii, 5, 90, 158, 165;
Aboriginal request for clear delineation
of responsibilities, 134–35; Aboriginal
views translated into techno-science,
168; appearance, not reality, of participatory decision making, xxiii, 142–46,
150–51, 160; "burdensome" (2008 report),
162–63; clear definition lacking, 133–35,
148–50; Comprehensive Land Agreement
"hazy" re consultation, 138; decision-
making methods of Dene (traditional),
30–31, 142–43, 170; Dene disenchantment/
frustration with participatory process,
101–2, 147, 170; Dene resigned that
MGP will proceed, 87, 170; elders
intimidated and not often consulted,
142; failure to consider Dene perspectives, 26, 73, 75, 76, 88–89, 138–46, 168;
government authority and decision
making, 92–93, 124, 125; hopes for
improvement, 160; impersonal nature
of, 140–43; JRP recommendations
ignored impact of project on Dene, xvii,
87–89, 171–73; justifying abrogation of
Aboriginal rights, 135; legitimation
crisis, 6–7; legitimation for government
decisions, xviii, 5, 7–8, 153–59, 160, 163;
manipulation of decision making by
outsider forces, 125–26, 142–43; narratives (stories) not taken seriously, 155,
158, 168; *not* a veto right for Aboriginal

peoples, 135, 148, 166; pattern of, 138–
39, 142–45; proponent-driven, not by
Sahtu Dene, 145–46; relationships with
communities not developed, 138–40;
reports written by proponents, 146;
"significance" of impact according to
proponents and Dene, 33, 74t, 76–80,
88–89, 143–46; third-party or industry
consultation not required, 135–37; tool
for proponents to obtain permits, 146,
147; unequal economic benefits, 99, 160,
170; valorization of future envisaged by
Euro-Canadians, 163–64. *See also* access
and benefits agreements (ABAs); Berger
Inquiry; Mackenzie Gas Project hearings; participatory resource management
consultation with Aboriginal peoples,
legal requirements: Aboriginal claims
becoming more assured, xii–xiii; clear
definition lacking, 133–35, 148–50;
Delgamuukw case (1997), 132, 133–34, 148;
Haida Nation and *Taku River* cases, 133;
international pronouncements, xi, xii–
xiii; justifying abrogation of rights, 135;
Mikisew Cree First Nation v. Canada
(2005), 133, 134, 148, 149–50; *not* a veto
right for Aboriginal peoples, 135, 148, 166;
required where rights or lands affected,
130–32; *Sparrow* case (1990), 6, 132–33,
148–49; "Sparrow test" (pre-2004), 6,
132, 148–49; third-party or industry
consultation not required, 135–37
*Convention on Indigenous and Tribal
Peoples* (International Labour
Organization), 165
Coon Come, Matthew, xiii, 162
Cooperation Plan for the Environmental
Impact Assessment and Regulatory
Review of a Northern Gas Pipeline
Project through the NWT, 36
Coulthard, Glen, xx
Council of Yukon Indians Agreement
(1990), xiv
Cournoyea, Nellie, 173
Cree: Alberta tar sands and, 80; consulta-
tion re James Bay Hydroelectric Project
lacking, 6; James Bay and Northern

Quebec Agreement (1975), xii–xiii, 95, 162; *Mikisew Cree First Nation v. Canada* (2005), 133, 134, 148, 149–50; participation in consultation to establish relationships, 167; perspectives of impacts of industrial activities, 80; on use of land after industrialization, 187n3

Cruikshank, Julie, 11, 65

Culhane, Dara, 43, 65

Declaration on the Rights of Indigenous Peoples (2007), xi, 165

Deh Gah Got'ine Dene Council, 174

Delgamuukw case (1997), 132, 133–34, 148

Déline: Déline District Land Corporation, 97, 98i; Déline Land Corporation (local), 17, 24, 85–86, 97, 98i, 109; employment sectors, 17, 19; Great Bear Co-op, 18i, 19; Grey Goose Lodge, 17; language-retention rate, 17; Northern Store (grocery store), 19; population, 14, 17, 103; research beneficial for author and community, 24. *See also* Sahtu Settlement Area, land corporations

Déline Land Corporation (local): on economic opportunities *vs.* disadvantages of pipeline, 85–86; members not distinguished between Dene and Metis, 109; ownership of Grey Goose Lodge, 17; report on licensing and permitting processes, 24; representatives on district land corporation, 97, 98i

Déline Renewable Resource Council, 68

Dene. *See* Sahtu Dene

Dene Tha' First Nation v. Canada (2006), 133, 148

Dene/Metis Western Arctic Land Claim (1990), 96

Devlan Exploration, 22

Diavik diamond mine, 35

Diduck, Alan, 43–44

Dokis, Carly, xvi; attendance at JRP hearings, 25, 173; experience living with Dene hosts, 23–26, 140–42; focus of book, xvi; research for Sahtu Dene communities, 24–25; research methodology, 25–26

Dombrowski, Kirk, 127–28

Durkheim, Émile, 31

Eagle, Noah, 80

Eastern Siberia–Pacific Ocean Pipeline, 165–66

Elias, Peter, 15, 89–90

Ellis, Stephen, 47, 154

Enbridge Northern Gateway Pipeline, 7–8

EnCana Corporation, 20

energy consumption: increase and oil and gas exploration, vii–viii; pipeline efficiency *vs.* tankers for gas, viii–ix

environmental impact statements (EIS): contents, 33; "disarticulation" of landscape, 73–76; failure to appropriately consider Sahtu Dene perspectives, 26, 73, 75, 76, 88–89; Indigenous people's difficulty with, 44; predicting and managing impacts, and providing mitigation, 66; prepared by proponents, 88; readability, 43–44; significance of MGP (according to Imperial Oil), 33, 74t, 76–80, 88, 145–46

Ernie MacDonald Land Corporation (in Norman Wells), 97, 98i

Escobar, Arturo, 63, 64

Far North Oil and Gas Review, 169

Feit, Harvey, 80, 167

Finding Dahshaa: Self-Government, Social Suffering, and Aboriginal Policy in Canada (Irlbacher-Fox), 8

Fisher, Walter, 90

Fort Good Hope, 14, 102–4; Fort Good Hope Metis Land Corporation, 97, 98i, 112–13; Yamoga Land Corporation, 97, 98i, 112–13. *See also* Sahtu Settlement Area, land corporations

Fort Good Hope Metis Land Corporation, 97, 98i, 112–13

Fort Norman Metis Land Corporation (in Tulit'a), 97, 98i, 109–12

From Talking Chiefs to a Native Corporate Elite (Mitchell), 126

Gell, Alfred, 163–64
Grant, Miriam, 10
Gwich'in Agreement (1992), xiv, 96
Gwich'in Tribal Council, 174

Habermas, Jürgen, xviii, 6–7, 163
Haida Nation v. British Columbia (2004),
    7, 133, 135
Halfway River First Nation v. British
    Columbia (1999), 134, 148
Hallowell, Irving, 72
Handley, Joe, 111
Hansen, Ken, 143–44
Hensel, Chase, 47
Husky Oil: activity in SSA, 20; consulta-
    tion with Tulit'a Land Corporation re
    Summit/Keele operations, 143–45, 155;
    problems with two land corporations in
    Tulit'a, 110–12; traditional knowledge
    study for Summit/Keele operations,
    155–56

impact benefits agreements. See access and
    benefits agreements (ABAs)
Imperial Oil: application for Mackenzie
    Gas Project (2004), 32; drilling rights in
    SSA, 20; estimated cost of MGP, 178n39,
    180n1; impact assessment of MGP, 33–
    35, 73, 74t, 75–76, 77–79, 88–89, 145–
    46; meetings with Dene, 57, 182n35;
    Peele River work camp, 106, 107i; pres-
    entations at Joint Review Panel hear-
    ings, 40–41; separation (disarticulation)
    of landscape vis-à-vis impacts, 73, 74t,
    75–76, 88–89
Indian and Northern Affairs Canada: access
    negotiations in SSA, 98; assessing/
    regulating pipeline development in
    NWT, 36; control of natural resources,
    99; sale of land prior to Aboriginal
    consultation, 152
Indian Brotherhood of the Northwest
    Territories (now Dene Nation), ix,
    95–96, 183n4
Indigenous peoples. See Aboriginal
    peoples
Ingold, Tim, 64

Inter-American Development Bank,
    165
International Finance Corporation, 165
International Frontier, 20
International Labour Organization's
    Convention on Indigenous and Tribal
    Peoples (1989), 165
Inuit Circumpolar Conference, 127
Inuvialuit Committee for Original
    People's Entitlement (COPE), ix
Inuvialuit Final Agreement of 1984, xiv,
    95–96
Inuvialuit Game Council (IGC), 36
Inuvialuit Regional Corporation, 173–74
Inuvialuit Settlement Area Board, 36
Irish Fishers' Knowledge Project, xii
Irlbacher-Fox, Stephanie, xviii, 8, 101,
    164

James Bay and Northern Quebec Agree-
    ment (1975), xii–xiii, 95, 162
James Bay Hydroelectric Project, 6
Joint Review Panel (JRP): appearance of
    participatory decision making, but not
    in reality, xxiii, 142–46, 150–51, 160;
    arrival in SSA (2006), 37–39; capitalist
    views of outsiders vs. Dene views of the
    land, 64–66; classical music out of place,
    41; concepts of knowledge (Indigenous
    and Western) incompatible, 46–47;
    concern about contamination causing
    sickness, 81–87; contrasted with Berger
    Inquiry, xvi–xvii, 4–5, 39, 42, 89, 168–
    70; Dene believed hearings after pipe-
    line plans in place, 57; Dene participation
    taken as "consent" for proposal, xvii, 5,
    90, 158; Dene resigned that project will
    proceed, 87, 173–74; Dene's difficulties
    with legalistic language and documents,
    43–45; Dene's symbolic claiming of
    space/identity in hearing room, 42–43,
    59–61; establishment, 35–37; failure to
    consider Aboriginal conceptions of
    animals, 76–77; formal layout of room,
    39–40, 40i, 41–42, 61–62; impacts of
    project on Dene not accurately con-
    sidered, xvi, 76–80, 86, 88–89, 171–73;

issues (non-pipeline) raised by Dene,
59–60; JRP's failure to incorporate
Indigenous forms of understanding, xvi–
xvii; procedural format, 40–41, 42–43,
61–62, 142–43; quantifiable data needed
by Dene to support their arguments,
90; recommendations' ignoring of
project impacts on Dene, xvii, 87–89,
171–73; recommendations non-binding
only, 8, 37; significance of MGP (according to Dene), 81–87; significance of
MGP (according to Imperial Oil), 33,
74t, 76–80, 88, 145–46
Joint Review Panel (JRP) and Dene culture: circumventing Dene law, 58–59;
Dene on inappropriateness of interfering in others' affairs, 51, 53, 56–57; Dene
relationship with land not appropriately
considered, xvi–xvii, xxiii–xxiv, 65–66,
76, 88–89, 168, 171–73; Dene skeptical
of non-local outsiders' "expertise," 9–10,
29, 49–50, 170; Dene view of primary
and secondary knowledge, 9–10, 48–50;
Dene's apprehension about speaking on
behalf of others, 45–46; Dene's dislike
of appearing ungenerous, 57–58; Dene's
use of humour, 60–61; dissent difficult
to express (considered disrespectful),
xvii–xviii, 58–59; hearings an example
of outsider interference, 56–57; JRP's
failure to incorporate Indigenous forms
of understanding, xvi–xvii

K'aalo Got'ine Dene, 102–3
Kakfwi, Steve, 111–12, 169
K'asho Got'ine Dene, 102, 103–4
K'asho Got'ine District Land
Corporation, 22, 97, 98i, 112–13
Kastenholz, Hans, 159
King, Hayden, xx
Kluane First Nation, 47, 76–77
Kuokkanen, Rauna, 15

Lamer, Antonio, 133–34
legitimation crisis, 6–7
legitimization practices. See consultation
with Aboriginal peoples

Lévi-Strauss, Claude, x
Long, Norman, 11
Louie, Clarence, 111

Mackay Range Development Corporation,
19, 100, 153, 184n8
Mackenzie Delta, ix, vii. See also Berger
Inquiry (Mackenzie Valley Pipeline
Inquiry); entries beginning with
Mackenzie
Mackenzie Gas Project (MGP):
Aboriginal Pipeline Group, 33–34;
anchor fields (Taglu, Parsons Lake,
Niglintgak), 32; appearance (not reality) of participatory decision making,
xxiii, 142–46, 150–51, 160; application
by Imperial Oil (2004), 32; approval by
National Energy Board, 173, 178n39;
arguments for and against, 33–35; cost
of project (estimates in 2004, 2007,
2013), 178n39, 180n1; Dene resigned
that project will proceed, 87, 173–74;
ethical, economic, political, environmental questions, xviii, xxiv; failure to
consider Sahtu Dene perspectives, 26,
73, 75, 76, 88–89, 138–46, 168; fate of
project rests with economic conditions,
xviii, 173; gas production dependent on
construction of pipeline, xxii; Joint
Review Panel established, 35–37; local
perspectives the theme of book, xxii;
significance of impacts, according to
environmental impact statement, 33,
73, 74t, 76–80, 88, 145–46; significance
of impacts on Dene, according to JRP,
171–73; transboundary and transjurisdictional nature, 35–36
Mackenzie Gas Project (MGP), impact
on Sahtu: "disarticulation" of landscape
impacts in environmental impact statement, 73–76; of earlier extractive projects, 50; evidence of contamination
and sickness, 81–87; impacts on Dene
not accurately considered, 76–80, 86,
88–89, 153; significance according to
Imperial Oil's environmental impact
statement, 33, 73, 74t, 76–80, 88–89,

145–46; significance according to JRP, 171–73; socio-economic impacts of project, xxii–xxiii, 33–35, 88

Mackenzie Gas Project hearings: Joint Review Panel (*see* Joint Review Panel [JRP]); question if development benefits communities, 124–25; question if subsistence and oil-based economies could co-exist, 124–25. *See also* Berger Inquiry (Mackenzie Valley Pipeline Inquiry); participatory resource management

Mackenzie Valley: major area of interest for oil/gas ventures, 22–23. *See also* Sahtu Dene; Sahtu region

Mackenzie Valley Environmental Impact Review Board (MVEIRB): approvals before co-management institutions, 35; Cooperation Plan for assessing and regulating energy developments, 36; De Beers Gahcho Kue diamond mine assessment ordered, 35; guidelines for environmental impact assessments, 73; Joint Review Panel established, 36–37; Mackenzie Gas Project assessment ordered, 35; referrals of applications from Sahtu Land and Water Board if community concerns, 151–52

Mackenzie Valley Pipeline Inquiry. *See* Berger Inquiry

Mackenzie Valley Resource Management Act, 151–52

Maps and Dreams (Brody), 65

McCrank, Neil, 162–63

McRae, Glenn, 167

Merry, Sally Engle, 9

Métis and Non-Status Native Association of the Northwest Territories (*later* Métis Nation), 95

Mikisew Cree First Nation v. Canada (2005), 133, 134, 148, 149–50

Miller, Bruce, 47–48

Mitchell, Bruce, 43–44

Mitchell, Marybelle, 126

Morrow, Phyllis, 47

Morrow, William, 96

Nadasdy, Paul: Aboriginal concepts evaluated by Euro-Canadian frameworks, 168; on asymmetric power relations in co-management, xv–xvi; on Canadian property and ownership laws and Aboriginal participation in legal processes, 131; on differences between experience and science in co-management, xv; on geographical and political divisions in Aboriginal lands, 113–14; on human-animal relationships, 72; on incompatibility of Indigenous and Western concepts of knowledge, 47; on JRP's failure to consider Aboriginal conceptions of animals, 76–77; on use of traditional knowledge in environmental management, 154

National Energy Board: approval of MGP, 173, 178n39; preparation for assessing and regulating pipeline development in NWT, 36

National Forest Strategy document (1992), xiv

nature/land: capitalist view and, 64–66, 162; colonial view of appropriate uses of land, 64–65; concept of nature relational and historically contingent, 64; Sahtu Dene view of nature/land, 65–66, 69–72, 83–84, 90, 172–73. *See also* Sahtu Dene, relationship with the land

Neyelle, Charlie, 79–80, 172

Nielsen, Leslie, 111

Nisga'a Treaty, 161, 162, 186n1

Norman Wells, 14, 20, 97, 98i. *See also* Sahtu Settlement Area, land corporations

Northeastern Quebec Agreement (1978), 95–96

Northern Frontier, Northern Homeland (report of Berger Inquiry), ix–x. *See also* Berger Inquiry (Mackenzie Valley Pipeline Inquiry)

Northern Store (grocery store), 19, 180n6

Northrock Resources, 20

Norwegian, Rocky, 111

Notzke, Claudia, xiii, 15

Nunavut Agreement (1993), xiv

Ocean Ranger oilrig, vii
O'Faircheallaigh, Ciaran, 44, 166–67
oil and gas activities, impact on Dene:
capitalist view of nature, 64–66, 162;
Dene view of nature/land, 65–66, 69–
72, 83–84, 90, 172–73; evidence of
contamination and sickness, 81–87
oil and gas companies: AEC West, 22;
Apache Canada, 22; Canadian Natural
Resources Limited, 22; consultation
with Aboriginal groups, approach, 135–
36; Devlan Exploration, 22; EnCana
Corporation, 20; Husky Oil, 20, 110–12,
143–45, 155–56; International Frontier,
20; Northrock Resources, 20; Paramount Resources, 22; Petro Canada, 22,
113; Syncrude Aurora Mine, 80; training
for staff re Aboriginal cultures, 136. *See
also* Imperial Oil
oil and gas transportation: challenges in
the North, viii, 23, 32–33; pipeline
advantage over tankers for gas, viii–ix;
reserves in Canadian North, 23; US *vs.*
Canadian settlements with Indigenous
peoples, viii. *See also* oil and gas transportation; pipelines
Olivier de Sardan, Jean-Pierre, 11
O'Meara, Dina, 173
Our Common Future (report of Brundtland
Commission), xi

Palmer, Andie, 43, 131
Paramount Resources, 22
participatory resource management:
accountability, fairness, transparency
lacking, 159–60; aim of environmental
assessment boards, 10; arguments for,
xii; Berger's support for, 4; "coloniality"
or domination of Eurocentric viewpoints, 164; co-management initiatives
(*see* resource co-management initiatives);
criticism of older methods, xi–xii;
culture and participation in decision
making, 11–12; decision-making authority remains with state, xviii, 5, 7–8,
10–11, 148, 160, 163; decision-making

methods of Dene (traditional), 30–31,
142–43; environmental management
principles, xii; failure to consider Sahtu
Dene perspectives, 26, 73, 75, 76, 88–89,
138–46, 168; hopes for improvement,
160; ideal situation, 159; Indigenous
input becoming stronger, xii–xiii; "industry" in Canadian North, 8–9; legitimation method for government, xviii–
xix, 5, 7–8, 153–59, 160; marginalization
of Aboriginal knowledge, xv–xvi, 168;
power relations asymmetric, xv–xvi, 12,
160; process now "handmaiden of state,"
5; quantifiable data need to be produced
by Dene, 90; Sahtu Land and Water
Board authority, 108, 136–37, 139, 151–
52; unequal economic benefits, 99,
160, 170. *See also* access and benefits
agreements (ABAs); consultation with
Aboriginal peoples; Berger Inquiry
(Mackenzie Valley Pipeline Inquiry);
Joint Review Panel (JRP)
Pasternak, Shiri, xx
Petro Canada, 22, 113
pipelines: advantages over tankers, viii–
ix; Canol Pipeline (1942), 35; Enbridge
Northern Gateway Pipeline, 7–8; Interprovincial Pipeline (now Enbridge), 20,
179n2; Norman Wells Pipeline (1985),
35, 125; Prudhoe Bay to Valdez, viii. *See
also* Mackenzie Gas Project (MGP);
oil and gas transportation
Prentice, Jim, 32
Prudhoe Bay oil field, vii

Renn, Ortwin, 159
resource co-management initiatives:
Aboriginal involvement as "cultural
performance," 9; Aboriginal knowledge
marginalized, xv–xvi, 168; Aboriginal
participation taken as "consent" for
proposal, xvii, 5, 90, 158, 165; Aboriginal
peoples limited to advisory role, 5;
agreements in 1980s and 1990s, xiv–xv;
aim of environmental assessment boards,
10; categorized by extent of Aboriginal

involvement, xiii–xiv; colonial-based interventions in Aboriginal lives, xvi, xvii, xix, 8; "coloniality" or domination of Eurocentric viewpoints, 164; culture and participation in decision making, 11–12; decision-making authority remains with state, xviii, 5, 7–8, 10–11, 148, 160, 163; definition, xiii; Dene skeptical of non-local "expert" knowledge, 9–10, 29, 49–50, 170; endorsement by Royal Commission on Aboriginal Peoples, xiv; Eurocentric conceptions of knowledge imposed, xix; experience *vs.* science, xv–xvi; hopes for improvement, 160; "industry" in Canadian North, 8–9; legitimation crisis, 6–7; legitimation method for government decisions, xviii–xix, 5, 7–8, 153–59, 160; new "orthodoxy" in jurisdictions, xiv–xv; power relations asymmetric, xv–xvi, 12, 160; prior to mid-1970s, 6; unequal resource- and royalty-sharing arrangements, 99, 160, 170. *See also* access and benefits agreements (ABAs); Berger Inquiry (Mackenzie Valley Pipeline Inquiry); consultation with Aboriginal peoples; Joint Review Panel (JRP); Sahtu Land and Water Board authority

Royal Commission on Aboriginal Peoples (1997), xiv

Rushforth, Scott: on association between authority and primary knowledge, 29; on conceptions of knowledge, 48; Dene skeptical of non-local "expert" knowledge, 9–10, 29, 49–50; on harvesting areas of Sahtu Got'ine, 103; on mixed economy in the Sahtu, 16

Sahtu Dene: Angus, 86–87; author experience living with Dene hosts, 23–26, 140–42; Charlie Neyelle, 79–80, 172; communities in SSA, 14–15; culture (*see* Sahtu Dene culture); David, 53–54, 105–6; decision-making methods, 30–31; Dene groups, 102–4; Dene law (code of conduct), 53–59, 182n6; domestic and mixed economies, 15–17, 121–25; ʔehtseo

(Grandfather) Ayah, 52, 58–59; Frank, 51–52, 140–42; hand games and their importance, 28–31, 170; Jamie, 37–39; Jimmy, 26–28; new ways of speaking necessary in participatory resource management, 11–12; primary and secondary forms of knowledge, 48–50; resignation that project will proceed, 87; Sahtu Settlement Area, 13m, 14; skeptical of non-local "expert" knowledge, 9–10, 29, 49–50, 170; support for industrial development, 12, 85–86, 120–21; tension between supporters of development and of traditional way of life, 16, 121–25; Thomas, 24; transition to life in communities, 15–16, 122. *See also* Sahtu Dene and Metis Comprehensive Land Claim Agreement (1993); Sahtu Dene culture; Sahtu Dene, relationship with the land

Sahtu Dene, relationship with the land: all parts of environment equally essential, 73, 75; Comprehensive Claim Agreement and (*see* Sahtu Dene and Metis Comprehensive Land Claim Agreement); "country or Dene food," 66–69, 84–85; Dene as part of land, 66, 76; environment as social and moral system, 65–66, 69–72, 83–84, 90, 172–73; "going out on the land," cost of, 83, 122–24; "going out on the land," importance, 24, 68–69; history and engagement with land, 3, 12, 14, 23–24; land as only real security, 105–6; land as source of food, 23–24; land not "owned" (as in common law), 101, 106–7; not appropriately considered by JRP, 65–66, 76, 88–89, 168, 171–73; part of Dene identification and culture, 3, 23–24, 76; perception of land compared with outsiders', 64–66; respectful relationship with animals, 70–72, 80, 83–84; youth's time on the land limited, 123

Sahtu Dene and Metis Comprehensive Land Claim Agreement (1993): communities do not hold veto rights, 149; corporatization, 126–28, 170–71;

criticism difficult to voice openly, 128–
29; Dene and Metis both included, 96;
Dene voted for ratification, 129, 171;
description, 91; disappointment of Dene
in agreement, 101–2, 147, 170; government authority and decision making,
92–93, 124, 125; legal requirements for
Aboriginal consultation, 130–31, 132–38;
manipulation of decision making by
outsider forces, 125–26; mining companies not required to consult, 137;
motives of government vs. Dene for
signing, 95, 101; oil and gas industry
central to economic development, 171;
Sahtu Land Use Plan's delayed implementation, 128–29, 185n47; subsurface
and surface ownership, 22, 92–93, 92m,
124; system of resource co-management,
91; terms, 96–97; Treaty 11 and, 94–95,
97; unequal economic benefit arrangement, 99, 160, 170. See also Sahtu Dene
and Metis Comprehensive Land Claim
Agreement, impact on Dene life; Sahtu
Settlement Area (SSA); Sahtu Settlement
Area, land corporations
Sahtu Dene and Metis Comprehensive
Land Claim Agreement, impact on Dene
life: conflict between protecting Dene
rights and commodifying resources,
115–16; division of Tulit'a community,
109–12; geographical boundaries and
Dene groups, 107–9; geographical
boundaries formalized, 102–7; non-local
participatory processes, 9–10, 29, 49–
50, 170; tensions between communities,
112–15
Sahtu Dene culture: apprehension about
speaking on behalf of others, 45–46;
building relationships and trust, 140–
42; decision making, 56; Dene law of
relationships, 70–72, 172; Dene view of
primary and secondary knowledge, 9–10,
48–50; dissent difficult to express due
to culture, xvii–xviii, 58–59; generosity
and sharing cultural norms, xvii, 53,
55–58, 67–68; "going out on the land,"
importance, 24, 68–69; hand games,

28–31, 170; land use patterns flexible
but acknowledged, 106–7, 114; non-
interference in others' affairs, 51, 53,
55–57; prophecies about future, 51–52;
respectful relationship with animals,
70–72, 80, 83–84; sharing of Dene foods,
67–68; silence valued, 141–42; use of
humour, 60–61
Sahtu Designated Organizations (SDOs).
See Sahtu Settlement Area, land
corporations
Sahtu Got'ine Dene, 102–3
Sahtu Land and Water Board authority:
application process for permits, 139, 151;
applications submitted prior to ABA,
139; concerns of public and referrals to
MVEIRB, 151–52; duty of proponents
to consult, 136–37; responsible for
issuing land use and water permits,
108, 151
Sahtu Land Use Plan, 128–29
Sahtu Secretariat Incorporated (SSI), 98,
98i
Sahtu Settlement Area (SSA): communities and transportation, 14–15, 26–27;
community governance, 100–1, 184n10;
establishment (see Sahtu Dene and
Metis Comprehensive Land Claim
Agreement [1993]); formation, 13m, 14,
91, 92m; Fort Good Hope, 14, 102–4;
geography in 2006, xxi, 13m, 14; history,
3; mixed economy in the Sahtu, 15–17;
Municipal Lands ownership and management, 97; Norman Wells, 14, 20; oil
and gas exploration, 16, 23; Sahtu Land
and Water Board authority, 108, 136–37,
139, 151–52; Sahtu Settlement Lands,
ownership and title, 97, 108, 184n6.
See also Colville Lake (K'áhbamitué);
Déline; Sahtu Settlement Area, land
corporations; Tulit'a
Sahtu Settlement Area, land corporations:
access and ownership of subsurface rights,
98–99; Ayoni Keh Land Corporation
(Colville Lake), 24–25, 97, 98i, 104, 112–
13; bureaucratic (not local) approach to
decision making, 94; community-level

corporation management, 100; Déline
District Land Corporation, 97, 98i;
Déline Land Corporation (local), 17,
24, 85–86, 97, 98i, 109; district-level
corporation management, 100; Ernie
MacDonald Land Corporation (in
Norman Wells), 97, 98i; Fort Good
Hope Metis Land Corporation, 97,
98i, 112–13; Fort Norman Metis Land
Corporation (in Tulit'a), 97, 98i, 109–
12; K'asho Got'ine District Land Corporation, 22, 97, 98i, 112–13; members
divided into Dene or Metis, 93–94,
100, 109; membership by enrolment,
100, 109; primary role, 99–100; privileged form of management, 115–16;
replacement for chiefs and councils,
93; royalty-sharing arrangements with
Ottawa, 99, 160; Sahtu Designated
Organizations for administering transfers, 97; Sahtu Secretariat Incorporated
(SSI) coordinating body, 98, 98i; Sahtu
Trust administration of royalties, 99;
Tulit'a District Land Corporation, 97,
98i, 143–45; Tulit'a Land Corporation
(local), 97, 98i, 109–12; Tulit'a Unity
Accord (with Fort Norman Metis Land
Corporation), 110–12; Yamoga Land
Corporation (Fort Good Hope), 97,
98i, 112–13. See also access and benefits
agreements (ABAs); Sahtu Settlement
Area, land corporations
Sandlos, John, xv
Saul, John Ralston, xix
Savishinsky, Joel, 57
Scott, James C., 109
Seed, Patricia, 65
Shi'ta Got'ine Dene, 102–3
Smith, David, 29
social impact assessment (SIA) in Alberta,
163–64
Sparrow, R. v. (1990), 6, 132–33, 148–49
"Sparrow test" (pre-2004) on justification
for interfering with Aboriginal rights,
132–33, 148–49
Stetson, George, 164
Stevenson, Mark, 154

Supreme Court of Canada: *Delgamuukw*
case (1997), 132, 133–34, 148; *Mikisew*
case (2005) on duty to consult, 133, 134,
148, 149–50; reluctance to define "consultation" re Aboriginal rights/lands,
134; *Sparrow* case (1990) on legal duty
to consult, 6, 132–33, 148–49; on Treaty
11 claims by Dene, 96; *Tsilhqot'in* case
(2014) on Aboriginal title, 5–6
sustainable development, xi
Syncrude Aurora Mine, 80

*Taku River Tlingit First Nation v. British
Columbia* (2004), 6, 133, 135
terra nullius and industrialization, 65
Thom, Brian, 114
Thomas, David Hurst, 65
traditional ecological knowledge (TEK),
x–xi
traditional knowledge studies: arguments
for and against Aboriginal participation,
158–59; definition of "traditional" difficult, 154–55; Dene fear of appropriation of stories, 158; Dene relationships
with land not addressed in report, 157–
58; "disarticulation" of landscape and
impacts, 156–57; final report prepared
by proponent, 157; format and content,
154, 155–57; narratives (stories) minimized, 155, 158, 168; proponents' ex-
pectation of one study to cover many
years, 157–58; quality and production
methods vary with land corporations,
153, 155; requirement for land use permits, 153–54
Trudeau, Pierre Elliott, ix
Tsilhqot'in Nation v. British Columbia, 5–6
Tulit'a: employment sectors, 19; Fort
Norman Metis Land Corporation, 97,
98i, 109–12; Hand Game Tournament
and events surrounding it, 28–31, 170;
language-retention rate, 19; Mackay
Range Development Corporation, 19,
100, 153, 184n8; Northern Store (grocery store), 19; oil and gas exploration/
production, 19–20; photograph, 18i;
population, 14, 19, 102–3; research

beneficial for author and community, 24–25; Tulit'a District Land Corporation, 97, 98i, 143–45; Tulit'a Land Corporation (local), 97, 98i, 109–12; Tulit'a Unity Accord (with Fort Norman Metis Land Corporation), 110–12. *See also* Sahtu Settlement Area, land corporations

UN Brundtland Commission Report (1987), xi
UN Economic and Social Council, *Declaration on the Rights of Indigenous Peoples* (2007), xi, 165
Usher, Peter, 92–93

Village Journey (report of Alaska Native Review Commission), 127
Vincent, Sylvie, 93

Waswanipi Cree Trappers Association, 167
Webler, Thomas, 159
Westman, Clinton: Cree perspectives of impacts of industrial activities, 80; on Cree *vs.* Syncrude on use of land after industrialization, 187n3; criticism of traditional land use studies in Alberta tar sands, 155; social impact assessments, fears of opportunity costs, and mass loyalty, 163–64, 165
White, Graham, 46

Yakeleya, Norman, 111, 144
Yakovleva, Natalia, 165–66
Yamoga Land Corporation (Fort Good Hope), 97, 98i, 112–13

NATURE | HISTORY | SOCIETY
GENERAL EDITOR: GRAEME WYNN

Claire Elizabeth Campbell, *Shaped by the West Wind: Nature and History in Georgian Bay*

Tina Loo, *States of Nature: Conserving Canada's Wildlife in the Twentieth Century*

Jamie Benidickson, *The Culture of Flushing: A Social and Legal History of Sewage*

William J. Turkel, *The Archive of Place: Unearthing the Pasts of the Chilcotin Plateau*

John Sandlos, *Hunters at the Margin: Native People and Wildlife Conservation in the Northwest Territories*

James Murton, *Creating a Modern Countryside: Liberalism and Land Resettlement in British Columbia*

Greg Gillespie, *Hunting for Empire: Narratives of Sport in Rupert's Land, 1840–70*

Stephen J. Pyne, *Awful Splendour: A Fire History of Canada*

Hans M. Carlson, *Home Is the Hunter: The James Bay Cree and Their Land*

Liza Piper, *The Industrial Transformation of Subarctic Canada*

Sharon Wall, *The Nurture of Nature: Childhood, Antimodernism, and Ontario Summer Camps, 1920–55*

Joy Parr, *Sensing Changes: Technologies, Environments, and the Everyday, 1953–2003*

Jamie Linton, *What Is Water? The History of a Modern Abstraction*

Dean Bavington, *Managed Annihilation: An Unnatural History of the Newfoundland Cod Collapse*

Shannon Stunden Bower, *Wet Prairie: People, Land, and Water in Agricultural Manitoba*

J. Keri Cronin, *Manufacturing National Park Nature: Photography, Ecology, and the Wilderness Industry of Jasper*

Jocelyn Thorpe, *Temagami's Tangled Wild: Race, Gender, and the Making of Canadian Nature*

Darcy Ingram, *Wildlife, Conservation, and Conflict in Quebec, 1840–1914*

Caroline Desbiens, *Power from the North: Territory, Identity, and the Culture of Hydroelectricity in Quebec*

Sean Kheraj, *Inventing Stanley Park: An Environmental History*

Justin Page, *Tracking the Great Bear: How Environmentalists Recreated British Columbia's Coastal Rainforest*

Daniel Macfarlane, *Negotiating a River: Canada, the US, and the Creation of the St. Lawrence Seaway*

Ryan O'Connor, *The First Green Wave: Pollution Probe and the Origins of Environmental Activism in Ontario*

John Thistle, *Resettling the Range: Animals, Ecologies, and Human Communities in British Columbia*

Printed and bound in Canada by Friesens
Set in Garamond by Artegraphica Design Co. Ltd.
Copy editor: Deborah Kerr
Proofreader: Helen Godolphin
Indexer: Patricia Buchanan
Cartographer: Eric Leinberger